Diderot's Dream

Wilda Anderson

Diderot's
Dream

THE JOHNS HOPKINS UNIVERSITY PRESS
BALTIMORE AND LONDON

© 1990 The Johns Hopkins University Press
All rights reserved
Printed in the United States of America

The Johns Hopkins University Press, 701 West 40th Street, Baltimore, Maryland 21211
The Johns Hopkins Press Ltd., London

The paper used in this book meets the minimum requirements of American
National Standard for Information Sciences—Permanence of Paper for Printed
Library Materials, ANSI z39.48-1984.

LIBRARY OF CONGRESS CATALOGING-IN-PUBLICATION DATA

Anderson, Wilda, 1951–
    Diderot's dream / Wilda Anderson.
        p.   cm.
    Includes bibliographical references.
    ISBN 0-8018-3976-9
    1. Diderot, Denis, 1713–1784—Criticism and interpretation.
2. Materialism in literature.   3. Humanism in literature.
I. Title.
PQ1979.A88   1990
848'.509—dc20   89-43478 CIP

Frontispiece: Portrait de Diderot, by L.-M. Van Loo (Photo: Musées nationaux).

Contents

Acknowledgments

I would like to thank Carl Anderson, Rosalina de la Carrera and my colleagues Josué Harari, Gary Hatfield, and François Roustang for their generous willingness to read various stages of this manuscript. They have provided many helpful suggestions and a great deal of moral support. I would also like to thank Thomas Kavanagh and Jack Undank for their challenging criticism.

Eric Halpern of the Johns Hopkins University Press has been a patient and encouraging editor, and Irma Garlick and Therese Boyd, my copy and production editors, have significantly improved the manuscript and made the production a remarkably smooth process. To them all I express my appreciation.

Diderot's Dream

Introduction

Diderot has been of little interest for postmodern literary criticism. This is of course due in large part to the longstanding unavailability of reliable texts of his works, which the continuing publication of the new *Oeuvres complètes*, edited by Herbert Dieckmann, Jacques Proust, Jean Varloot, et al. is slowly remedying. Now that the texts are becoming accessible, however, some exciting work has been produced that reveals how similar some of Diderot's literary concerns were to those of interest today. *Jacques le fataliste*, with its continual displacing of the reader-writer relationship, *Le Neveu de Rameau*'s ruthless foregrounding of the creative power of its own ludic mechanisms, or the many works in which a play is set up between language and music or language and art provoke familiar meditations on the nature of literary writing and its relation to a problematics of representation. His corpus poses other problems, though, one of which is that a good percentage of it is not literary according to our understanding of the term. The works that have been eagerly embraced as revealing a prophetic literary modernity in Diderot do not seem to fit with the texts he wrote for the *Encyclopédie*, his technical or political essays, and especially the mathematical and natural philosophical treatises, which were, after all, grounded in a materialist philosophy that has long been outmoded. And yet, when his work is looked at from the perspective of this same dynamic materialism, a kind of coherence does emerge in it.

Demonstrating such coherence is usually thought to "kill" a work, to explain it away by removing its literary polysemy, that is, its potential for acting on and with the reader to produce a multiplicity of meanings, a characteristic most justly prized in Diderot's more familiar works. I do not believe that this flattening occurs in the case of Diderot, however, for the type of coherence that emerges does not reduce his works to monologic texts. On the other hand, it is true that overall, they do not generate an unlimited multiplicity of meanings, because they are highly directed and directing and were constructed to be so. Instead, they set up a partially open but partially constrained interaction with their readers that is one of their most characteristic qualities, whether the subject matter be literary, technical, or philosophical. I think that the constraint results from these texts' belonging to an intellectual project that for Diderot includes but transcends the literary: the French Enlightenment. First and foremost Diderot's texts were an Enlightenment activity, and only secondarily were they literary in a modern sense. Rather than dismissing them as nonliterary, though, it proves to be useful to allow them to be literary on their own terms, for Diderot's work provides a striking demonstration that "literariness" is a historically and culturally relative notion, not a universally fixed phenomenon. To understand it, we have to see it operating within the larger intellectual framework established by its practitioners. The first half of this work attempts to analyze the essential tie that Diderot posited between knowledge about the natural world and what I will call an operational poetics. This relation the modern definition of the poetic not only denies but reverses into an opposition constitutive of our overall conceptual field. Diderot's concept of the literary does not hold in this context, nor does ours in his.

Diderot does hold in common with us that an important path to understanding the nature of the literary experience lies in investigating how a work says by doing, not just in distilling what it says. He differs, I think, in not viewing literature's self-reflexivity as what distinguishes it from the other forms of activity of and within the material world. He accepts literature as a fundamentally self-reflexive exercise, but only because *all* forms of activity fit his sense of the "poetic," making textual activity and material creation continuous with and, in his terms, "about," each other.

It is through this activity that literature brings concepts about both the mental and material domains into being. Because for Diderot concepts are cognitive events that occur within a textual experience inseparable from the readerly activity, the conceptual coherence that supports his work cannot be extracted from the texts and schematized apart from them. Diderot's materialism can really be penetrated only with the texts in hand, for he does not explain; he demonstrates. His textual procedures work best if they are seen in solidarity with the intellectual worldview, determined by his materialism, that prescribes them. Unfortunately, that worldview itself has to be extracted from the texts using the procedures it determines. Given that Diderot's materialism is grounded in a series of philosophical and natural philosophical assumptions that do not hold for the modern reader, its frankly archaic nature can translate for a modern reader into a form of conceptual inaccessibility. Happily, the way around this difficulty—to follow modern practices of active critical reading—coincides with Diderot's own textual program. Although our practices are grounded in different ideas of language and the world, like Diderot we delve into texts and play their structures and strategies against themselves and each other. In this way it is possible, in spite of his philosophical remoteness, to bring into relief the fundamental concepts structuring Diderot's thought by revealing their crucial interdefinitions. Accordingly, one intended function of this book is to serve as a sort of instruction manual for reading Diderotian texts—neither telling all that one can make him say nor attempting to exhaust the implications of his work. It does try to elaborate the basic principles and their interrelationships that structure the cognitive activity of the reader interacting with his texts, in other words, the conceptual field that makes these texts operational.

To function as an introduction to Diderot's conceptual universe, this book need not provide coverage, in the normal sense, of his corpus. Instead, what I have tried to do is provide a maximum of tools using a strategic selection of texts. Most of the works I discuss are among his best known, but others are less often read because they seem irrelevantly didactic or unliterary. Read together, however, I think this particular group of texts provides a powerful and succinct overview of Diderot's intellectual project. To use one of his favorite images, they form the resonant network that provides the tension and dynamism for the wider body of his work. The project of this book—to excavate the conceptual field underlying Diderot's vocabulary—therefore requires that it proceed by detailed textual readings of a series of works. A general picture of where these readings are heading may help the reader keep the interpretive project in mind, even though the full explanatory overview will take on meaning only as the conceptual components themselves are derived in the course of the exposition.

The goal of part I of this book is to try to regenerate something of the textual project of Diderot's idiosyncratic materialism. I think that his project appears strange because he derived his materialism from a denial of the mind-body opposition, whereas for a modern reader the opposition of body to mind is part of the concept of mechanistic materialism. Chapters 1 and 2 focus on two texts—the *Interprétation de la nature* and *Le Rêve de d'Alembert*—that more or less frame Diderot's key productive period. I attempt to show how his materialism determines the cognitive procedures called upon in his texts to transmit basic concepts such as material vibration, music, the nature of personhood, and interpersonal reactions. It also leads him to replace the familiar opposition between action and reaction with the notion of interaction. Resulting from a view of the world as a totalizing sum of mind-matter events that is nonetheless driven by an open-ended dynamic, these concepts set up the definitions of intellectual and social activity that underlie his other works.

One by-product of the replacement of action-reaction with interaction will prove to be his highly idiosyncratic notion of literature. Diderot's texts not only set up an active and open-ended dynamic with their anonymous readers but, even more, do so with the texts of his predecessors and his contemporaries. Diderot's archaic materialism, by denying the mind-body opposition, leads him to adopt what looks like a very modern position: he also denies that the opposition between literary creation and literary commentary is valid. Therefore it is useful to keep in mind while reading this book that some of his most conventionally literary works come to life only when they are read as equally critical: they are virtuoso polemical performances driven by the latent presence of another author's challenge.

In chapter 3 I try to accent the originality of Diderot's conceptual machine by showing how, from within the project of the *Encyclopédie*, he opposed it to that of a contemporary representative of the Enlightenment, d'Alembert. Diderot and d'Alembert were the coeditors of the *Encyclopédie*; they were equally passionately committed to the Enlightenment as the social harnessing of the Age of Reason. In practice, though, the seeming similarity of their intellectual presuppositions broke down, and the original project of the *Encyclopédie* diverged into two antithetical programs. Diderot's meditations, in the famous article "Encyclopédie," demonstrate this split. This article constitutes a quite striking example of what will come to be the characteristic Diderotian writing stance resulting from his notion of all activity as interaction, for it is a direct response to d'Alembert's "Discours préliminaire." In it Diderot eloquently presents his idea that philosophical endeavor is characterized by the essential inseparability of intellectual and social activity. In so doing, he extends his discussion of writing to propose that what he will call the natural literary writing of the true materialist is a privileged tool for bringing about social and physical change. Diderot's interaction with d'Alembert reveals the deep internal inconsistencies between two competing construals of the Enlightenment by unmasking the different epistemologies behind their identical vocabularies. At the same time, it spurs Diderot on to far-reaching speculations, specifically foreshadowing the work on language and esthetics that I will discuss in the second half of this book.

Part II of the book then shifts focus from this "theoretical" or intellectual focus of Diderot's materialism to its programmatic consequences. The group of texts that most economically reveals the social side of his conceptual field turns on the interdependence of sexual, esthetic, economic, and ethical institutions.

Chapter 4, which deals with the *Supplément au voyage de Bougainville*, dismantles the myth of the noble savage. Diderot's *Tristes tropiques* proposes an economics of sexual and linguistic exchange much more radical than Lévi-Strauss's rereading of Rousseau and, in so doing, clears the stage for the antiutopian moral esthetics of the *Salon de 1767*, the subject of chapter 5. In the *Salon*, Diderot acknowledges that art can result in the corruption that, for example, Rousseau denounces in the "Discours sur les sciences et les arts," but he argues that this is only one side of art: its decadence, its perversion. That perversion is necessary, paradoxically, to the renewal of genuine art, to the reconstitution of the dynamic *modèle idéal*. Although it is perhaps the ultimate realization of Diderot's materialist theories, the *modèle idéal* is one of Diderot's most evasive ideas. Not a fixed model of beauty, it is rather an intuitive relationship that the artist establishes with the material world he is trying to depict. Because the world is always changing, the *modèle idéal* must always change, or, better, the function of the unattainable *modèle idéal* is to drive, like a carrot before a horse, the process of continual adaptation of man to the world and the world to man. Moreover, the *modèle idéal* is not limited to the fine arts but extends to any domain; the speculative interaction with nature that it provokes characterizes for Diderot the creative genius in any field.

The last text dealt with in this book is, perhaps, the most intractible of all Diderot's works, unless it is approached through the pathways marked out by the *Supplément* and the *Salon de 1767*. In the way that the *Rêve de d'Alembert* caps off and elegantly demonstrates the structure of Diderot's materialism, the *Neveu de Rameau* demonstrates and sums up the implications, both ethical and social, that this materialism has for human behavior. To make this clear, Diderot has to show what meanings can hold for personhood or the psychological individual within a relational and materially dynamic world picture. For Diderot the modern distinction between public and private does not hold; a more useful opposition would be man interacting or man not interacting. Seemingly cynical and pessimistic, the *Neveu de Rameau* may perhaps better be characterized as uncompromisingly humanistic in materialist terms, for it argues for interacting with the world in such a way as to make self-interest dovetail with the interest of the social group and the interest of the social group dovetail with self-interest. Only when this has been achieved does the Diderotian notion of virtue have any meaning. The question is how to interact in the most mutually beneficial way in a world where virtue is not a personal quality but an activity, the fundamental social activity. The *Neveu* shows that ultimately it is, as the article "Encyclopédie" and the *Salon de 1767* had suggested, this peculiar definition of virtue, rather than the idea of power, that founds Diderot's notion of the political.

Diderot is probably the least understood philosopher of the Enlightenment. His dream, as with so many others who came before him, was to provide a coherent philosophy to explain the world. Like his contemporaries, the other natural philosophers, he hoped by doing so to teach his readers how to act in that world. What makes his dream special is that he hoped to do this not by telling them what to do but by showing them how to figure it out for themselves. Yet surprisingly, his tradition had no intellectual sons, only nephews— only lateral descendents. This is partly because his view is so profoundly critical. His notion of continuation is antidisciplinarian: his readers are to rewrite their predecessors, to shift the questions raised, to continue the activity of thinking critically rather than promulgating a body of ideas. A second reason depends on the first: Diderot's prescribed processes for the textual transformation of knowledge, determined by his materialism, can make his philosophy so painstaking to extract and schematize that it becomes difficult to perceive it as an intellectual program. This book is intended to provide one possible path around such difficulties. I hope that upon reaching the end, my reader will have found the texture of Diderot's thought sufficiently well evoked for both its coherence and its relation to later intellectual traditions to make apparent Diderot's place as one of the most ambitious thinkers of the Enlightenment.

Part I

Diderot's Materialism

Vibrant Organization

ONE

The Philosopher's Task

D iderot grounded all of his writing, even his most literary, in a materialist theory of physical matter in motion. He began to develop this theory in the late 1740s and elaborated upon it for the rest of his life. Although the elaborations took on slight changes in perspective or focus, he kept his essential picture of how the material universe functions remarkably stable—especially for a writer so typically characterized as the embodiment of all that is fruitfully paradoxical, unstable, or capricious. Indeed such a characterization can seem realistic when one reads his works out of the context of his materialism, although critics will probably always be tantalized and challenged by the uncollapsible intricacies of *Le Rêve de d'Alembert, Jacques le fataliste, La Religieuse* and its "Préface annexe," *Le supplément au voyage de Bougainville*, or "Est-il bon, est-il méchant?"

Despite the effort he apparently expended on it, Diderot's theory of the material world seems to invite charges of plagiarism like those leveled at him periodically in his own time, especially with respect to the sources of the articles of the *Encyclopédie* (quite understandable and finally excusable) and to the sources of his plays (a plagiarism that is, for many, much less easily digestible). He had a reputation for insouciance regarding his own and prior authors' or thinkers' originality. For the materialist theory, Diderot openly combined parts of the sometimes contradictory works of Spinoza and Leibniz and drew on Newton as well as Descartes. He revived components of Aristotle's theory of forms, linked his own work almost symbiotically with Condillac's, and owed much to Buffon, all the while engaging in close argument with the ideas of La Mettrie and Helvétius.

Nevertheless, Diderot's theory was stable and coherent and was his own in a peculiar and personal way.

This stability and coherence can be hard for a modern reader to recognize, however. Diderot's work sometimes seems inaccessible or paradoxical to us because it was deeply rooted in the dynamic between epistemology and science particular to the French Enlightenment. Saying of an author from our culture that the capriciousness of a literary work demonstrates the unity of the material universe or that the greatest originality in a world of continual change is produced by plagiarism would naturally be considered paradoxical. Not so concerning Diderot, but without examining his French Enlightenment roots, we cannot properly grasp his key concepts and how they interdetermine one another. Once we understand them, we can see that these seeming paradoxes, like most (perhaps all) of Diderot's paradoxes, point neither to the open-ended or ludic quality of his literary writing nor to his "modernity."

I must point out here that I am using the terms *epistemology, science,* and *paradox* in their commonly accepted modern senses. The word *epistemology* did not yet exist for the Enlightenment; *science* meant an ordered body of knowledge, and *paradox* meant only "argument or proposition that goes against commonly admitted opinion."[1] This simple example suggests how much initial groundwork in defining terminology we must go through to be able to understand Diderot's texts. Although the problem always exists when reading historically distant material, for Diderot's works the difficulty is exacerbated: anything like a straightforward lexical substitution or explication fails, and even getting the *épistémè* or the worldview of his age straight falls short. The reason is illuminated in the problem of definition, especially in the project of the *Encyclopédie*, in which definition was one of the essential and most polarized tasks and one that promoted much disagreement and fruitful discussion—especially for Diderot. His solutions hardly conform to the clean picture presented by Foucault, for example, in *Les Mots et les choses*.[2]

1. For "Paradoxe," see Paul Robert and Alain Rey, *Le Grand Robert de la langue française,* 2d ed. (Paris: Le Robert, 1986), 7:70. For "Science," see Denis Diderot and Jean LeRond d'Alembert, *Encyclopédie, ou Dictionnaire raisonné des sciences, des arts et des métiers, par une société de gens de lettres* (Paris/Lyon: Briasson, David l'aîné, Le Breton, Durand, 1751–67), 35 vols. s.v. "Science," by d'Alembert, 14:787–793.

2. Michel Foucault, *Les Mots et les choses* (Paris: Gallimard, 1966), chap. 3.

To resolve the paradoxes about his writing (in both the modern and the eighteenth-century senses of *paradox*), we need first to show how for Diderot the meanings of concepts like "definition" or "his own" or "personal identity" were determined heavily by the way he understood the world to function. His definitions of thought and of intellectual production were, in fact, utterly bound to his notion of the activity of all matter. In turn, we can plausibly say that his concept of the motion of all matter was given meaning only by his understanding of what constitutes the activity of thought. As a result, our simplest lexical tools for exploring the operation of Diderot's texts must be excavated from these texts' long-buried theoretical and thematic foundations. We must outline the basic construct of his materialist theory to be able to understand what Diderot meant by intellectual endeavor and by language and its products. In doing so, we shall also illuminate our own traditions of critical lexical investigation.

We find sketches of Diderot's basic position on materialism as early as 1749 in the *Lettre sur les aveugles* and continue to find them among even his last writings. Eventually he elaborated his position especially well in the *Principes philosophiques sur la matière et le mouvement* (1770) and in the *Eléments de physiologie* (begun around 1778). The most striking example of its literary demonstration and application constitutes one of Diderot's most justly admired pieces: the *Rêve de d'Alembert*, written in 1769, to which I will return in chapter 2. Generally, however, the work on the *Encyclopédie* in the period 1749–54 is held to be the agent that crystallized the essential structure of his theory. I think, however, that his breakthrough work is the *Pensées sur l'interprétation de la nature*, published in 1753–54, and written during the same period as many of the *Encyclopédie* articles. From this work I will derive the focus of part I.[3]

3. The classic and indispensable reference works on Diderot's scientific or natural philosophical writing of this period are still the following: Jean Mayer, *Diderot Homme de science* (Rennes: Imprimerie Bretonne, 1959); Jacques Proust, *Diderot et l'Encyclopédie* (Paris: Armand Colin, 1967); Jean Varloot, intro. to the *Rêve de d'Alembert*, in Denis Diderot, *Le Neveu de Rameau. Le Rêve de d'Alembert*, ed. Roland Desné and Jean Varloot (Paris: Messidor/Editions Sociales, 1972; reprint, 1984), 185–227; the critical apparatus in DPV: Denis Diderot, *Oeuvres complètes*, 19 vols. to date, ed. Herbert Dieckmann, Jacques Proust, and Jean Varloot (Paris: Hermann, 1975–), vols. 5–8 (the *Encyclopédie*) and vol. 17 (the *Rêve* and related texts); and especially the complex and masterly notes of Varloot and Herbert Dieckmann in DPV, vol. 9 (the *Pensées sur l'nterprétation de la nature* and contemporary philosophical writings).

The *Interprétation*, like the *Encyclopédie*, places itself directly under the aegis of Francis Bacon. The title (reminiscent of three of Bacon's own titles) and the epigraph (a repetition of one of Bacon's) make clear that the format of the work and the attitude that the reader is to adopt, as well as many of the author's own positions, owe much to Bacon's work, especially the *New Organon*.[4] Briefly stated, the reader of the *Interprétation* is plunged into a context of impartial empirical observation of nature. And yet, this move was not merely an efficient way for Diderot to situate his reader intellectually. It was also a way for him *not* to place his work. By posting his allegiance back to Bacon, Diderot avoided any initial polarization either toward Descartes or Newton, or relative to any of his contemporaries whom he alluded to in the body of the text. Still, he did focus attention on one aspect of his work that might otherwise be overlooked or at least underrated and that is crucial to our discussion here: the rhetorical tradition, or rather a tradition of rhetorical innovation linked to intellectual creation, of which Bacon can be seen to be emblematic. The *Pensées sur l'interprétation de la nature* is about nature, but it is even more concerned with interpretation and with the status of interpretation as an event in the material world being studied. Diderot intended form and strategy in this piece to be taken seriously as embodiments—or even demonstrations—of the subject matter under discussion.

The work is divided structurally into several somewhat autonomous sections. The first third or so, up to *Pensée* XXXII, presents a discussion of intellectual procedures. This section appears at first glance to be a theoretical or epistemological musing. Metaphysical is the way it is sometimes characterized in deference to the still accepted mythical etymology of Aristotle's word *metaphysics*: that which stands above or beyond physics, which justifies it or explains it.[5] The second section is entitled "Exemples." It begins to deal with its real subject matter only in *Pensée* XXXVI (the *cinquièmes conjectures*). It is

4. For a quick overview of the Diderot-Bacon relationship, see Jean Varloot's "Appendice" to the *Interprétation* in DPV 9:103–111.

5. For example, DPV 9:29, n. 11 to the critical edition of the *Interprétation*. But for a rapid discussion of the untenability of this etymology, see Gary Hatfield, "Metaphysics and the New Science," in David Lindberg and Robert Westman, eds., *Reappraisals of the Scientific Revolution* (Cambridge: Cambridge University Press, forthcoming). Whether it is historically a correct derivation or not, it is particularly apt with respect to Diderot's rather strategic use of the term in this work and in the article "Encyclopédie."

a speculative discussion of particular problems in what I will here call material philosophy, which Diderot sometimes called experimental philosophy, sometimes natural philosophy. After the examples, Diderot seems to return to his "metaphysics," but this time using a physical model derived from his experimental speculations to provide an abstract structure for the mental operations of his philosopher. He then proceeds to another "example," an "experiment" to test a "hypothesis," but this time the hypothesis is not about a concrete laboratory experiment of the recognizable sort. His experiment is to analyze the *Essai sur la formation des corps organisés* of Maupertuis as a way of demonstrating how the natural method of philosophy should operate critically. The results of this "experiment" lead him to state a series of "conclusions," which appear to be maxims and polemical statements about the social situation of natural philosophy but which are in fact a pretext to combat the logical support of several types of political and religious prejudice. The *Interprétation* ends, like the *Optics* of Newton, with a series of questions. These questions stand in a curious relation to the rest of the text read linearly; they escalate out of the context of the essay of Maupertuis into a series of seemingly wild and lyrical speculations that point directly to the subject matter and to the style of the much later *Rêve de d'Alembert*. Moreover, through their implicit referral of the reader back to the beginning of the *Interprétation* and the warnings to the reader, they also anticipate the structure and rhetorical functioning of the experiment-experience of *reading* the *Rêve* (a question I shall return to in chapter 2).

The original title of the *Interprétation* was *Pensées sur l'interprétation de la nature*. The word *pensées* was dropped in the expanded edition of 1754, but the point of writing the work in the well-known and ideologically loaded *pensée* structure, a series of detached thoughts generated by the association of ideas, is clearly referred to in the address to the reader on the first page. In words that seem banal but are in fact carefully worked out to accord with the eventual conceptual definitions in the text, Diderot claims to have structured his work for young people who "se disposent"—who not only are tempted by or intending to study natural philosophy but who literally are arranging or situating themselves with respect to, are attuning themselves to, its study. Although Diderot's construction sounds modest, it hides a much more ambitious project that becomes visible to his reader only when he understands the material aspects of intellectual activity. The *Interprétation* was intended not to instruct (instill fixed or rote knowledge) but to exercise the students, to force them into guided intellectual activity or motion. "Il m'importe peu que tu adoptes mes idées, ou que tu les rejettes, pourvu qu'elles emploient toute ton attention."[6] This epistle to the reader in fact tells him that he is to participate actively. The first *Pensée* elaborates:

> C'est de la nature que je vais écrire. Je laisserai les pensées se succéder sous ma plume, dans l'ordre même selon lequel les objets se sont offerts à ma réflexion, parce qu'elles n'en représenteront que mieux les mouvements et la marche de mon esprit.
>
> Ce seront ou des vues générales sur l'art expérimental, ou des vues particulières sur un phénomène qui paraît occuper tous nos philosophes, et les diviser en deux classes. Les uns ont, ce me semble, beaucoup d'instruments et peu d'idées; les autres ont beaucoup d'idées et n'ont point d'instruments. L'intérêt de la vérité demanderait que ceux qui réfléchissent daignassent enfin s'associer à ceux qui se remuent, afin que le spéculatif fût dispensé de se donner du mouvement; que le manoeuvre eût un but dans les mouvements infinis qu'il se donne; que tous nos efforts se trouvassent réunis et dirigés en même temps contre la résistance de la nature; et que, dans cette espèce de ligue philosophique, chacun fît le rôle qui lui convient. (27–28)

It is of nature that I will speak. I will let my thoughts follow one another under my pen, in the very order that the objects offer themselves to my reflection, because they will all the better represent the movements and the progress of my mind.

These will be either general views on the art of experimentation or particular views on a phenomenon that seems to occupy all our philosophers and divide them into two classes. Some have, it seems to me, many instruments and few ideas; the others have many ideas and no instruments at all. A concern for truth would require that those who reflect finally deign to associate with those who are active, so that the speculative be excused from activating itself; that the maneuver have a goal in the infinite movements it is used for;

---

6. DPV 9:26; all citations of the *Interprétation* are by page number to this edition and volume.

   In order to avoid irrelevant controversy, I would like to remind my reader that here, as nearly everywhere else, Diderot assumes that his readers are male. They are either his philosophical contemporaries or the "nephews," as he calls them, who will carry on the work of the Enlightenment.

that all our efforts end up united and directed together against the resistance of nature; and that, within this kind of philosophical league, each fill the role that is appropriate to him.

The first sentence is bivalent. Diderot was writing not only about nature but also out of or from nature—in other words, writing naturally. The second sentence reaffirms the duality: nature itself, manifested as "les mouvements et la marche de mon esprit," will produce both the content and the order of the work. The reader's task will be correspondingly double: not only must he absorb the information that Diderot provides about the subjects under discussion, but he must also continually analyze for himself, as an illustration of the subject matter, the way Diderot's thoughts link themselves together. This means, as we shall see, that the reader is effectively drawn into a sort of Socratic dialogue; he must juxtapose the succeeding *Pensées* and figure out what the idea, the implicit question, must have been that provoked the next *Pensée* from its predecessor.

The subject matter under discussion also proves to be nature—the approach to studying nature used by two opposed groups: abstract thinkers and instrumentalists. Diderot would have them league together against nature. It is not obvious when reading *Pensée* 1 the first time, but the "naturalness" of the *pensée* structure and the "nature" that is being studied seem to be two separate phenomena. One is a characterization of mental activity, the other a characterization of the material world. The words even suggest that nature as constituted by the material world seems to stand apart from, because it resists, the mental activity of its observers. The falsity of this dichotomy underlies the whole project of the *Interprétation*. We encounter it first in the domain of mental activity as the opposition between abstraction and experiment.

This is the concern of part 1 of the *Pensées*: Diderot argued eloquently against the isolation of the mathematician from the material world. The mathematician, the geometer especially, represented for him the systematizer *par excellence* whose work dooms him to an ivory tower first of fame (earned for the dazzling symmetry of his construction) and then oblivion (because this symmetry is never borne out by nature).

But what is the alternative? To study the material world instead of focusing on the processes of the logic of mathematics? In other words, to be the instrumentalist of experimental philosophy rather than the idea-oriented thinker of geometry? *Pensée* VI foreshadowed the argument that would underlie the thrust of the article "Encyclopédie" the following year and opened a veiled attack on the description of the project of the *Encyclopédie* in the *Prospectus* and the "Discours préliminaire" as primarily a storehouse of empirically derived facts. The construal of empirical knowledge as fixed facts had already been undermined in the address to the reader of the *Interprétation*. Therefore, experimental philosophy so construed is not the alternative to geometry, and not only because it is impossible for one man or group of men to enumerate all possible knowledge about the material world. To attempt such a task would be presumptuous and wrong-headed. Moreover, even if it could be accomplished, the stock of knowledge would be useless as a tool, since no one could master enough of it to synthesize a coherent picture of the world. Limits must be placed not only on the systematists but also on the activities of the experimentalists. These limits must be established out of our sense of the useful. The useful (a term never directly defined in the *Interprétation*) requires that the proliferation of facts be tamed by the use of systematic thought and that the tendency to self-referentiality of systematic thought be counteracted by contact with the results of observation. One without the other has no chance of enduring. The true natural philosopher must be both instrumentalist and systematist. Diderot again focused not on product but on procedure: "Tout se réduit à revenir des sens à la réflexion, et de la réflexion aux sens: rentrer en soi et en sortir sans cesse. C'est le travail de l'abeille" (34; "Everything can be reduced to moving from the senses to reflection and from reflection to the senses: to go into oneself and come out, without cease. It is the bee's labor"). The *va-et-vient* of Diderot's bee-philosopher between idea and experiment has two consequences: it allows him, of course, to construct usable descriptions of nature. Even more crucially, it protects him against the blinding effect of astonishment in the face of the phenomena of nature.[7] Astonishment

7. This passage is usually read as praise for the pedagogical mastery Diderot's friend Rouelle showed in his chemical demonstrations at the Jardin du Roi. But it can also be read as a subtle criticism of the common Enlightenment notion that experimental science alone is sufficient to counteract the dramatic effect of miracles in producing religious superstition. A balancing component of analogical thinking is required to turn observation into independence-preserving judgment.

is the inability to see beyond the immense variety to the hidden but inherent unity of nature—a unity made up not of structure but of action: "[la nature] n'a peut-être jamais produit qu'un seul acte" (35; "Perhaps [nature] has produced but a single act"). This unity is hypostatized out of the myriad observed phenomena by the use of systematic analogy: "en physique expérimentale, on apprend à apercevoir les petits phénomènes dans les grands; de même qu'en physique rationnelle [systematic thinking], on apprend à connaître les grands corps dans les petits" (39; "In experimental physics we learn to see small phenomena in the large; just as in rational physics we learn to know large bodies in the small").

The person capable of seeing through to the hidden unity and working with it is the genius. He is able to observe, to reflect, and to experiment. It seems—and this is a point to which I will return in the chapter on the article "Encyclopédie"—that Diderot distinguished between local genius as the intense talent for a particular discipline (like Rameau the uncle's gift for music and music theory) and comprehensive genius as the combination of a profound intellectual grasp with an uncanny ability to relate one's work to the rest of nature's functioning. The creator sees beyond. As a result he innovates rather than just discovering; this is what it means to have his work characterized as *utile*.

Nonetheless, Diderot continued to insist on a slight superiority for the experimental in the study of nature. Experiment has its own image: that of the *tâtonnement*, the almost vibratory continual touching and retouching that constitutes investigation by direct intervention, a natural procedure that is "une étude innocente qui ne demande presque aucune préparation de l'âme" (45; "Innocent study that requires almost no preparation of the soul").[8]

8. The similarity to Condillac's position in the *Traité des sensations* of the same year is unmistakable. Condillac's statue can accede to knowledge only through touch. However, the differences between both the suppositions and the goals of the *Traité des sensations* and Diderot's *Interprétation* are just as striking. For example, each work described touch as the source of the process of distinguishing. For Condillac the touching had to be continuous over self and other surfaces (the statue conceptualizes "otherness" and "limit" only when the sensation felt by his touching hand in its serial motion across surfaces ceases to be mirrored by his body surface's corresponding sensation of being touched). From this Condillac derived the model of the serial analysis of discrete objects, which he used as the basis for a logic of induction and deduction. But Diderot sees touching as vibratory, thus providing a dialectical interaction between an already functional self and an active world. Condillac

Moreover, because Diderot's *tâtonnement* demands that the philosopher repeatedly reestablish contact with the physical world, it not only keeps him from falling into the "fureur des conjectures" (45; "mania for conjectures") of the systematizers but also—and I think that this is in the end the crucial consideration—provokes reactions from nature, often unsuspected ones. The symbiotic relationship thus created between experimenter and nature is what Diderot was leading up to at the end of the first part of the *Pensées*. This is the high point and the most important moment in part 1 of that work for understanding Diderot's recasting of the notion of empirical fact.

Il en est de même en physique expérimentale, de l'instinct de nos grands manouvriers. Ils ont vu si souvent et de si près la nature dans ses opérations, qu'ils devinent avec assez de précision le cours qu'elle pourra suivre dans les cas où *il leur prend envie de la provoquer par les essais les plus bizarres.* Ainsi le service le plus important qu'ils aient à rendre à ceux qu'ils initient à la philosophie expérimentale, c'est bien moins de les instruire du procédé et du résultat, que de *faire passer en eux cet esprit de divination par lequel on* subodore, *pour ainsi dire, des procédés inconnus, des expériences nouvelles, des résultats ignorés.* (48)

The instinct of our great demonstrators works the same way in experimental physics. They have so often and so closely observed nature in her operations that they guess with fair precision the course she might take in the cases where they are tempted to provoke her through the most bizarre experiments. Thus the most important service that they can render to those they initiate into experimental philosophy is less to instruct them in procedure and result *than to induce in them this spirit of divination through which one sniffs out [subodore], so to speak, unknown procedures, new experiments, unknown results.*

The image of the great natural philosopher with his hand on the pulse of nature, pushing and tapping nature to react, to respond, is a dramatic one. Diderot's emphasis was explicit. What the natural

---

was trying to invent a plausible story for the origin of linear logic in sensation. Diderot was interested not in origins (which imply a reproducible process and thus a world of essentially unchanging laws) but in the way to adapt most efficiently to a world in continual transformation.

philosopher is to transmit to new minds are not particular laboratory procedures or the experimental results, but a complex intellectual practice that enables the natural philosopher to reach the real goal of his study, the meaning that lies behind the laboratory procedure or the experimental result, the hidden nature that allows itself to be perceived only one surface at a time. This "esprit de divination" is a fluid or dynamic form of hypostatization. It allows the natural philosopher to posit what is unseeable immediately or in totality. The thrust of the philosopher's work, however, must not be to divine a stable structure that he then transmits as his contribution (although at this point in the text, the quest for an architecture of truth statements is not yet rejected). He works to produce a state of mental attention, of sensitivity, that will allow him to interact with nature in a forceful but reciprocal way. His impression of nature will continually change, continually adapt itself, accommodate itself to the new information he provokes through clever guesses and extrapolations from his previous impressions.

The natural philosopher does indeed see nature as a unified whole, as the previous *Pensées* had indicated, but from the last two *Pensées* in this part we begin to realize that what Diderot meant by "the unity of nature" was not the standard, accepted clockwork machine of Cartesian materialists or Newtonian astronomical mechanics, a mechanism whose structure and physical laws are stable and unchanging, and hence subject to being exhaustively described once and for all.

Only at this point, in spite of all the hints he has dropped, do we have to take seriously the idea that Diderot's unity of nature may be nonparadoxically antireductionist. Contemplation of the hypostatized unified nature suggests not minimalist natural laws, but "les essais les plus bizarres"; only the natural philosopher proves able to project and make comprehensible the results. To those without the "touch," the experiments seem bizarre; to those who have not achieved the perception of nature's unity as complex, their results are astonishing.

The word *bizarre* has occurred several times previously in the *Interprétation*, always in strategic positions (for example, in *Pensées* xxiv, xxv). Whether Diderot was describing the behavior of natural philosophers or characterizing his own text, *bizarre* usually has signaled a move or a connection that is not logically motivated—perhaps one that is not logically supportable at all. The description of the successfully trained natural philosopher finally provided in *Pensée* xxx shows us that *bizarre* all along had been implicitly used to designate what *appears* incongruous or arbitrary to the uninitiated eye. *Pensée* xxx makes it clear that the perception of something as being bizarre is a local reaction, that "[le vulgaire] ne sait pas que ce qui éclaire le philosophe et ce qui sert au vulgaire sont deux choses fort différentes, puisque l'entendement du philosophe est souvent éclairé par ce qui nuit, et obscurci par ce qui sert" (41; "The common man does not know that what enlightens philosophy and what is useful for the common are two very different things, since the understanding of the philosopher is often enlightened by what harms and clouded by what is useful").

Besides, the most bizarre is yet to come: the last *Pensée* in the "metaphysical" part is both bizarre itself and about the functioning of the bizarre. The subject is, "comment cet esprit [de divination] se communique-t-il?" (47; "How is this spirit of divination communicated?"). The answer is through natural philosophers, who to communicate it will have first descended into themselves to study and understand this "esprit de divination." Only when a natural philosopher can both use it for his own exploratory purposes and understand it fully in its own right as a natural phenomenon will he be able not just to describe it but also to transmit it. What he transmits is the ability to *subodorer*, to create the seemingly bizarre in order to provoke the hidden truths with the confidence that well-founded guesses seem arbitrary or bizarre only because the truth they are going to reveal has not previously been uncovered.

> S'il trouvait, par exemple, que c'est une facilité de supposer ou d'apercevoir des oppositions ou des analogies, qui a sa source dans une connaissance pratique des qualités physiques des êtres considérés solitairement, ou de leurs effets réciproques, quand on les considère en combinaison; il étendrait cette idée; il l'appuierait d'une infinité de faits qui se présenteraient à sa mémoire; ce serait une histoire fidèle de toutes les extravagances apparentes qui lui ont passé par la tête. Je dis *extravagances*: car quel autre nom donner à cet enchaînement de conjectures fondées sur des oppositions ou des ressemblances si éloignées, si imperceptibles, que les rêves d'un malade ne paraissent ni plus bizarres ni plus décousus? Il n'y a quelquefois pas une proposition qui ne puisse être contredite, soit en elle-même, soit dans sa liaison avec celle qui la précède ou qui la suit. C'est un tout

si précaire et dans les suppositions et dans les conséquences, qu'on a souvent dédaigné de faire ou les observations ou les expériences qu'on en concluait. (48–49)

If, for example, he found that it is a capacity to suppose or perceive oppositions or analogies having its source in a practical knowledge of the physical qualities of beings considered in isolation, or in terms of their reciprocal effects when they are considered in combination; he would extend this idea, he would support it with an infinity of facts presenting themselves to his memory; this would be a faithful history of all the apparent extravagances that had passed through his head. I say *extravagances*: for what other name can one give to this chain of conjectures founded on oppositions or resemblances so farfetched, so imperceptible, that the dreams of a sick man seem no less bizarre or disjointed? Sometimes there is not a single proposition that cannot be contradicted, either in itself or in its link to the ones that either precede or follow it. It's a totality so precarious both in suppositions and consequences, that often no one bothers to perform either the observations or the experiments that follow from it.

The philosopher who can transmit an appreciation for this precarious understanding will be able not merely to astonish but, unlike Socrates, to communicate this gift for apparent divination to his students.[9]

The summary presentation of part 1 of the *Interprétation* that I have just given is misleading in two ways. The first is that Diderot's ideas are more complex and less straightforward than this description would suggest. In fact, on their first pass through the text, readers of the *Interprétation* are often struck by the bizarreness and seeming

9. Notice that the similarity often claimed between the "elitism" of Diderot's natural philosopher and the willful obscurity of the Paracelsians and other early alchemists is unfounded. Owen Hannaway, in his *Chemists and the Word* (Baltimore: Johns Hopkins Press, 1976) argues that the alchemists' silence was intended to withhold knowledge of the material world from those *not touched with the religious revelation of the relationship of God to the material world*. Diderot constructs his world without a god, so the use of the term *divination* is an ironic extension into the domain of the purely material, as we shall see, and, rather than being a warrant for elitism, provides the natural philosopher with an obligation to teach his ability to divine, to the extent that they can learn it, to others. The alchemist is morally required to be a solitary thinker; Diderot's natural philosopher can operate only when he is interacting with nature, a nature that includes his interlocutors as well as language.

arbitrariness of Diderot's argument as well as by the unclear meaning
of several key terms. Diderot makes it difficult for his reader to produce a coherent reading from a single linear traversal of the work.
Nonetheless, an initial reading is possible along the thematic lines
that I have outlined. Indeed, to a certain extent, this reading is representative of the standard modern critical construal of this text. The
second way that my reading is misleading is complementary to the
first. It is that I have not yet provided a sense of the rhetorical operation of this part of the work and the consequences it has even for
the initial reading; nor have I described the interplay between structure and content, between style of presentation and message. One of
the most striking characteristics of Diderot's presentation of his
"metaphysics" is its strong dependence on metaphors to describe the
functioning of the intellect and its relationship to the material world.
Indeed, the metaphoric density of this first part is one of the reasons
why the *Interprétation* is sometimes dismissed as not being a serious
piece of speculative philosophy. Its literary qualities cause readers to
consider it to be amateur science rather than science, prescientific, to
use Bachelard's term, rather than scientific.[10] These judgments are off
the mark. Diderot's text is a good deal more ambitious than it is
often understood to be and does indeed qualify as an example of speculative philosophy that must be taken seriously. True, it does not constitute a work of "science." But the reason is not because Diderot
could not produce such a work (which may be correct). Instead it is
because he did not intend to perform an act of science. This work is
intended to be a critique of science in the form of a *demonstration of
the nature of natural philosophy*. Because science (as seen by Diderot
as well as by modern scientists) deals with the same subject matter as
natural philosophy, many authors either lump them together or con-
strue natural philosophy as a misguided precursor of the modern
physical sciences. I think Diderot, on the other hand, took natural
philosophy to be a way of understanding the world that was fundamentally in opposition to that of science.[11] The difference between

10. Gaston Bachelard, *La Formation de l'esprit scientifique* (Paris: Vrin, 1926; reprint, 1975),
chap. 2.
11. This notion gives even more weight to Charles Coulton Gillispie's comments on
Diderot's relationship to chemistry in his still seminal article "The *Encyclopédie* and the Jac-
obin Philosophy of Science: A Study in Ideas and Consequences," in Marshall Clagett, ed.,
Critical Problems in the History of Science (Madison: University of Wisconsin Press, 1969),

Diderot's notions of natural philosophy and science can be under-stood only if we explore the all-important "literary" operations called into service in the text.

The content of part II defines these literary qualities—the carefully chosen rhetorical and poetic dynamics—of the text and makes them the necessary choice for the expression of his message. A single read-ing of the text would mask this, however. This is a work whose multi-ple parts vibrate back and forth against each other, continually forcing the reader to modify his previous conclusions as to what Di-derot had established in any of them. In that sense, the reading of part I that I have provided above can only be considered provisional, a stepping-off point from which to approach part II; it must later be substantively (I use the word nonmetaphorically here) revised in the context of the conjectures of part II. The most direct way to evoke this construction is not to attempt an exhaustive account of Diderot's speculations on the material domain but to pass directly to the most essential conjecture in part II and in its light do a strategic rereading not of the entire part I but of its *frame*, the initial addresses to the reader, *Pensées* I and XXXI.

We know that one of Diderot's main targets in part I was the "fureur de conjectures" of the abstract systematizer. Yet in part II, entitled "Exemples," his examples are precisely the "extravagances," "rêveries," the "conjectures fondées sur des oppositions ou des ressem-blances si éloignées, si imperceptibles, que les rêves d'un malade ne paraissent ni plus bizarres ni plus décousus" (the "conjectures founded on oppositions or resemblances so farfetched, so imper-ceptible that the dreams of a sick man seem no less bizarre or dis-jointed") mentioned at the end of *Pensée* XXXI (49). These conjectures from the mind of the well-trained natural philosopher become in fact the sign of his mastery. In the "Premières conjectures," though, Dide-rot had told us that: "c'est cette habitude de déraison que possèdent dans un degré surprenant ceux qui ont acquis ou qui tiennent de la nature le génie de la physique expérimentale; c'est à ces sortes de rêves qu'on doit plusieurs découvertes. *Voilà l'espèce de divination qu'il faut apprendre aux élèves, si toutefois cela s'apprend*" (50; "it is this habit of

255–89. See also my "1754: From Natural Science to Scientific Discourse," in *The New His-tory of French Literature*, ed. Denis Hollier (Cambridge, Mass.: Harvard University Press, 1989).

folly that those who have acquired or who are naturally endowed with the genius of experimental physics possess; it is to these sorts of dreams that we owe various discoveries. *This is the kind of divination that we must teach students, if indeed it can be taught*"). How are we to understand him? How are we to understand this *bizarrerie* of Diderot's?

The key passages are to be found in the "Cinquièmes conjectures," *Pensée* XXXVI. There Diderot addressed the topic of motion in matter.

The two principal theories that Diderot had to contend with concerning the role of motion in the material universe were those of Descartes and Newton. Descartes held the *plenum* to be in constant but reactive motion. The visible qualities of matter are the macroscopic manifestation of the combined effects of the shape of their minimal constituent particles and the motion induced in them by contact with other particles. Newton saw the physical world as a *void* in which point-centers of mass attract each other across sometimes immense distances and therefore cause displacement, or in which one mass transmits inertia and therefore displacement to another by colliding with it. Some of the commentaries on the *Interprétation* see it as Cartesian, others read it as Newtonian.[12] I think that in some ways, Diderot's picture was a mixture of the two even though its overall structure was Newtonian. However, the real issues are not to be found in his similarities or dissimilarities with either of these prior thinkers. Diderot was not primarily interested in displacement as the translation of a body from one place to another, so he posed the problem of motion in another way. He derived his general model of motion from his theory of shock within elastic bodies. Focusing on vibration rather than displacement eventually allowed him to generate his story of vibration as an organizer of matter rather than on motion as a displacer of matter. It also allowed him a very fluid and supple definition of *body*—of what it is that constitutes an individual entity of one sort or another.

Diderot first defined resonance, using the model of a vibrating cord with a fixed point in the center. Not only do the two halves both vibrate, but they vibrate in unison. The form and amplitude of motion on one moving side is reproduced in the other moving side

12. Cf. Aram Vartanian, *Diderot and Descartes* (Princeton, N.J.: Princeton University Press, 1953). See also DPV, vol. 9, the critical notes in the appendix to the text, 103-11.

because of the fixed point of contact between the two. Diderot generalizes this phenomenon to a multiple system, one that is not first a constellation of discrete point-masses linked by cords in space but a series of fixed points *within a "solid"*[13] *mass*:

> Ce phénomène, qu'on croit particulier aux cordes vibrantes, a lieu d'une manière plus ou moins forte dans toute percussion; . . . il tient aux lois générales de la communication du mouvement; . . . il y a dans les corps choqués des parties oscillantes infiniment petites, et des noeuds ou points immobiles infiniment proches; . . . ces parties oscillantes et ces noeuds sont les causes du frémissement que nous éprouvons par la sensation du toucher dans les corps, après le choc, tantôt sans qu'il y ait de translation locale, tantôt après que la translation locale a cessé; . . . cette supposition est conforme à la nature du frémissement qui n'est pas de toute la surface touchée, à toute la surface de la partie sensible qui touche, mais *d'une infinité de points répandus sur la surface du corps touché vibrants confusément entre une infinité de points immobiles*; . . . apparemment dans les corps continus élastiques, la force d'inertie distribuée uniformément dans la masse, fait en un point quelconque la fonction d'un petit obstacle relativement à un autre point; . . . en supposant la partie frappée d'une corde vibrante infiniment petite, et conséquemment les ventres [of the actual wave] infiniment petits, et les noeuds infiniment près, on a selon une direction, et pour ainsi dire, sur une seule ligne, une image de ce qui s'exécute en tout sens, dans un solide choqué par un autre. . . . (57–58, my emphasis)

This phenomenon, thought to be specific to vibrating strings, takes place more or less in all percussion, . . . it comes from the general laws of the communication of movement; . . . in all shocked bodies there are infinitely small oscillating particles and nodes or infinitely close points; . . . these oscillating particles and nodes are the causes of the shivering that we experience through the sensation of touch in bodies after the shock, sometimes without there being local translation, sometimes after the local translation has ceased; . . . this sup-

---

13. This is not the term that Diderot uses—he basically does not characterize the mass at all other than through his mechanical description of it. I am using inaccurate but suggestive provisional characterizations, such as "solid," "fluid," "dynamic," etc., to allow the modern reader to see what is at stake in the descriptions. Diderot would not use *solid*, for example, in the way we do; the succeeding description will show what his understanding of the internal structure of a solid is, and at that point his own definition can take over from my characterizations.

position conforms to the nature of this shivering, which belongs not to the whole surface touched but *to an infinity of points spread on the surface of the touched body, vibrating confusedly between an infinity of immobile points*; ... apparently in continuous elastic bodies, the inertial force distributed uniformly in the mass serves the function, at one particular point, of a little obstacle relative to another point; ... if we consider the struck part of a vibrating string infinitely small, and consequently the waves infinitely small and the nodes infinitely close, we have, in one direction and, so to speak, in a single line, the image of what is happening in all directions in one solid shocked by another.

A crucial point to notice here is the existence of an infinity of vibrating points and an infinity of immobile points. This seems to make no sense if, working from the standard construal of matter as an accumulation of solid particles, we think of these points as being little particles that behave like solid objects themselves within the larger solid object. How can there be an infinity of them unless they are infinitely small and thus not material particles? Or was Diderot just using *infinity* metaphorically? In fact, the "noeuds" that serve the function of the "obstacles," the fixed points, are not solid objects or particles themselves at all. They act like them, but they are actually local events created by the reaction of the inertia contained in the solid to the shock introduced from without. These tiny events look like objects (in that they have location), but they are not objects in the same way that we think of the solid particle as being an object.

This redefinition of the nature of an object is so central for understanding Diderot's extrapolations of his material mechanics into his theory of knowledge and literature that a small digression to make the consequences clear is warranted. Think of a wave on the ocean. If you look at it from a boat, you see what appears to be an object moving across the surface of the water. But if you look inside the wave to follow the motion of the actual matter of the water, you see that as the wave passes through them, the molecules of water move in a circular or elliptical path with respect to the floor of the ocean. They do not follow the path of the wave moving toward the shore. The wave is not a mass of water moving along; it has no material substance of its own;[14] it momentarily affects the relative configurations

14. The wave has no material substance, although it does have its own energy. I shall return to this question later, for although Diderot defines his event-objects as containing

of the molecules it passes through. Most of us would say that the wave is not a real object in the sense that the water molecules are; rather, the wave-object is an illusory object displayed by the motion of the water itself. Motion, then, is in common sense terms an event that happens to matter; it is not constitutive of matter's nature. For most of Diderot's Newtonian contemporaries—and even for us (Einstein and wave mechanics notwithstanding)—matter is conceived of as being by nature static. Even when we liquefy or vaporize a substance, we think of its dynamism as coming from energy added from without, and we do not change our basic notion of the matter itself as being essentially static. Moreover, the idea of stable identity, an identity that endures across time, is linked to this way of conceiving substance.[15] Unless they are acted upon, material things stay both where they are and what they are. Descartes saw motion as being continually imposed by God on a passive universe.[16] Newton saw motion as resulting from force, again conceptualized as a manifestation of God, and therefore originating outside the closed material world. For him, moreover, force has a stable nature similar to that of matter (only by defining it in this way could he make it quantifiable). However, for Diderot, the wave-object I have described yielded an extended definition of what it means to be an object. This new type of "object" is a phenomenon resulting from motion, or rather, one whose existence and discreteness can both be understood only as being an event that results from a combination of brute matter and a certain type of motion—that of shock and oscillation.

Another component that must be added to the picture Diderot presents is that of elasticity. For without a notion like elasticity, his system can have no physical instantiation of organization. What he meant by elasticity was the tendency of a body within a discrete com-

---

dynamism, I do not think that his notion of contained motion is the same as the modern notion of energy. Whence my disagreement with both Jacques Chouillet's basic thesis in his *Diderot. Poète de l'énergie* (Paris: Presses Universitaires de France, 1984) and Jean Varloot's emphasis on energy in his otherwise unsurpassed introduction to the *Rêve* in Diderot, *Le Neveu. Le Rêve.*

15. See the useful discussion of a related issue in Sylvain Auroux, "Diderot encyclopédiste: Le Langage, le savoir et l'être du monde," *Stanford French Review* 8 (1984): 175–88.

16. For a concise discussion of the Cartesian problematic, see Gary Hatfield, "Force (God) in Descartes' Physics," *Studies in History and Philosophy of Science* 10 (1979): 113–40.

plex object to maintain its position inside the configuration of the complex object. If the complex object is hit with a shock, the internal body, initially thrown out of its site, tries to return to its place. Diderot tried to show this by describing a planetary system by analogy with a solid elastic body. The bodies within it can be torn out of their configuration by force introduced from outside, but their mutual attractive (gravitational, we would say) interactions tend to try to reassert the original distribution. If they cannot, or if another body is introduced, a new organization accommodating the new inertia or attraction or both arises. "En ce sens général et abstrait, le système planétaire, l'univers n'est qu'un corps élastique: le chaos est une impossibilité; car il est un ordre essentiellement conséquent aux qualités primitives de la matière" (60; "In this general and abstract sense, the planetary system, the universe, is nothing but an elastic body: chaos is an impossibility; for there is an essentially consequent order to the primitive qualities of matter").

It would seem a straightforward extrapolation of this picture to cast Diderot's universe as one having at least a potential equilibrium state, in which eventually every force and mass might be brought into a stable balance or periodic motion, were enough time allowed. The fact that the universe may be essentially a graduated scale of complexes of "objects" that are themselves elastic systems right down to the elemental molecules[17] does not distinguish it fundamentally from a mechanistic view of the material world, whether construed according to Cartesian or Newtonian mechanics. What does distinguish it, however, is the ambiguity of object as *event* rather than as stable matter, for this means that the picture of a graduated architecture of configurations can be misleading. At any point in time, a "snapshot" would show an architectural structure, but this structure, by its very nature, could not endure if the events manifesting themselves at that moment as objects could not themselves endure as objects. For them to change position but remain themselves is one thing. It is another for objects to stop being objects at all.

In this text on the qualities of matter, the consequences of the ambiguity or, rather, of the double-sided definition of the concept of object are left implicit until the end. I will return to them later. How-

17. Diderot uses Buffon's notion of molecule here, not the modern one—he means the minimal particle that carries identifying characteristics and can act and react. Therefore it need not necessarily be thought of as a solid fixed particle.

ever, Diderot extended them tangentially and suggestively by in effect moving from the model of celestial mechanics with its discrete and stable, cleanly interacting, simple point masses to the world of chemical affinities.[18] Chemistry provided him with precisely the link between the macroscopic and microscopic manifestations of motion that he needed to elaborate an all-encompassing material theory.

> [Le modèle interplanétaire de l'interaction] ne concerne proprement que les corps élastiques simples, ou les systèmes de particules de même matière, de même figure, animées d'une même quantité et mues selon une même loi d'attraction. Mais si toutes ces qualités sont variables, il en résultera une infinité de corps élastiques mixtes. J'entends par un corps élastique mixte, un système composé de deux ou plusieurs systèmes de matières différentes, de différentes figures, animées de différentes quantités et peut-être même mues selon des lois différentes d'attraction, dont les particules sont coordonnées les unes entre les autres, *par une loi qui est commune à toutes et qu'on peut regarder comme le produit de leurs actions réciproques.* (62; my emphasis)

> The planetary model of interaction properly describes only simple elastic bodies, or systems of particles of the same matter, the same shape, animated by the same quantity and moved according to the same law of attraction. But if all these qualities are variable, an infinity of mixed elastic bodies results. By mixed elastic body I mean a system composed of two or more systems of different matter, different shapes, animated by different quantities and maybe even moved according to different laws of attraction, whose particles are coordinated to each other, *by a law that is common to them all and that one can consider as the product of their reciprocal actions.*

This law that they have in common is not the equivalent of a rigid architecture but is more like a temporary local equilibrium state. In other words, its mode of existence is related to that of the *noeuds* in

18. Diderot did not make explicit that this was what he was doing. At the time, though, he had been following Rouelle's demonstrations at the Jardin des Plantes to help Rouelle write a textbook; much of what he was describing in the *Interprétation* was an extension of the theory of affinities (as implicit in Geoffroy's 1715 tables) into the domain of the mechanical behavior of complex systems. See my "Diderot's Laboratory of Sensibility," *Yale French Studies* 67 (1984): 72–94, for a more detailed discussion of the workings of affinity theory and its elaboration in the *Rêve de d'Alembert*.

the vibrating shocked solid. Curiously, this law was the closest thing that Diderot came up with to define the individual identity of a body. In the chemistry of the time, a chemical principle (what the affinity theory chemists called an element) embodied one quality. A combination of principles, a chemical *mixte* or compound, in other words, would show itself to the observer as the mutual interaction of these qualities and the "average" or result would define the specificity of that *mixte*. Diderot attempted here to ground this definition of chemical compound in his theory of oscillations. He did it by recasting the affinity theory in his own terms. This theory had been developed partly to account for how qualitative analysis in chemistry could operate: how certain substances tend to combine more with some substances than with others, even to the extent of pulling substances out of compound with others for which those substances have less affinity. Obviously, the phenomenon described is a dynamic one. Diderot tried to explain it in terms of the specific and characteristic ability of the internal elasticity of each compound (and of each compound's compound components) to withstand shock. He said that, as affinity is a form of "attraction" that manifests itself when substances are brought into contact, affinity can shock them by the force of its pull. (Diderot stated that there may be many different forms of attraction, not just that between quantities of mass, that is, gravity.) This shock brings into existence new configurations that are the sums or at least functions of the prior-existing identity states. This description of chemical interaction allowed him to incorporate the dynamic as the creator of temporary events into the theory of chemical principles and therefore to redefine as also being events everything but the very simplest qualities. (Even there, as with the notion of molecule, that Diderot posited an endpoint to the analysis is uncertain.) Once he had defined these identity-events within identity-events as the dynamic reality behind the illusorily static architecture of the world, he had synthesized mechanics and chemistry, the macroscopic and the microscopic, the world of qualitative appearance and the world of dynamism. He could then extrapolate back out to *le grand tout* to account for the dynamic diversity of the physical universe.[19] This entire construct could still be subsumed, how-

---

19. One caveat: Diderot left room for what I will here call the meaningless event, the event that happens without internal determination, as well as the physically necessary and

ever, to the reactive universe Diderot ascribed to Descartes or Newton. Where is the dynamic self-sufficiency? Did Diderot still need a god continually to reaffirm motion at every moment (like Descartes) or at least initially to provide the impetus that set the world moving (like Newton and Leibniz)? Diderot's answer to the questions I am raising is implicit in part v (the final section) of the *Interprétation*. Because part v anticipated and foreshadowed the *Rêve de d'Alembert*, I must wait until I discuss the *Rêve* in detail to discuss his answer systematically as well as to show its relationship to the problem of defining the notion of functional psychological identity.

Diderot returned almost immediately from this quite technical discussion of the mechanical operation of the material world to his discussion of the working of philosophy. He alluded (sufficiently cryptically that the reader has to stop and think to make the jump

---

therefore meaningful event. If, for example, a complex body were struck (whether by inertial physical force or by the presence of a strong chemical affinity in another body) and one of its components were expelled (whether mechanically or chemically), the expelled component could come to rest (mechanically or chemically) in contiguity with another object with which it might not be able to establish a stabilizing relationship. For example, a rock might sit next to another rock; a salt might be mixed with another salt after evaporation of the solvent but without a chemical bonding occurring. The system then would be one not of coordination (*coordination* seems to mean essential mutual organization) but of composition. "La séparation ne sera jamais spontanée où il y aura *coordination*; elle pourra l'être où il n'y aura que *composition*. La *coordination* est encore un principe d'*uniformité*, même dans un *tout* hétérogène" (64; "Separation will never be spontaneous where there is *coordination*; it can be so only where there is mere *composition*. *Coordination* is still a principle of *uniformity*, even in a heterogeneous *whole*"). In other words, mere contiguity produces no identity. The system must pass to a state of continuity, of dynamic internal organization, for functional identity to be present.

However, although the process described is certainly dynamic, it still includes no principle of intention, of self-motivated change, of causality. The caveat above does leave room for spontaneity, but spontaneity is not sufficient to provide a principle of change or of motion. Spontaneity allows change to occur; it is not the principle of change.

Whence my basic disagreement with the theses of the books of Jeffrey Mehlman (*Cataract. A Study in Diderot* [Middletown, Conn.: Wesleyan University Press, 1978]) and Pierre Saint-Amand (*Diderot: Le Labyrinthe de la relation* [Paris: Vrin, 1984]). Both introduce the notion of chance, of spontaneity, and attempt to refer Diderot's notion of change back to Lucretius and Leibniz. But chance is not an active principle for change. Nor does it require a fundamentally dynamic view of the material universe. Diderot certainly knew these earlier authors, but as with so many others, he drew on their notions that, placed in the very different epistemological construct he elaborates, result in a picture of the material universe that is emphatically his own.

back to *Pensée* xxx) to the *délire philosophique* with which he had begun the *conjectures*. The reader is constrained to return to the earlier discussion to pick up the association of ideas, and in so doing he confronts again the last two *Pensées* of part I. This initial structure— moving from metaphysics in the first part to physics in the second— was a standard and accepted rhetorical format whose most acute example for Diderot's contemporaries would probably still have been Descartes's *Discours de la méthode*. Like Descartes's work and (I suspect) unlike that of most of his merely tradition-following fellow authors, the message of Diderot's *Interprétation* is essentially located in the epistemological discussion, in other words, in the first part. But what this means for Diderot and what it means for Descartes could not be farther apart. Unlike Descartes's argument, which proceeds (and which is intended to justify epistemologically his proceeding) from the beginning relentlessly to the end of a chain of reasoning, the *Interprétation* (like so many of Diderot's other works) requires its reader to reread part I in the light of the material speculations of part II to understand what was already at stake in the first part in terms of a model of mental functioning. The vocabulary he had used in part I, seemingly a series of metaphoric clichés, takes on new meanings by analogy with the physical models in the speculative experimental examples. What we had thought were metaphors we now have to take literally. Suddenly, therefore, the very structure of the work also takes on a new meaning: what does it imply to have the work structured as a series of fragments linked by the association of ideas? What is the nature of this association of ideas? What is the *marche naturelle de l'esprit* if not the natural affinity that certain ideas have to others, to call them out in a necessary (though not perhaps the only necessary) order? In structuring his text this way, as an elastic event-object itself, in forcing the reader to participate in the process of associating ideas by having to search out the links between the succeeding *Pensées*, Diderot draws his reader into the dynamic resonating system of speculation. Compound thinking takes place, the reader thinking along in harmony (literally—he resonates in unison) with Diderot. In this programming of the reader is contained both the resolution of the irony implicit in the beginning of *Pensée* xxxix (this is only a *délire philosophique* if one is not attuned to the natural development of this argument by an understanding of the material dynamic of all argument) and the answers to the questions concerning the use of the *bizarre* and the *rêveries*, as the master natural philosopher teaches his student how to philosophize. Now the reader can understand just how serious Diderot was in his initial address when he said that he was going to "[l']exercer": the best proof of the content of his particular form of instruction is contained only in the experience of undergoing it. We also see that the way to transmit this ability to philosophize naturally follows the same pattern: Diderot puts the reader vicariously through the natural processes being discussed. The reader is simultaneously the subject of the experiment and its observer.

Of course, one problem remains: if the reader's organization cannot resonate to these shocks and vibrations, all the master's efforts cannot force him to become a natural philosopher. The reader will remain contiguous, not continuous, with the ongoing process, and the natural philosopher's demonstrations and arguments will remain for him nothing but a *délire philosophique*. Still, when the procedure works, what position is better or more efficient to be in to learn what it means to observe in harmony with the world? What more natural way to learn natural philosophy? From Diderot's point of view, what other possible way can there be to learn natural philosophy?

We see here one of the first characteristics that distinguished Diderot's natural philosopher from the scientist. Like the mathematician of part 1 of the *Interprétation*, the scientist believes himself to be a being of matter working on the substance of the incorporeal, the intellectual, as though mind and matter were unconnected. Although he is not studying the incorporeal itself, the scientist still maintains himself intellectually distinct from his world so that he conceives his actions to be interventions in the domain of the material, not interactions with it. He analyzes only what he does to the world when he acts upon it, not what the world does to him in return. The natural philosopher is more likely to reach an understanding of the functioning of the world precisely because he sees that his understanding of it is one more material manifestation of the world's interacting with itself, and he can take his own actions into account.

And yet, is Diderot's a metaphorical description of mind? The world of mind and the world of matter may be describable in terms of identical structures, but does that mean that they are part of the same entity? This question provides the real link between the end of

the *Exemples* (*Pensées* XXXII–XXXVIII) and the resumption of the epistemological discussion that constitutes part III. The question can be
formulated only after the reader has reread and reflected upon part I
in the light of part II. In this third part, then, Diderot did call upon
the structuring metaphors of his physics to argue a continuity of
effect in the two domains. A researcher's interest in a phenomenon is
a kind of affinity that he has for a question. "On s'attache naturellement aux recherches à proportion de l'intérêt qu'on y prend" (71;
"One becomes attached to one's research in proportion to the interest
that one takes in it"). Systems deriving from coordination are like
mixtes; they are transitory events with local meaning and significance
that themselves also bring about other forms of coordination and
thus new "objects," whether these objects are new hypotheses—
mental systems—or other material beings. Thus arises the importance of the model of *le tâtonnement* from part I. A form of vibratory
touching, simultaneously mental and physical, it sets up a symbiotic
resonance between the body and mind of the natural philosopher
and his subject of study, nature. Immediately the thought arises: if
the natural philosopher's act of observation is a form of resonance,
then it is subject to the same laws outlined in *Pensée* XXXVII for other
material coordinated elastic systems. The philosopher must be acted
upon by the world he is observing just as much as he acts upon it.
His mind (and body—I shall return to this issue in my discussion of
the *Rêve*) is subject to reorganization and perhaps even to dissolution
from contact with the world for the same reasons that the world is
being organized by contact with him: it is touching him as much as
he is touching it. The result of this contact should ideally be that the
world and the philosopher fuse into a larger coordinated and thus harmonious whole:[20] the natural philosopher knows the world only by
actively becoming a part of it, by following its procedures and structuring himself and his actions according to its responses. In return,
the world must also be structured by the intervention of the natural
philosopher. His actions in it, if harmonious, are definitely natural.
We see, though, that *natural* can no longer be defined as being conceptually opposed to things that are produced by men. The crucial

20. Note that coordination defines Diderot's notion of harmony: resonance according to
coordination produces harmony, a definition that, we shall see, has consequences both for
his understanding of the nature of music (in, for example, *Le Neveu de Rameau*) and for his
construal of physiology (especially in the *Rêve*).

consequence of this definition of the natural is that for the natural philosopher, nature and culture cannot be assumed to constitute an opposition. They may form a mutually interactive couple from certain strategic perspectives, but this formulation is only local and strategic. Culture must be seen as a part of nature, as a product of nature, although a particularly dynamic component.[21] Part IV of the *Interprétation* completes a shift like that from part I to part II in that it furnishes a concrete example of the theory Diderot worked out in part III. The example is not concrete in the sense of treating specific problems of the world's material operation, though. Rather, it discusses the specific operation of a natural philosophical text about the world, the *Essai sur la formation des corps organisés* of Maupertuis.[22] In part IV, Diderot leads his reader to investigate Maupertuis's theory as though it were a material object; he is to interact with it according to the procedures he has just learned and see what consequences this will have for his understanding of Diderot's theory.

Maupertuis's book is about the sources of change in a mechanical universe. Diderot was interested in Maupertuis's model basically for what it could provide him in the way of mechanical formulations for what we would now call biological questions, although neither Diderot nor Maupertuis separated biological issues from the physicochemical issues addressed above. According to Diderot, Maupertuis's world never changes its essential nature; only superficial changes in the "ways of being," or modes of things, can occur. These modes are desire, aversion, memory, and intelligence (78), which Diderot characterized as typically attributed not to all matter but only to the animal domain. Diderot's Maupertuis, then, turned the universe into one giant feeling and thinking being, similar to Spinoza's god-universe. Maupertuis in his response to the *Interprétation* denied that Diderot's reading was correct and rather astutely perceived that Diderot was

21. In this sense, Diderot means by the distinction between "artificial" and "natural" only the human or nonhuman provocation of an object-event; in the larger view artificial objects form a subset of the natural objects. From this continuity Diderot will derive the permutation of his mechanophysical materialism into his idiosyncratic model of cultural dynamism and historical development, as we shall see in the discussion of the *Supplément au voyage de Bougainville* in chap. 4.

22. The published form of Maupertuis's thesis dates from 1754. The critical apparatus to the *Interprétation* in DPV, vol. 9 was invaluable for my analysis, because it provides both the relevant passages from the *Essai* and the relevant replies from Maupertuis's *Réponse aux objections de M. Diderot*.

really using Maupertuis's text to put forward indirectly his own ideas about the sources of the dynamic.

What Diderot used to draw his ideas out of those of Maupertuis was the act of "testing" Maupertuis's theory by analogical extrapolation. The notion that Diderot set forth was that of an infinite gradation of sensibility, sensibility being the capacity (inherent in all matter) to sense. In some entities it is in a latent state, in others active; in some (for example, men) it exists in great quantity, but in others (the organic molecules) it hardly exists at all.

> En conséquence de cette sensibilité sourde [in the lowest molecules], et de la différence des configurations, il n'y aurait eu pour une molécule organique quelconque qu'une situation la plus commode de toutes, qu'elle aurait sans cesse cherchée par une inquiétude automate, comme il arrive aux animaux de s'agiter dans le sommeil, lorsque l'usage de presque toutes leurs facultés est suspendu, jusqu'à ce qu'ils aient trouvé la disposition la plus convenable au repos. . . . Et il eût défini l'animal en général, *un système de différentes molécules organiques qui, par l'impulsion d'une sensation semblable à un toucher obtus et sourd que celui qui a créé la matière en général leur a donné, se sont combinées jusqu'à ce que chacune ait rencontré la place la plus convenable à sa figure et à son repos.* (84-85)

> As a result of this mute sensibility in the lowest molecules and of the difference in configurations, there would have been for a particular organic molecule only one most suitable situation that it would continually seek out of some automatic disquiet, as it happens that animals move in their sleep when the use of almost all their faculties is suspended, until they have found the disposition most appropriate to rest. . . . And this would describe animals in general, *a system of different organic molecules that, through the impulsion of a sensation similar to a dull and mute touch that the one who created matter in general gave to them, combine until each has found the place the most suitable to its shape and rest.*

Diderot here, in his extrapolation from Maupertuis, called directly upon the description of affinity-ruled elastic systems that he had before only applied metaphorically to the realm of the living. Here, he explicitly made the connection between the nature of psychological drive or living impulse and the dynamism of the physicochemical complexes. Although he was pretending only to be showing the limits and weaknesses of Maupertuis's text, to be showing its inherent structure without adhering to the conclusions he drew from it, and to be suggesting ways to strengthen the argument that would derive naturally from Maupertuis' own development of ideas, in fact Diderot used Maupertuis to extend his own physical chemistry into the domain of living beings.

I would like to emphasize quickly that Diderot was not engaged in biological (or even physiological) reflection. In the system he was developing, for all that he expressed his adherence to the doctrine that the domain of the living is essentially different from and distinct from that of the *matière morte* (and here his adherence was an ironic strategic diversion pretending to placate the Sorbonne), the living is only an extension of the nonliving. In fact, the quotation above already suggested that the living differs from the nonliving only in the quantity of sensibility that it either incorporates or activates. Diderot became more adamant and detailed in his defense of this position as the years went by. The activity of the living is like that of elastic constructions; it is just a subset of the phenomena structured by the laws of elastic dynamics. Baldly stated, biology as a separate or specific discipline cannot exist, for there is nothing distinct about the living. Diderot was providing a mechanics of the living as part of the overall mechanics of all matter. What we call the organic was for him the organization that results within a complex subjected to the vibration and resonance that organize any elastic system.

This position unifies the whole text. Diderot could support it only through suggestion and proceeded to do so at the very end of the *Interprétation* by appending "questions" that resemble the "inquiries" at the end of Newton's *Optics*. Here he suggested all the questions that the *Rêve de d'Alembert* will later elucidate: questions about how the living develops and interacts with the nonliving, how one passes from the living to the nonliving and how the one transforms into the other. The reader, however, must answer them himself by engaging in the give and take of observation and speculation, for Diderot, true to form, patterned the questions as an elastic system of hypothesis and conjecture, of judgment and testing, of speculation and fact. This question system was another of the systems in his greater system of the *tout*. Philosophy is continuous with nature; its structure is tied to that of the material world. Just as there can be no meaningful movement without the mutual attractions of the parts of a material mechanical system like a chemical compound,

Si les phénomènes [the components of a philosophical system] ne
sont pas enchaînés les uns aux autres, il n'y a point de philosophie.
Les phénomènes seraient tous enchaînés, que l'état de chacun d'eux
pourrait être sans permanence. Mais si l'état des êtres est dans une
vicissitude perpétuelle; si la nature est encore à l'ouvrage, malgré la
chaîne qui lie les phénomènes, il n'y a point de philosophie. Toute
notre science naturelle devient aussi transitoire que les mots. (94)

If the phenomena [the components of a philosophical system] are not
linked to one another, there is no philosophy. If the phenomena are all
thus linked, then the state of each could be impermanent. But if the
state of the beings is in perpetual vicissitude, if nature is still at work,
then in spite of the chain that links the phenomena, there is no philosophy. All of our natural science becomes as transitory as words.

Here *enchaînement* has two possible meanings. Phenomena are
linked to each other physically to form the world, and phenomena
are linked to each other logically. The logic is merely the statement
or recognition of the physical links. Neither type of link can exist
without the other. This passage, however, must be carefully interpreted. It does not mean that change is impossible. It means that no
meaningless—that is, inconsequential—spontaneous change is possible. The universe is dynamic; it evolves; the *enchaînement,* too,
must pass through time in order to account for the successive states
of the material dynamic whole. This is what Diderot meant later
when in the *Rêve* he said, "Tout change, tout passe, il n'y a que le tout
qui reste" (259; "Everything changes, everything passes away, only the
whole remains"). Natural philosophy's place is, literally, to take part
in this dynamic. Its own operations form part of the organization of
the system of the dynamic world.

However, just as not every imaginable change or movement can
take place in the functioning material world, not every conjecture or
hypothesis has effect or meaning. The natural philosopher does not
speculate in a vacuum; he does not create any coherent theory that
pleases him. He must interpret. In other words, he must move continually between observation and interaction with the physical world
and a parallel organizing action in his intellectual construct. So an
interpretation is not a theory, exactly. It is a way of situating oneself
in the ongoing evolution of the physical world so that one both perceives change and its principles and participates in it.

This procedure, as I have tried to show, is continually called upon throughout the *Interprétation*; the musings about intellectual procedures spring from a model of material activity, and the concept of the activity of matter is tested by observation of the activity of thought. Each return to the preceding, supposedly opposite domain adds a dimension to the reader's understanding of the one he is at that moment considering; in his mind (or in his thought processes) they draw closer and closer together until the questions at the end leave it to the reader to make the final leap into the universe of material thought proper. That leap will not have a solid landing point for many years, until Diderot begins writing a project that at first seems intended for a different audience with different concerns. Yet as we shall see, it serves as the long-awaited complement to the *Interprétation*. This work is the *Rêve de d'Alembert*.

Good, Solid Philosophy

A s a much later work than the *Interprétation*, the *Rêve de d'Alembert* provides a good perspective for isolating the crucial elements in Diderot's early materialist writings that continued to structure his thought. Moreover, it was the detailed extension of his materialism into the domain of the living that led to the *Rêve*.[1] The *Rêve* and the *Interprétation* thus complement each other as the two crucial texts on Diderot's materialism that form the perfect frame, both conceptually and chronologically, for the Diderotian casting of the project of the *Encyclopédie* that will be the subject of chapter 3 of this book and for the permutation of his materialism into a socioeconomic theory of the esthetic that is the subject of chapters 4, 5, and 6.

The *Rêve de d'Alembert* is often said to be Diderot's most coherent statement of his materialist philosophy. He did, of course, write several more classically philosophical accounts, like the *Eléments de physiologie* and the *Principes philosophiques de la matière et du mouvement*, but only in the *Rêve* did all of the pieces really come together. Although critics typically say that the *Rêve* works remarkably well despite being one of his most literary works, what we already know

1. In the introduction to his as yet unsurpassed critical edition of the *Rêve de d'Alembert* (the latest version being in Denis Diderot, *Le Neveu de Rameau. Le Rêve de d'Alembert*, ed. Roland Desné and Jean Varloot [Paris: Messidor/Editions Sociales, 1972; reprint, 1984]), Jean Varloot points out the overlap with the work on the *Encyclopédie*, especially articles such as "Spinosiste," "Naître," and "Leibnizianisme." This introduction remains one of the clearest presentations of the content of Diderot's materialism and its antecedents and is marred only by Varloot's lack of interest in what the literary components bring to the theory and his determination to see Diderot's primary interest for the modern reader to be as a forerunner of Marxist-Leninist forms of historical materialism.

about Diderot's reconceptualization of theory in the *Interprétation* as a dynamic process of interactive interpretation leads us to posit that the *Rêve* succeeds precisely because Diderot chose for it a rhetorical vehicle perfectly adapted to his dynamic materialism. The *Rêve* realizes in practice the integral worldview that the "questions" at the end of the *Interprétation* had foreshadowed, but it is forced into a complex dialogue structure to do so. The "literariness" of the *Rêve* proves to be, as tends to be the case with Diderot, essential for its functioning as a successful philosophical exercise for its reader. First to the "theory."

The Irritable Polyp

In the *Interprétation*, Diderot had warned his reader that anyone who read his book "Spinozistically" was misreading him. Beyond that, he did not emphasize the profound atheism his materialism was to make possible. His warning could just as well precede the *Rêve*:

> P.S. Encore un mot, et je te laisse. Aie toujours présent à l'esprit que la *nature* n'est pas *Dieu*, qu'un *homme* n'est pas une *machine*, qu'une *hypothèse* n'est pas un *fait*; et sois assuré que tu ne m'auras point compris, partout où tu croiras apercevoir quelquechose de contraire à ces principes. (*Interprétation*, 26)

> P.S. One more word, and I leave you. Always keep in mind that *nature* is not *God*, that a *man* is not a *machine*, that a *hypothesis* is not a *fact*; and be assured that you will not have understood me at all wherever you think you see something contrary to these principles.

In the *Rêve* he does not subtly hide away the issue of his atheism in an ambiguous postscript; rather, he addresses the issue directly and forcefully. The question of the necessity or rather the nonnecessity of a divine being has to be resolved before any materialism will be able to hold its own logically.

Diderot's use of the term *god* contains two notions, sometimes alternately, sometimes simultaneously. The first is that of a god as the principle of activity. The second is the network of related images of a god as all-present and all-knowing. The two notions are not of equal importance, as a god might just possibly be the principle of the dynamic without being all-knowing. I will begin with the notion of the dynamic, the dominant notion for Diderot, and return to the less evidently godlike second option.

As was discussed earlier, for both Descartes and Newton the material world consists of passive substance without inherent dynamism. God adds dynamism from without to provoke movement as reaction. God serves as the agent; the world only reacts. In opposition to Descartes and Newton—and I think precisely because he wished to push the implications of their mechanistic views of the universe to their logical limits—Diderot eliminated a god from his vision of the world so as to be able to construct a picture of a material world sufficient unto itself. He wanted to see what an uncompromising materialism would look like. To give matter the capacity not only to react but to act on its own, however, he had to introduce an inherent principle of dynamism.

Now Diderot, as well as most of his contemporaries, seems to have assumed that acting and thinking are linked: a consciousness must will action if action is to be distinguished from a reaction. The critical distinction between passive matter and active matter therefore hinges on positing a passage from inert matter to feeling and thinking matter—which raises again for Diderot the question of how to abolish the mind-body dualism that posed the only real threat to his absolute materialism. If his mechanochemical theory in the *Interprétation* was to be all encompassing, it had to be able to account for the behavior of living matter, including mental behavior and the phenomenon of consciousness. This issue determined his focus in the *Rêve*: although the *Rêve* eventually touches on the nature of the material changes specific to living beings, such as sexual reproduction, its discussions essentially focus on the material instantiation of mental events such as feeling, thinking, and memory, and their modes of transmission.[2]

As in the *Interprétation*, Diderot knew well that his explanations of mental operations had to take into account the actions of his char-

2. In contrast to most of Diderot's commentators, I hesitate to describe his point of view as biological, because the distinction between the living and the nonliving is one that Diderot only partly adhered to, as we shall see. Moreover, he was developing a picture of a mechanical world whose forms of motion are what I will call organic, but the picture does not take the organic as being strictly biological. He himself, as Varloot mentions in his introduction to the *Rêve*, used the term *physiological* when referring to the specificity of the living. As the notion of biology is really a nineteenth-century invention, its connotations for Diderot's work could be confusing to the reader, so I will in general avoid the term.

acters and his reader if he expected to maintain his reader's conviction that the natural philosopher is implicated in the material world as he describes it. More of that later, however, since preparatory to discussing the event-nature of the *Rêve*, we need to provide, as a springboard, a more typical analytic presentation of the "actual theoretical content" of the conversations.

The work begins by confronting the issue head on:

D'ALEMBERT J'avoue qu'un être qui existe quelque part et qui ne correspond à aucun point de l'espace; un être qui est inétendu et qui occupe de l'étendue; qui est tout entier sous chaque partie de cette étendue; qui diffère essentiellement de la matière et qui lui est uni; qui la suit et qui la meut, sans se mouvoir; qui agit sur elle et qui en subit toutes les vicissitudes; un être dont je n'ai pas la moindre idée; un être d'une nature aussi contradictoire est difficile à admettre. Mais d'autres obscurités attendent celui qui le rejette. *Car enfin cette sensibilité que vous lui substituez*, si c'est une qualité générale et essentielle de la matière,—il faut que la pierre sente.

DIDEROT Pourquoi non?[3]

D'ALEMBERT I admit that a being that exists somewhere and who corresponds to no point in space; a being without extension who takes up space; who is entirely within each part of this extension; who differs essentially from matter and is unified with it; who follows it and moves it, without being moved; who acts on it and undergoes all its vicissitudes; a being of which I haven't the slightest idea; a being of such a nature is difficult to accept. But other obscurities await those who reject it. *For after all, this sensibility that you substitute for it*, if it is a general and essential quality of matter—the stone must feel.

DIDEROT Why not?

It is not clear at the outset of the passage which definition of *god* Diderot was really attacking. When he followed with his famous analogy between active and inert sensibility and kinetic and potential energy using Falconet's statue as the man-shaped stone, however, it was the notion of god as the source of the dynamic that stood revealed as the target. In the stone, sensibility is inert. Grind the

3. DPV 17:89–90; all citations of the *Rêve* are by page number to this edition and volume.

stone up, ferment it into humus, grow a plant in it, feed the plant to a human being, and the material of the stone that has passed into the body of the human does indeed feel, even think. The sensibility that was latent—only potential—in the statue-stone has been forced into a structure in which it becomes active. Diderot then offered another analogy: d'Alembert's own progress from unformed masses of molecules in his mother's and father's bodies through his embryonic development and birth to his eventual career as a decidedly thinking geometer is like the history of the powdered statue. This is how an egg develops into a chicken. Diderot may not quite be able to show the mechanism of the transformation of unfeeling matter into feeling matter, but anyone can clearly witness that the event takes place.

But the mind-body proponents can still pose a critical question: Are the mechanisms not always the same? Do the rules for transformations stay the same, so that someone somewhere may be conceived of as having laid them down? For the Newton of the Prolegomenon to the second book of the second edition of the *Principia Mathematica*, the notions of law and lawgiver imply each other and are corollaries to the idea of a world of static matter set into motion by an exterior dynamic source. As was already worked out in the *Interprétation*, if essential staticity and the god principle are dispensed with, the notion of law cannot be maintained. So for Diderot, the structure of the mechanism of change was, rather than a universal and ahistorical law, a historically contingent event. Natural law and the resulting practice of thinking deterministically are only local possibilities, local eddies in the coordination of the material world, not reliable for predicting the behavior of the world across long periods of time. So tomorrow's chicken may be different from today's.

D'ALEMBERT Et pourquoi les mêmes éléments épars, venant à se réunir, ne rendraient-ils pas les mêmes résultats?

DIDEROT C'est que tout tient dans la nature, et que celui qui suppose un nouveau phénomène, ou ramène un instant passé, recrée un nouveau monde. (99)

D'ALEMBERT And why should the same disparate elements, happening to reunite, not bring about the same results?

DIDEROT It's because everything is linked in nature, and he who imagines a new phenomenon, or brings back a past moment, re-creates a new world.

We are not told the reason until much later, when Mlle. de l'Espinasse quotes to Dr. Bordeu the almost mystical chant of the dreaming d'Alembert: "Dans cet immense océan de matière, pas une molécule qui ressemble à une molécule, pas une molécule qui se ressemble à elle-même un instant: *Rerum novus nascitur ordo*, voilà son inscription éternelle" (128–29; "In this immense ocean of matter, there is not one molecule that resembles another molecule, not one molecule that resembles itself for an instant: *a new order of things is born*—such is its eternal inscription"). How can we understand such a world of constant change? What can "identity," either for substance or persona, mean in such a context? How can there be any continuity, a category needed to conceptualize identity? To answer, Diderot made a clever detour. The historicization of the material world that we saw above rested on undermining the notion of absolute or ahistorical natural law. As a corollary, this historicization also eliminated natural law as the guarantor or embodiment of epistemological continuity, of the "readability" of the development of the material world through the sequence of events in its past or into its future—in other words of determinism. The universal and enduring stability of law produced by natural law has been replaced by another type of continuity, this one having a historical nature with its origin firmly planted within the world of matter, though Diderot first presents it, provocatively, in mental terms.

DIDEROT Pourriez-vous me dire ce que c'est que l'existence d'un être sentant, par rapport à lui-même?

D'ALEMBERT C'est la conscience d'avoir été lui, depuis le premier instant de sa réflexion, jusqu'au moment présent.

DIDEROT Et sur quoi cette conscience est-elle fondée?

D'ALEMBERT Sur la mémoire de ses actions.

DIDEROT Et sans cette mémoire?

D'ALEMBERT Sans cette mémoire il n'aurait point de lui, puisque ne sentant son existence que dans le moment de l'impression, il n'aurait aucune histoire de sa vie. Sa vie serait une suite interrompue de sensations que rien ne lierait.

DIDEROT Fort bien. Et qu'est-ce que la mémoire? d'où naît-elle?

D'ALEMBERT D'une certaine organisaton qui s'accroît, s'affaiblit et se perd quelquefois entièrement.

DIDEROT Si donc un être sentant et qui a cette organisation propre à la mémoire, lie les impressions qu'il reçoit, forme par cette liaison une histoire qui est celle de sa vie, et acquiert la conscience de lui, il nie, il affirme, il conclut, il pense. (99–100)

DIDEROT Can you tell me what the existence of a sentient body consists of, with respect to itself?

D'ALEMBERT It's the consciousness of having been itself, from the first instant of its reflection until the present moment.

DIDEROT And on what is this consciousness based?

D'ALEMBERT On the memory of its actions.

DIDEROT And without this memory?

D'ALEMBERT Without this memory it would have no self, since, sensing its existence only at that moment, it would have no history of its life. Its life would be a disjunctive series of sensations that nothing linked.

DIDEROT Very good. And what is memory? What does it come from?

D'ALEMBERT From a particular organization that grows, weakens, and sometimes disappears altogether.

DIDEROT If, then, a sentient being having this organization particular to memory links the impressions that it receives, forms through this linking a history of its life, and acquires consciousness of itself, it denies, it affirms, it concludes, it thinks.

What is this organization? As we might suspect from any of Diderot's earlier works, and especially the *Interprétation*, it is a spatial and dynamic organization existing within matter. Even so, it must have a substrate to exist in, and that substrate has a particular structure as well. The metaphor that Diderot used to model the mind was that of a living clavichord (101–3). It was the network of fibers contained in the image of the clavichord that was, however, what Diderot felt to be essential to grasping the physiological reality. The fibers that make up the organs of a living body resonate, like the struck strings of a clavichord, to all analogues of touch recognized by the senses whether the origin of the sensation was outside or inside the body. Notice that again, as in the *Interprétation*, the dominant paradigm Diderot used to describe sensation was not vision but touch. As had Condillac in the *Traité des sensations*, he even assimilated the effective operation of vision–the least material of the senses–to its being patterned on the cognitive processing of touch sensations–the most material. A touch causes a fiber, like a string in the clavichord, to resonate, to produce the mental equivalent of a sound understood as vibration. Moreover, if sensations are motion-events or vibrations occurring within the network of fibers, then the motion of a sensation occurring in one fiber can, as does sound in a well-tuned clavichord or in a tuning fork, cause sympathetic vibration. It can thus provoke another "sound"-sensation in a neighboring fiber.

This model had two advantages for Diderot. The first was that it allowed him to get around the problem of the time-linearity of sensation and thus of thought, which had posed serious logical problems for his nonmaterialist predecessors as well as for himself in attempting to generate an explanation of the structure of consciousness. Diderot modeled thought as material events occurring in a spatial network, thus permitting the coexistence of two sensations. This coexistence allowed the phenomenon of a sensation-of-sensing to occur at the same time that the immediate sensation took place, and even to be explained as an event materially provoked by the occurrence of the immediate sensation. In other words, consciousness, always already a double structure of the sensing of sensation, could be modeled. Consciousness of the sensation plus sensation yielded the further complex event-object named "idea." Another advantage of Diderot's spatializing of thought was that he was not limited to a binary architecture. Not only could two thoughts occur at the same time, but a single thought could be seen to provoke the simultaneous occurrence of a multiplicity of mental events. Therefore in the *Rêve*, Diderot has finally provided a model for the physiological instantiation of the *productive* analogical thinking central to the project of the *Interprétation*. For how could one make judgments without being able to hold at least two ideas in the mind at once so as to compare them? The second advantage was that this model allowed Diderot to complexify the relationships between thoughts. They were no longer merely deductive or inductive logical relationships. The concept of resonance implies orders of harmony and dissonance; hence judgments at the least of identity, similarity, and difference all have their direct corporeal realizations in the mechanical operation of the fiber network.

Now, the "clavichord" of a human mind may be born delicately and finely tuned, whence comes a sensitive intelligence. It may be from its beginnings attuned to certain harmonies and relatively insensitive to others, whence arises a talent for one type of thinking and less talent for another.[4] The most important consequence of this model was that the clavichord's physical functioning allows us to understand in material terms how it could learn. Its internal organization—the coordination of its constituent elements—had inevitably to be either disturbed or refined by each event it experienced. Bordeu, d'Alembert, and Mlle. de l'Espinasse extend this idea in the second section of the work. The fiber network (although no longer expressed through the metaphor of a clavichord but as a spider web with a spider in the center processing the incoming vibrations and sending vibrations out) provided the physical structure not only for sensation but also for memory. If the fiber network is refined by learning a pattern, a touch from without or within may reprovoke the same "sound" that caused the patterning, thus voluntarily or involuntarily bringing back the parallel experience of a previous similarly resonating event. These are the "actions, les réactions habituelles" (119) (that is, involuntarily programmed into the object by past experience) that d'Alembert dreams of. This memory, an organization that is the physical residue of the organism's history, determines the way it reacts to the world. In this sense, memory patterns according to the past what the organism can think about future

4. The most famous example of the network occurs not in the *Rêve* but in the *Neveu de Rameau*. Diderot used the same model to describe the "truncated" but extremely well-organized fiber network of the musical genius Rameau, who could not, great musical ability notwithstanding, get along with people. His nephew, on the other hand, had fibers so knotted that he could hardly think clearly, and his erratic behavior displayed the unharmonious and unpredictable resonances between seemingly unpatterned fibers. I will return to the social and esthetic consequences of unharmonious networks in my discussion of Rameau the nephew in chapter 6.

sensations. This learning is therefore the basis of a material transformism that is the physiological instantiation of memory. Such a model will help us to understand why Diderot's statement that "pas une molécule qui se ressemble à elle-même un instant" (128; "not one molecule that resembles itself for an instant") does not imply the impossibility of memory. Each material object's internal physical structure is the result of its past history. For human beings, this smacks of a Lamarckian transformism.

> BORDEU Supposez une longue suite de générations manchotes; supposez des efforts continus; et vous verrez les deux côtés de cette pincette [formed by the shoulder blades] s'étendre, s'étendre de plus en plus, se croiser sur le dos, revenir par-devant,—peut-être se digiter à leurs extrémités, et refaire des bras et des mains. La conformation originelle s'altère ou se perfectionne par la nécessité et les fonctions habituelles. Nous marchons si peu, nous travaillons si peu, et nous pensons tant que je ne désespère pas que l'homme ne finisse par n'être qu'une tête. (137)

> BORDEU Imagine a long series of generations of one-armed men; imagine their continual efforts; and you will see the two sides of this pincer [formed by the shoulder blades] extend, extend more and more, cross in back, come around front—maybe grow new fingers at the extremities, and reconstruct arms and hands. The original conformation alters or perfects itself through necessity and habitual functioning. We walk so little, we work so little and we think so much that I do not give up hope that one day man will end up being all head.

Notice that Diderot's historical change provided for the endurance of a sort of mental or psychological identity. The structure of the "clavichord" is only gradually changed and complexified from that of its origin. The "clavichord" does not remain identical to itself; in other words, it is not the exact same material object at different points in time. Certainly it is temporally continuous with itself, and the differences in its makeup are explainable in terms of the events it undergoes. In the same sense, the memory content, the particular coordination or tuning of its components with respect to each other, is itself not permanent or untransformable. A good deal of the discussion between d'Alembert and Dr. Bordeu in the second part concerns the consequences that various catastrophic events can have on the material organization of the fiber network and the effects that changes in an individual's organization bring about in his memory, psychological functioning, and perception of his own identity. (Bordeu discusses cases where the flow is interrupted: his patients either lose all memory and have to build new identities by living new experiences or pass in and out of states of awareness of their actions.) Psychological identity and continuity certainly exist in this system, but "identity" does not imply "identical" in Diderot's world.

This is a strange kind of identity, then, one that results from organization but is not unchanging. To what kind of object does it pertain? To one whose shape can endure even though its actual substance changes. Organic beings all embody this kind of identity, and animals, plants, and human beings are all conceived of as "objects." They are objects not in the way that static matter is, however, but in the way that the wave that I described in the discussion of the *Interprétation* constitutes an object. An organism is an object in continual interaction with its surroundings; it exists in a flow of material substance, continually taking in and sending out matter, all the while maintaining a provisional organization, an identity therefore, that we would certainly qualify as continuous. A wave object, and thus by extension an organism, is distinguished not by the stability of its matter but by the nondissolution of its configuration and the nondisruption of its activity.

Note that the wave is an object made up of a heterogeneous assortment of other event-objects. In the *Interprétation* this object-property did not pose a problem for, say, describing the mechanical interactions of astronomical bodies. Nor did it, once the concept of affinity was introduced, pose a problem for understanding chemical systems. However, in the *Rêve*, the supposedly distinctive nature of living organisms introduces the question of the origin as well as the nature of consciousness. How did Diderot logically turn an aggregate of inanimate objects into the single new object that is conscious of itself as existing? How did he go from inanimate to animate organization?

MLLE. DE L'ESPINASSE [reading from her transcription of d'Alembert's dream] Ecoutez...Un point vivant...Non, je me trompe. Rien d'abord; puis un point vivant...A ce point vivant, il s'en applique un autre, encore un autre; et par ces applications successives, il résulte un être un; car je suis bien un; je n'en saurais douter...(en disant cela, il se tâtait partout)...Mais comment cette unité s'est-elle faite? . . . Tenez, Philosophe; je vois bien un agrégat, un tissu de petits êtres sensibles; mais un animal?...un tout?...un système un, lui, ayant la conscience de son unité? je ne le vois pas...non, je ne le vois pas. (117)

MLLE. DE L'ESPINASSE [reading from the text of d'Alembert's dream] Listen...a living point...No, I'm wrong. First nothing, and then a living point...To this living point another is joined, then another; and by these successive additions, a unified being results; for I am certainly unified; I can't doubt that...(in so saying, he felt himself all over)...But how does this unity come about? . . . Listen, Philosopher, I do see the aggregate, a tissue of tiny sensible beings; but an animal?...a whole?...a unified system having consciousness of its unity? I can't see it...no, 1 can't see it.

He did not, at least not in direct exposition. Diderot's text avoids the issue with two detours. The first is the material explanation of memory that we saw above. One can understand how memory might be materially coded or captured in the organization of a living organism, but that does not give us an origin for the living. The other detour is the swarm of bees (120–22), the animal extension of the affinity-determined melting of a drop of mercury into another. A swarm of bees looks and behaves, when swarming, like an animal; eliminate their feet and have them physically continuous rather than just contiguous. One could not distinguish this polyp from an animal. Notice that this is a "behaviorist" and not an internalist characterization: would the bees have a single unitary consciousness that would be aware of itself as a single entity? Perhaps one could only answer this question by being the polyp.

The most effective way for Diderot to attack the issue of consciousness was to introduce his idea of sensibility, which served with respect to living beings the function that affinity did for chemical compounds in the *Interprétation*. Because sensibility operates both mentally and materially, it is a form of sensitivity to anything that touches the individual—whether that be a hand, an idea, or a tender scene. Sensibility is in effect the primary issue discussed in the second part of the *Rêve*. It is the instigator of interactions among the living, and the various ways in which it operates permitted Diderot to explain a good number of thorny natural historical questions. In this

light we can understand d'Alembert's protest in the very first lines of
the work that for Diderot sensibility replaces the god function: sensibility is the source of the structuring dynamic.[5] Sensibility serves as
the bridge between the animate and the inanimate. It is a state, a manifestation of the organization of matter, that can be transmitted by
motion and whose defining characteristic is that it propagates as resonance. This resonance in turn acts on surrounding objects and can
cause their patterning to respond, to resonate. Is a substance being
transmitted? No, not in an everyday sense.[6]

One might immediately ask, Is this the first suggestion of a vitalistic principle? Clearly not, and this is the answer to nineteenth-
century qualifications of Diderot as a vitalist: sensibility seems to be
a function of density of organization. The difference between the
stone that does not think in Falconet's statue, whose outward shape
represents a man, and the stone that no longer carries that shape but

5. Diderot's phenomenon, sometimes also called irritability, was postulated as existing in
a latent state even in inanimate objects. Commentators are often uncertain whether to call
this sensibility a substance of its own, a form of energy-made-substance that can be combined with other substances, or whether it is a type of organization. As has been noted
(Varloot's introduction is again the most explicit on this problem), the text appears to waffle
on this issue. I suspect, though, that the opposition is ill posed. Given Diderot's notion that
matter is inherently composed as much of organization as of substance, or rather that substance is the appearance taken on by an organization-event, the question is one of which
way it is practical to look at it in which circumstances. See also Jean-Claude Guédon, "Chi-
mie et matérialisme, la stratégie anti-newtonienne de Diderot," *Dix-huitième Siècle* 11 (1979):
185–200.

6. This is the crucial addition that the *Rêve* makes to the theory presented in the *Interprétation*, as the bridge between the notions of matter and organization in action.

A modern reader is tempted to make the analogy between "sensibilité" and a chemical
principle understood as a simple substance with a permanent essential identity. A chemical
principle, however, need not be thought of as a simple substance. Diderot did indeed
embrace the idea of a world of heterogeneous chemical substances, but he nowhere seemed
to have been interested in whether one could ever reach the endpoint of the analysis of matter into its principal components, into what we would call its chemical elements. This is in
part because his notion of matter excluded the notion of fixed chemical identity. One of the
principal characterizing "components" of any matter lay for him in its organization not
only in what are easily perceivable as complex objects but also in what we call "simple" substances. Organization is, as I have tried to show, a state, or a hierarchy of coordination
states. Neither the simple state (does it exist?) nor the hierarchy of states is ever fixed; chemical identity, like any other identity, can only be the temporary manifestation of one of
these coordination states at a particular place and for a finite period of time. Of course,
some states are more stable than others, therefore it makes sense to talk of chemical elements as being fixed when discussing their combination into less stable organizations such
as compounds. Still, this is only a way of speaking, a kind of mental abbreviation.

does think when some of its substance is incorporated into the human being is that the human being is extremely organized with respect to dynamic functioning. In other words, no difference in *kind* is induced by combining an inorganic substance with a vitalistic principle (a model that merely reproduces the mind-body opposition in material terms). The "inorganic" (that is, not very organized) is nonliving because it is not at that moment highly organized and thus not obviously responding dynamically to the movement around it. Inorganic and organic are two extremes on a spectrum of density of organization. The inorganic is not so much nonliving as not very living. In fact, even to pose the problem in this way is to misunderstand the audacity of Diderot's vision, in which the living is just organized inorganic, one corner of the mechanophysical *grand tout*. I would be tempted to say that rather than biologizing the material world, Diderot realizes a coherent mechanization of the living with his introduction of the notion of sensibility understood as irritability.

Irritability is a function of the coordination of dynamic components, an organization that the vibrations central to the thesis of the *Interprétation* can produce or destroy at any time, as they continually organize and disorganize the matter of the universe. A problem remains: does Diderot's dynamic motion only organize? Diderot never dealt with this question in the *Rêve*, but he seemed to have an implicit answer, not only here but in all his works dealing with the nature of the dynamic. Although this answer was not formulated in theoretical form, we can say that Diderot's motion did more than organize, for his concept of motion was dual: some motion organized and other motion disorganized. He did theorize motion that disorganized, but it had an essential place in his work as the obstacle that those who want to increase organization have to face. It produces catastrophes (when it destroys organization on all levels altogether), monsters (when the balances and harmonies between objects are distorted—*La Lettre sur les aveugles*, the "Suite de l'Entretien"), and misfits (when the locally organized individual is not in harmony with the pervading organization of his larger environment—the Nephew's description of himself in *Le Neveu de Rameau*). One of the functions that Diderot assigned to consciousness (itself a form of high-level organization) seems to be to choose ways of guiding the dynamic so as to maximize the creation of organization and minimize the equally likely disorganizing power of the dynamic. In actual-ity, the duality of Diderot's motion concept may have been insufficiently coherent to be formulated. A good way to describe it would be to say that it is like the intellectual thematic predispositions, models through which people habitually think, that Gerald Holton analyzes in his work on modern scientific thinkers.[7]

It is likely that Diderot originally derived his notion of identity as organization within flux from his reading of Bacon's essentialist transformation of Aristotle's concept of form.[8] For Aristotle form complemented change in living beings. "Living things were distinguished from non-living things by their ability 'to initiate movement and change without an external mover, that is, [by] the power of self-movement or self-change. The kinds of movement or change common to all living things were growth, the assimilation of diverse matter under the form of the organism, and the continuation of this process in the reproduction of the species.'"[9] Form as the essence toward which change tended was both the determinant of change and the principle for the attribution of identity through time to discrete beings. Mary Slaughter argues that the notion of analysis as the Enlightenment used it is dependent on a worldview that can conceive of singular essences transcending the apparent chaos of the dynamic. I extrapolate to posit that for Aristotle, making the dynamic system teleological meant that cause and identity assimilate each other. In effect, Aristotle dispensed with the categorial instability inherent in a world of change. Slaughter argues that Bacon dispensed with the dynamic side of Aristotelian physics to distill the essentialist position inherent in it and to provide the epistemological ground for analytic taxonomies and scientific nomenclatures.[10] Thus, although Diderot's theory of organization looks at first sight remarkably like a return to Aristotle's concept of form, it differs because Diderot's system is not teleological. It is open-ended. Diderot might

7. Gerald Holton, *The Scientific Imagination: Case Studies* (Cambridge: Cambridge University Press, 1978).

8. For an exceptionally clear discussion of the development from Aristotle to Bacon of the relationship of concepts of form to notions of identifying essences and the consequences of theories of linguistic structure, see M. M. Slaughter, *Universal Languages and Scientific Taxonomy in the Seventeenth Century* (Cambridge: Cambridge University Press, 1982), esp. chap. 1, pp. 32–37 and chap. 4, 95–96.

9. R. G. Collingwood, *The Idea of Nature* (Oxford: Oxford University Press, 1965), 97; quoted by Slaughter, *Universal Languages*, 32.

10. Slaughter, *Universal Languages*, 96.

certainly in some ways have been resurrecting the Aristotelian dynamic, but he rejected the Baconian-d'Alembertian analytic derived from its teleology, knowing that an analytic epistemology is not adequate to describe this world—as we shall see in discussing the project of the *Encyclopédie*. Diderotian categories did not transcend the effects of change: they were conditional intellectual states just as for him chemical elements could be understood only as conditional material states.

All forms of organization are conditional material states. The dynamic nature of the world means that disorganization may dissolve them.[11] It is important to see that even sensibility can function as a form of disorganizing motion.

> BORDEU Mais qu'est-ce qu'un être sensible? Un être abandonné à la discrétion du diaphragme. Un mot touchant a-t-il frappé l'oreille? un phénomène singulier a-t-il frappé l'oeil? et voilà tout à coup le tumulte intérieur qui s'élève, tous les brins du faisceau qui s'agitent, le frisson qui se répand, l'horreur qui saisit, les larmes qui coulent, les soupirs qui suffoquent, la voix qui s'interrompt, l'origine du faisceau qui ne sait ce qu'il devient; plus de sang-froid, plus de raison, plus de jugement, plus d'instinct, plus de ressource.
>
> MLLE. DE L'ESPINASSE Je me reconnais. (179)
>
> BORDEU But what is a sensible being? A being abandoned to the whims of its diaphragm. Does a touching word strike the ear? A singular phenomenon strike the eye? And suddenly interior tumult breaks out, all the threads in the network wave around, a shivering spreads, the being is seized with horror, its tears flow, it is suffocated with sighs, its voice breaks, the origin point of the network no longer knows what it is doing; no more sang-froid, no more reason, no more judgment, no more instinct, no more control.
>
> MLLE. DE L'ESPINASSE I recognize myself.

11. Diderot held heat to be one of the possible manifestations of disorganizing motion. We must note, however, that for him heat just as often, or perhaps even more often, produced organization. The heat applied to an egg brings about the motion in the internal matter that organizes it into a chick (continuing the allusion to Aristotle). Such a view—in which heat produces order rather than disorder—immediately rules out a thermodynamic reading of Diderot's materialism. Diderot's dynamic history was not a forerunner of an entropic view of the universe. This is another point of basic disagreement between my reading of Diderot's materialism and Jeffrey Mehlman's, in his *Cataract. A Study in Diderot* (Middletown, Conn.: Wesleyan University Press, 1978).

The drive or characteristic that Diderot identified in the ongoing change, however, is a move toward increasing organization. The world is not a yin-yang balance between order and chaos, between stability and catastrophe. Consciousness provides a desirable and statistically realized overall direction to the change that takes place in the material world. It moves toward organization, towards a form of coherence.[12] The *grappe d'abeilles* becomes the nerve fiber network linking the organs of a human body into one organism, the spider web with the spider in the center.[13] The difference is important.

MLLE. DE L'ESPINASSE   La différence, s'il vous plaît?

BORDEU   C'est que la conscience n'est qu'en un endroit... elle ne peut être que dans un endroit, au centre commun de toutes les sensations, là où est la mémoire, là où se font les comparaisons. . . .

MLLE. DE L'ESPINASSE   Et qu'est-ce donc que la mémoire?

BORDEU   La propriété du centre. Le sens spécifique de l'origine du réseau. (175–56)

MLLE. DE L'ESPINASSE   And the difference, please?

BORDEU   It's that consciousness is only located in one spot . . . it can be only in one spot, in the common center of all sensations, there where memory is located, there where comparisons are made.

MLLE. DE L'ESPINASSE   And what is memory, then?

BORDEU   The property of the center. The particular sense of the origin point of the network.

Memory is both the process of material analogy and the consciousness made possible by this processing. It provides the unity that makes the difference between aggregate and organism. It also makes

---

12. In this sense one might say that Diderot's world does, after all, have a teleological component. Still, it is very different from Aristotle's world, which was essentially stable but composed of a great number of teleologically identifiable local individuals. Diderot's world has no essential individuals but has an overall tendency toward organization, and an organization whose development is unforeseeable because the laws that guide change themselves change with the structure of the world.

13. Diderot will elaborate the consequences of the spider image in the *Salon de 1767*; the relationship to his aesthetic theories as more clearly worked out in that text will be taken up in chapter 5.

possible the further aggregation of the new unity with others of its scale into superorganisms, and on up towards a total vision of the universe. The bee swarm and the human nerve network are just small examples of the tendency of the total mass of matter to resolve itself slowly into one giant organism.

Does this get us finally to a Spinozistic vision of god? Not really. Bordeu draws the conclusion; his vision is of an all-encompassing god indeed, but a powerless and historically contingent god who "serait matière, dans l'univers, portion de l'univers, sujet à vicissitudes, il vieillirait; il mourrait" (143). The only god possible in this world is not a god from without, not a ruling or decision-making god. It is nothing but a result of the natural tendency of the material world to organize and unify consciousness. Bordeu's god would be (or would have been) nothing more than a giant, irritable polyp.

D'ALEMBERT Que voulez-vous donc dire avec vos individus?...Il n'y en a point. Non, il n'y en a point...Il n'y a qu'un seul grand individu; c'est le tout. Dans ce tout, comme dans une machine, dans un animal quelconque, il y a une partie que vous appellerez telle ou telle; mais quand vous donnerez le nom d'individu à cette partie du tout, c'est par un concept aussi faux que si, dans un oiseau, vous donniez le nom d'individu, à l'aile, à une plume de l'aile. . . . Qu'est-ce qu'un être?...la somme d'un certain nombre de tendances...Est-ce que je puis être autrechose qu'une tendance?...non. Je vais à un terme...Et les espèces?...Les espèces ne sont que des tendances à un terme commun qui leur est propre. . . . Et la vie? (138–39)

D'ALEMBERT So what do you mean by your "individuals"?... There aren't any. No, there aren't any...There is only one great individual; it is the whole. In this whole, as in a machine, in an animal of some sort, there is a part that you call one thing or another; but when you give the name of individual to this part of the whole, you're using a concept as false as if, in the bird, you gave the name of individual to the wing, to a feather in the wing. . . . What is a being?...the sum of a certain number of tendencies...Can I be something other than a tendency?...no. I develop to an endpoint...And species?...Species are only the tendencies toward a common endpoint specific to themselves . . . And life?

"Un terme": one of the most difficult questions to deal with when confronting Diderot's materialism is the apparent moral determinism that seems to follow from his materialism.[14] In this question of moral determinism lie the real issues of the irrelevance of a Diderotian god, no matter how material.

Let us digress briefly to consider the grounds on which a determinism can be based. Determinism opposes the idea of free will. One might even say that the mind-body problem could be shuffled to make the logical dependences be the following. It is unacceptable for humans not to be the responsible source of, in other words to will, their own actions. If their willing an action is merely a reaction to something and they are unaware of this, then their will is not free even though they move to initiate action. For will to be really free, a mind-body distinction must exist to ensure that the mind is not merely reacting to its environment. Even then, however, freedom relating to mental phenomena remains an issue. The first problem posed is the theological one: assuming a god exists, does that god determine a person's choice, or is that person not only responsible for but also the sufficient cause of his own decisions? Here arises the difficulty in succinctly opposing the notions of grace and guilt—they arise from different decisions about the relationship of a person's responsibility to his decision-making capabilities. If, however, God-the-lawgiver is also God-the-creator, why would he create a world in which his creatures could choose to do wrong? The logical incoherence can be eliminated by eliminating a god from the picture—the explicit or implicit positions of Helvétius or Maupertuis, for example, as Diderot implied in the discussion of their work in the *Interprétation*. A second problem then arises. Casting the world as total materialism in the reactive form that Helvétius and Maupertuis chose effectively, if not consciously, maintains the mind-body distinction, with the mind side of the world *along with all of its attributes, like decision and creation*, merely eliminated. The passivity of the mechanistic construal of materialism is not a necessary logical consequence of having chosen a materialist viewpoint, however. Although determinism is typically assumed to be the inevitable consequence of adopting an uncompromising materialism, it depends instead on an unperceived conceptual incompleteness in the *reactive* form of mate-

14. See, for example, Varloot's difficulties in his introduction to the *Rêve*; James Creech's Derridean attempt to sidestep it in his *Diderot: Thresholds of Representation* (Columbus: Ohio State University Press, 1986), esp. chap. 10; and Jack Undank's *Inside, Outside and In-Between* (Madison, Wis.: Coda Press, 1979).

rialism: a mind-body distinction is first established, and then mind is discarded. The opposition of action to reaction is only compatible with and a logical consequence of the separation of mind and body, not of the choice of a materialist or idealist viewpoint.

If one wants to decide whether Diderot is a determinist or not, either one has to accept reading him from a viewpoint conceptually determined by a mind-body distinction or, because Diderot refused this distinction, one has to situate the definition of *determinism* in the very different conceptual field that results from his refusal. Diderot himself did indeed use the term, but like so many of his other terms—*matter, motion, thought, structure,* or *organization*—it has to be redefined within his conceptual system. Perhaps the answer is that, denying the mind-body distinction, Diderot quite coherently denied that action and reaction are qualitatively distinct. No action is either entirely predetermined in a mechanical Laplacian sense or entirely innovative and undetermined. Activeness is a function of how much sensibility is either inert or mobilized in any event. Therefore one's assessment of any event as being reactive or active is always a quantitative judgment—there is a point beyond which one can effectively speak of an event as a reaction, or beyond which one can effectively speak of it as an action, just as there is a point beyond which one might as well speak of the uncomplex as inanimate or of the complex as living.

Still, as with the opposition of substance to organization, these are ways of speaking that use old terms defined from within an outmoded conceptual scheme. Diderot did not discard the old terms, as they remained perfectly useful as long as they could be adjusted to take their new conceptual context into account. For him, though, the way to redefine a word was not to specify new fixed meanings. That would be to fall into modes of thought still dominated by the static-law system he was trying to escape: why should definitions of terms be any more stable than the world the terms describe? The text argues that the process of redefinition must itself function in accordance with this world picture. An effective process of redefinition can come about only through the reader's direct experience of using these terms, of seeking coherence for them himself as he observes the operation of phenomena they are used to characterize.[15] With the

15. This is one cause of the opacity of Diderot's later texts even for readers who were his contemporaries. To really understand them required the consistent use of different definitions for nominally familiar terms, an unrealistic expectation especially given that many

user and not with Diderot must lie the judgment as to how long one can effectively act as though a definition were fixed; in other words, the user must decide how *provisionally fixed* (this is the definition of *stable*) any particular definition can be considered. His study of the nature of meanings should allow him to understand not only particular meanings but also the nature of meaning in such a world.

> Qui sait les races d'animaux qui nous ont précédés? qui sait les races d'animaux qui succéderont aux nôtres? Tout change, tout passe, il n'y a que le tout qui reste. Le monde commence et finit sans cesse; il est à chaque instant à son commencement et à sa fin; il n'en a jamais eu d'autre et n'en aura jamais d'autre. (128)

> Who knows the races of animals that preceded us? Who knows the races of animals that will succeed ours? Everything changes. Everything passes away. Only the whole remains. The world begins and ends ceaselessly. At every moment it is at its beginning and its end. There has never been another and there never will be another.

Even the notions of singular beginning and end are shown to derive from the definitions of cause and effect relevant only to the conceptual field ruled by the mind-body distinction. All such judgments can be only local, dependent on the viewpoint of the particular sensible organism interacting with the material world at that place and moment.

Diderot's Dream

As was clearly demonstrated in the *Interprétation*, a standard treatise format would not be appropriate for transmitting to a philosophically alert reader the multifaceted experience that Diderot wanted him to have. A text that merely expounded would be worse than useless in transmitting the above vision of the functioning of the material world, because its structure would rely on a logic reproducing the mind-body version of cause-and-effect structure that he was trying to eliminate. The text must induce in the reader the active-and-

---

texts, such as the *Rêve*, followed their semantic keys—in this case the *Interprétation*—by decades.

reactive state whose experience would be the most informative tactic Diderot could summon.

Therefore, although the *Rêve* explicitly presents the natural philosophical stakes of Diderot's *prises de position* concerning motion, a god, and the domain of the living, a summary of these positions (such as I have just tried to provide) can be expected to be misleading. The text in its operation continues the theorizing that begins *in medias res* and stops inconclusively with Dr. Bordeu's departure. The insights that an astute reader might have derived for himself without any help are in fact already furnished by the author, not in the explicit argument but in the way the text is put together and the way the characters interact. This formal overlay on the explicit argument points directly to Diderot's view that the kind of vibration that produces harmonic response, that induces dynamic organization out of resonance and therefore produces *sensibilité,* has orders or levels. If a form of vibration passes through a nonorganized group of objects (each already embedded in its own shape-producing flux), it can produce a secondary level of organization in the group. As a result, the group will become a new compound object. *Le Rêve de d'Alembert,* to present the phenomenon of the transmission of organization through vibration, explicitly discusses primary organization—everything that we have discussed so far—but it relies on demonstration to portray secondary levels of organization. Rereading the entire *Rêve* from this point of view discloses how the literary format stages an experiment in which the characters perform an unwitting demonstration and elaboration of the ideas they are discussing. As a result, to see the full scope of Diderot's vision we must turn to the literary construction of the *Rêve.*

The first dialogue, the "Entretien entre Diderot et d'Alembert," starts with two speaking voices engaged in what seems to be a discussion, a pure debate, between two disembodied minds. Near the end, however, the "d'Alembert" voice reveals indirectly that it belongs to a material body: the discussion has tired him out, and he wants to go home. The "Diderot" voice answers him, "Vous rêverez sur votre oreiller à cet entretien; et s'il n'y prend pas de la consistance, tant pis pour vous; car vous serez forcé d'embrasser des hypothèses bien autrement ridicules." D'Alembert ripostes: "Vous vous trompez. Sceptique, je me serai couché; sceptique je me lèverai" (111; "You will dream on your pillow of this conversation, and if it doesn't then take on consistency, it's too bad for you, for you will be forced to adopt hypotheses just as ridiculous in their own ways." "You are mistaken. A skeptic I will go to bed and a skeptic I will get up").

Of course Diderot is right, and d'Alembert does not understand the real implication of Diderot's words. He does not really rely on logical argument to convince d'Alembert; he works on d'Alembert's mind indirectly, using the physical state of dreaming.

What does it mean to dream? Dreaming is, for Diderot, a state of increased sensibility, wherein the conscious identity or individuality of the person is also weakened or even suspended.

MLLE. DE L'ESPINASSE Eh bien, le sommeil?

BORDEU Est un état de l'animal où il n'y a plus d'ensemble; tout concert, toute subordination cesse. Le maître est abandonné à la discrétion de ses vassaux, et à l'énergie effrénée de sa propre activité. ... Dans la veille, le réseau obéit aux impressions de l'objet extérieur. Dans le sommeil, c'est de l'exercice de sa propre sensibilité qu'émane tout ce qui se passe en lui. Il n'y a point de distraction dans le rêve. De là sa vivacité. C'est presque toujours la suite d'un éréthisme, un accès passager de maladie. (182–83)

MLLE. DE L'ESPINASSE All right, and sleep?

BORDEU Is a state of the animal in which there is no more ensemble; all concerted action, all subordination ceases. The master is abandoned to the discretion of his vassals and to the frenetic energy of his own activity. ... In a waking state, the network responds to impressions coming from exterior objects. In sleep, it is from the exercise of its own sensibility that everything going on within itself emanates. There is no distraction in the dream state. Whence its vivacity. It is almost always the result of a state of nervous excitation or a passing attack of disease.

This dream state in which d'Alembert spends the greatest part of the central dialogue is a physical condition of the living body brought about by the "passing attack" of the words of Diderot. They institute in d'Alembert a disorganized mental state that is so closely related to disease that Mlle. de l'Espinasse calls for the doctor. Although discourse provokes the "diseased" physical state in d'Alembert and not the contrary, this disease is just as infectious as any virus.

What was Diderot the author doing here? The Diderot and d'Alembert characters in the "Entretien" function as two living molecules put into contact by their discussion. They stay contiguous, but they do not either intellectually melt into or harmonize with each other. Then d'Alembert enters into a dream state that allows Diderot's ideas to penetrate his mind. Diderot reminds his friend in the last lines of their "Entretien" that "pulvis es, et in pulverem reverteris" (13; "you are dust and will return to dust"). The irony of the allusion is that the reference is not to the biblical meaningless dust of the dead but to the dust of Falconet's statue whose being ground into dust is merely the preliminary requisite to its being incorporated into a much greater and more powerfully thinking being. D'Alembert's monologue is actually a dialogue with a dreamed Diderot, with the contaminating dust of Diderot's thoughts; the text that Mlle. de l'Espinasse reads to Dr. Bordeu is a continuation of the first discussion. Sometimes it is almost impossible to distinguish between the words of the dreaming d'Alembert and those of the dreamed Diderot; sometimes the voices are so mixed together that they produce the effect of an aggregate voice. "MLLE. DE L'ESPINASSE: Il a continué...Eh bien, Philosophe, vous concevez donc des polypes de toute espèce, même des polypes humains?...Mais la nature ne nous en offre point" (124; "MLLE. DE L'ESPINASSE: He continued...All right, Philosopher, you conceive then of polyps of all sorts, even human polyps?...But nature shows us none"). Bordeu proceeds to give two or three rare examples of human polyps—such as Siamese twins—to prove that his research shows d'Alembert to be wrong, even if such examples seem to be out of the ordinary or even monstrous. The finesse of Diderot the author, on the other hand, is to present d'Alembert's own dream as being itself already a polyp and to show that the de l'Espinasse-Bordeu conversation provoked by the reading of the dream text produces a similar phenomenon, a very common one, not at all extraordinary or monstrous.

Mlle. de l'Espinasse wrote down everything that d'Alembert said, thinking that his mad speech would reveal his physical state to the doctor and allow Bordeu to "cure" his patient. The major section of the text is called the "Dream" proper, but its focus is the conversation between Bordeu and Mlle. de l'Espinasse, with the sometimes sleeping d'Alembert and the dreamed Diderot as background participants. The conversation between Dr. Bordeu and Mlle. de l'Espinasse demonstrates the growing organization of their two minds into one. Bordeu "completes" d'Alembert's fragmented mumblings; in this way, he without realizing it is aligning himself too with Diderot's original ideas and d'Alembert's elaborations upon them. As Mlle. de l'Espinasse says, "Je puis donc assurer à présent à toute la terre qu'il n'y a aucune différence entre un médecin qui veille et un philosophe qui rêve" (122; "I can now assure the whole earth that there is no difference between a doctor who is awake and a philosopher who dreams"). By chatting with Mlle. de l'Espinasse he draws her in too. He focuses as well on her thoughts. Each point in the discussion changes the structure of the knowledge that each character had previously had and brings their minds into congruence, to function for a moment, at the center of the work, as one single supermind that can think thoughts that each alone perhaps would not have been able to produce. Implicitly, therefore, Diderot demonstrated that sensibilities have been brought into synchrony, have been "compounded" and that this produces and is produced by a conversation—by "une action, une réaction habituelles...et cette action et cette réaction avec un caractère particulier... tout concourt donc à produire une sorte d'unité qui n'existe que dans l'animal" (119; "a habitual action and reaction...and this action and this reaction have a particular characteristic...everything comes together therefore to produce a sort of unity that exists only in the animal"). Our interlocutors, like the bee swarm image in the conversation between Diderot and d'Alembert, have not lost their own identities, but they have managed to construct a larger identity that includes them all—all four of them.

Bordeu and de l'Espinasse, however, are not aware of this aspect of their conversation, for they are paying attention to something quite different. Diderot did not mean his vibration model to be only a metaphor. What takes place on the plane of the mental can occur simultaneously in the material world. The exemplary event for understanding the theoretical necessity of the transition from the world of argument to the world of literary expression occurs close to the beginning of the dream transcription sequence. The passage is worth quoting in its entirety:

> Le vase où [Needham] apercevait tant de générations momentanées, [Diderot] le comparait à l'univers; il voyait dans une goutte d'eau l'histoire du monde. Cette idée lui paraissait grande, il la trouvait tout à fait conforme à la bonne philosophie qui étudie les grands corps dans les petits. Il disait, dans la goutte d'eau de Needham tout s'exécute et se passe en un clin d'oeil. Dans le monde le même phénomène dure un peu davantage; mais qu'est-ce que notre durée

en comparaison de l'éternité des temps? moins que la goutte que j'ai prise avec la pointe d'une aiguille en comparaison de l'espace illimité qui m'environne. Suite indéfinie d'animalcules dans l'atome qui fermente, même suite indéfinie d'animalcules dans l'autre atome qu'on appelle la Terre. Qui sait les races d'animaux qui nous ont précédés? qui sait les races d'animaux qui succéderont aux nôtres? Tout change, tout passe, il n'y a que le tout qui reste. Le monde commence et finit sans cesse; il est à chaque instant à son commencement et à sa fin; il n'en a jamais eu d'autre et n'en aura jamais d'autre. Dans cet immense océan de matière, pas une molécule qui ressemble à une molécule, pas une molécule qui se ressemble à elle-même un instant: *Rerum novus nascitur ordo*, voilà son inscription éternelle. (128)

The vase in which [Needham] saw so many momentary generations, [Diderot] compared to the universe; he saw the history of the world in a drop of water. This idea seemed grand to him; he found it completely in keeping with the good philosophy that studies large bodies in small ones. He said, in Needham's drop of water everything is carried out and happens in the wink of an eye. In the world the same phenomenon takes a little longer; but what is our duration in comparison to the eternity of time? less than the drop that I picked up with the point of a needle compared to the unlimited space that surrounds me. Indefinite series of animalcules within the fermenting atom, same indefinite series of animalcules in the other atom that we call the Earth. Who knows the races of animals that preceded us? who knows the races of animals that will succeed ours? Everything changes. Everything passes away. Only the whole remains. The world begins and ends ceaselessly. At every moment it is at its beginning and its end. There has never been another and there never will be another. In this immense ocean of matter, not one molecule resembles another molecule, not one molecule resembles itself for an instant: *A new order of things is born*—such is its eternal inscription.

D'Alembert has just given the most lyrical if not the most coherent presentation of the unified self-transforming universe, a presentation that will resonate in his mind with the idea of sexual union, for a very specific reason. The *poussière* of Diderot's argument, to use Diderot's own metaphor, is in the first part of this passage finally being "combined" and fermented (like the statue) with d'Alembert's perception: it is as if d'Alembert sees through Diderot's eyes, as if he is finally induced by the touch of Diderot's resonant imaging to enter into a form of intellectual coupling with the Diderot mind. The voice is a compound voice which, as soon as the coupling occurs, shifts from a straightforward description to a lyrical, literally an impassioned, apostrophe. This lyricism expresses an expanded intellectual vision possible only to the larger mind formed out of the two more limited philosophers' minds; it is the voice of a sort of intellectual ecstasy,[16] which then degenerates back into the sighing of the once again separate dreamed Diderot.

> Puis il ajoutait en soupirant: O vanité de nos pensées! ô pauvreté de la gloire et de nos travaux! ô misère, ô petitesse de nos vues! Il n'y a rien de solide, que de boire, manger, vivre, aimer et dormir. (128)

> Then he added, sighing: Oh, the vanity of our thoughts! oh, the poverty of glory and our labors! oh, the misery and the pettiness of our opinions! There is nothing solid, except to drink, eat, live, love, and sleep.

The extraordinary but predictable result is that the mind-event of course also occurs on the physical level.

> Mademoiselle de l'Espinasse! où êtes-vous? —Me voilà. —Alors son visage s'est coloré. J'ai voulu lui tâter le pouls; mais je ne sais où il avait caché sa main. Il paraissait éprouver une convulsion. Sa bouche s'était entr'ouverte. Son haleine était pressée. Il a poussé un profond soupir; et puis un soupir plus faible et plus profond encore. Il a retourné sa tête sur son oreiller et s'est endormi. (128)

> Mademoiselle de l'Espinasse! Where are you? —Here I am. —Then his face flushed. I tried to take his pulse; but I don't know where he had hidden his hand. He seemed to have a convulsion. His mouth was open. His breathing was hurried. He sighed deeply and then more weakly but deeper still. He turned his head on his pillow and fell asleep.

The intellectual coupling causes a sympathetic material resonance in d'Alembert; his sleeping mind makes the straightforward parallel

---

16. The same language, even more forcefully making the link between sexual and intellectual ecstasy, reappears in Dorval's absorption scene in the *Entretiens sur le fils naturel,* which I will discuss in chapter 3, and in the musical-physical interchanges between Suzanne Simonin and the lesbian Mother Superior in *La Religieuse.*

that Mlle. de l'Espinasse is to his body what Diderot was to his mind, and he reaches out for (an obviously equally dreamt) Mlle. de l'Espinasse, producing through masturbation the equivalent ecstatic experience. On the other hand, Mlle. de l'Espinasse has not understood what happened, but her detailed description of the event is sufficient for Dr. Bordeu to understand, and also to understand that she has herself been physically seduced by the vision of d'Alembert's orgasm (perhaps the intellectual as well as the physiological one) without her having to understand what it was that she was witnessing. "Je le regardais avec attention, et j'étais toute émue sans savoir pourquoi. Le coeur me battait, et ce n'était pas de peur" (128–29; "I looked at him with attention, and I was very moved without knowing why. My heart was beating, and it wasn't from fear"). In other words, a physical resonance in Mlle. de l'Espinasse is provoked by her physical presence focused on and by her receptivity to the vision of d'Alembert because she is worried about him. Her sensibility allows a material communication of "vibrations" that put her sexually in harmony with d'Alembert but bypass her cognitive participation in the event. Her body understands both events, even though her mind as yet understands neither.

As a result of Mlle. de l'Espinasse's unwitting recital of the effect of d'Alembert's masturbation on her emotional and physical state, Bordeu is drawn into the growing complex of reactive bodies; he reacts to her physically as well as intellectually. With the melding of the two minds goes an analogous attraction of the two bodies that nearly but not quite results in Dr. Bordeu's seduction by Mlle. de l'Espinasse.

MLLE. DE L'ESPINASSE Qui est-ce qui leur a dit que [la] nature ne pourrait former un faisceau avec un brin singulier, qui donnerait naissance à un organe qui nous est inconnu?

BORDEU Ou avec les deux brins qui caractérisent les deux sexes? Vous avez raison. Il y a plaisir à causer avec vous. Vous ne saisissez pas seulement ce qu'on vous dit, vous en tirez encore des conséquences d'une justesse qui m'étonne.

MLLE. DE L'ESPINASSE Docteur, vous m'encouragez.

BORDEU Non, ma foi; je vous dis ce que je pense.

MLLE. DE L'ESPINASSE Je vois bien l'emploi de quelques-uns des brins du faisceau; mais les autres que deviennent-ils?

BORDEU Et vous croyez qu'une autre que vous aurait songé à cette question?

MLLE. DE L'ESPINASSE Certainement.

BORDEU Vous n'êtes pas vaine. . . . (146)

BORDEU C'est cela. Venez que je vous embrasse.

MLLE. DE L'ESPINASSE Très volontiers.

D'ALEMBERT Docteur, vous embrassez Mademoiselle. C'est fort bien fait à vous.

BORDEU [They are discussing the hypothetical development of the embryo that would become Mlle. de l'Espinasse] Vous voyez . . . qu'il est à propos de vous dépouiller de votre organisation actuelle, et de revenir à un instant où vous n'étiez qu'une substance molle, filamenteuse,—informe, vermiculaire, plus analogue au bulbe et à la racine d'une plante qu'à un animal.

MLLE. DE L'ESPINASSE Si c'était l'usage d'aller toute nue dans les rues, je ne serais ni la première ni la dernière à m'y conformer. Ainsi faites de moi tout ce qu'il vous plaira, pourvu que je m'instruise. (148)

MLLE. DE L'ESPINASSE Who told them that nature couldn't make a network with a special thread that would give rise to an organ unknown to us?

BORDEU Or using the two threads that characterize the two sexes? You are right. It is pleasurable to talk with you. You not only grasp what you've been told, but you draw conclusions of an accuracy that astonishes me.

MLLE. DE L'ESPINASSE Doctor, you're leading me on.

BORDEU No, in faith; I'm telling you what I think.

MLLE. DE L'ESPINASSE I can see the function of some of the threads of the network; but what happens to the others?

BORDEU And you think that someone other than you would have thought of this question?

MLLE. DE L'ESPINASSE Certainly.

BORDEU You aren't vain.

BORDEU That's right. Come here and let me kiss you.

MLLE. DE L'ESPINASSE Very willingly.

D'ALEMBERT Doctor, you're kissing Mademoiselle. You're doing yourself proud.

BORDEU [They are discussing the hypothetical development of the embryo that would become Mlle. de l'Espinasse] You see . . . that it is useful to strip you of your present organization and go back to the moment when you were just a soft, stringy substance—shapeless, wormlike, more analogous to a bulb or the root of a plant than to an animal.

MLLE. DE L'ESPINASSE If it was customary to go naked in the streets, I would be neither the first nor the last to conform. Therefore do with me what you please as long as I learn.

What is a double entendre, after all, if not a specific form of harmony or resonance, that is established by one meaning but calls up another analogically? Especially a harmony between sexual and intellectual activity? The more their ideas converge, the closer Bordeu moves to Mlle. de l'Espinasse; he begins to align his argument with hers, to intersperse her words with his. Finally he goes so far as to mix his ideas with hers, to take her hands, then to embrace her and kiss her. He leaves at the end of the "Dream" to tend a patient but returns hastily to lunch with Mlle. de l'Espinasse, and their conversation gives us the "Suite de l'Entretien."

In rhetorical terms, the "Suite" is not a *suite de l'entretien*, since Diderot and d'Alembert are both absent, and two entirely different people are engaged in conversation. But if it is read in terms of the transmission of physical and philosophical resonances—of the fermentation[17] of the combination of Diderot's philosophical dust through d'Alembert with Bordeu and Mlle. de l'Espinasse—the "Suite" constitutes a follow up in the sense of a consequence of the ideas with which Diderot had jolted d'Alembert.

17. Fermentation implied at the time that an inanimate substance became, under the influence of heat, organized and then animate, so the word is neither here nor in the statue argument a metaphor.

The physical interaction between Bordeu and Mlle. de l'Espinasse continues to intensify until the moment when Bordeu finally realizes that the subject they are discussing (the sexual creation of mixed-category beings—in other words, monsters, satyrs, who will themselves "create" sex) is both a continuation of their earlier discussion and an indirect mode of seduction. He takes this long to see that the subject they had been discussing is manifesting itself in their own behavior. When he does, he leaves precipitately.

Because for Diderot mind and body were not distinct, the events in each domain are continuous with the course of events in the other. Ideas are physical vibrations; thought is indeed material. Bordeu sees at last the sexual seduction aimed at him, but was never aware of the somewhat monstrous coupling that created the polyp mind of the end of the second section. He certainly participated in and enjoyed the semisexual interaction with Mlle. de l'Espinasse, but was he really aware of it? He emphasizes several times that the *pureté de ses moeurs* allows him to discuss sexual subjects with Mlle. de l'Espinasse without moral risk (in other words without proceeding to physical action). He sees this as resulting from his ability to be "all mind"— only a diagnosing doctor who sees the phenomenon and analyzes it but is not affected by it. In other words, he trusts his training to keep the physical and the intellectual interactions from weaving together. Yet Diderot's choice of Bordeu is more subtle than has been generally acknowledged. He is, indeed, the famous doctor whose description of himself in Diderot's text is an evocation of the cold, controlled sensibility of the *Paradoxe sur le comédien*. However, he was also the author of the extraordinary article "Crise" in the *Encyclopédie*, which has the genial doctor, the superior diagnostician, work his wonders through the profound communication he establishes by feeling with his fingers (by his ability to *subodorer*) the entire coordination of the patient's body through the vibration of his pulse. Bordeu's use of the pulse is a mechanism of profound sensibility, however controlled, that works by touch, by contact, not by maintaining distance. In the *Rêve*, Bordeu, in spite of his vision of himself, is at least as responsive to Mlle. de l'Espinasse as she is to him. He simply does not realize it, because he knows to beware of invasion on the physical level, but he has been seduced by the growing acuity of her responses to him on the intellectual level. Ironically, it is on the intellectual level, where he diagnoses, that he has so superbly trained himself to be sensitive.

Mlle. de l'Espinasse, who defines herself late in the second part as a creature of all sensibility, all physical response and no intellectual control, is drawn by her physical response to d'Alembert into a physical response to Bordeu, which guides her into an intellectual performance clearly outdistancing Bordeu's expectations.

This weaving together of material communication with verbal (mental) communication allows us to understand the full weight of the choice of rhetorical format for the *Rêve*. What is literature and what is the action of writing literature in a world in which even thoughts are material? What does this literature look like? It looks like *Le Rêve de d'Alembert*. We find the analogical, interrupted, and changing discussion that is the explicit content of this work. "Nous ne composons pas, nous causons" (171; "We are not discoursing; we're chatting"), says Mlle. de l'Espinasse to Dr. Bordeu when he complains about the lack of logic in the conversation. We find above all the experiment on d'Alembert that is activated by Diderot at the end of the "Entretien" and whose results we, the readers, have observed, seemingly from the outside. We can now define this experiment as a nonscientific experiment, if by "scientific" we mean to indicate a procedure that attempts to reveal stable or noncontingent truths. We are involved with a poetic experiment, but what we call poetic is explicitly defined in this text in materialist terms.

MLLE. DE L'ESPINASSE Que pensez-vous du mélange des espèces?

BORDEU Votre question est de physique, de morale et de poétique.

MLLE. DE L'ESPINASSE De poétique!

BORDEU Sans doute; l'art de créer des êtres qui ne sont pas, à l'imitation de ceux qui sont, est de la vraie poésie. (196–97)

MLLE. DE L'ESPINASSE What do you think of the mixing of species?

BORDEU Your question concerns physics, morals and poetics.

MLLE. DE L'ESPINASSE Poetics!

BORDEU Without a doubt; the art of creating beings that are not in imitation of those that are, is true poetry.

This materialist definition of poetics in conjunction with the extended definition of matter as dynamic allows us to understand the full importance of conversation for Diderot. Conversation is a transmission of many forms of vibration, mental, emotional, physical; its function is to promote the materializing of social groups that produce further organization—whether that organization then takes the form of speculative knowledge, as in the conversations in the *Rêve*, political action, as it might in the *Encyclopédie*, or new human beings, as could have been the case in the "Suite de l'Entretien."

Notice that in this example an unorganized set of people has, through their conversation, become partially organized. But the conversation, once Diderot allows d'Alembert to leave him, has no consistent guiding principle. Unpredictable interjections by d'Alembert disrupt the conversation between Bordeu and Mlle. de l'Espinasse and tear apart the tenuous stability of the supermind. They are able to fend him off for a while, but eventually the object breaks down into its component pieces. The dynamic can both construct and dissolve organization. For the event to maintain the organization that produced the Bordeu–l'Espinasse couple, something else was needed.

MLLE. DE L'ESPINASSE Dans la grappe d'abeilles, il n'y en aurait pas une qui eût le temps de prendre l'esprit du corps.

D'ALEMBERT Qu'est-ce que vous dites là?

MLLE. DE L'ESPINASSE Je dis que l'esprit monastique se conserve, parce que le monastère se refait peu à peu, et quand il entre un moine nouveau, il en trouve une centaine de vieux qui l'entraînent à penser et à sentir comme eux. Une abeille s'en va; il en succède dans la grappe une autre qui se met bientôt au courant. (165)

MLLE. DE L'ESPINASSE In the swarm of bees there isn't one bee that would have time to take on the mind of the body.

D'ALEMBERT What are you saying there?

MLLE. DE L'ESPINASSE I am saying that the monastic spirit maintains itself because the monastery reconstitutes itself little by little, and when a new monk enters he finds a hundred old ones who lead him to think and feel as they do. One bee leaves, it is followed in the swarm by another who quickly catches on.

Diderot's materialism incorporated an idea of a natural good, and that idea is quite simple: it is what increases or produces balanced organization against the chance occurrence of chaos. As Bordeu so clinically states, ethical categories can only be transient, because like natural laws, they too have to change to accommodate the physical changes in the world, to suit the new organization and dynamism it embodies at any moment. Today's virtue may be tomorrow's vice (as we shall see in the *Supplément au voyage de Bougainville*); even more striking, today's vice may be tomorrow's virtue (this is the upshot of the argument presented by *le Neveu de Rameau*). Mlle. de l'Espinasse's "esprit monastique," however, makes possible both the maintenance of continuous organization and a mechanism for accommodating change. Even then, one condition holds: some guiding consciousness must prevent the centrifugal ending of the *Rêve*. For the *Rêve's* polyp mind was only the aggregation of a swarm; it attained functionality, but not consciousness of itself as a thinking being—it formed no memory. The web needs a spider in the center integrating the whole into a single experience. The *vieux* in the monastery turn the swarm of monks into a sort of consciousness—into an "animal." Unlike Mlle. de l'Espinasse's hypothetical and sad little universe-god, the irritable and doomed universal polyp, this model—monastery, academy of sciences, *Encyclopédie*—is not merely a single living and thus necessarily mortal consciousness. It is immortal because the holders of the memory are not only multiple but successive: the *vieux* exist in a series, training their replacements, their nephews, before they themselves wear out. As with any Diderotian event-object, the monastery is a coordination (again, not a fixed organization) persisting within a flow of material, the flow here consisting of people.

Although it is not at first glance obvious, the *vieux* function does exist in the *Rêve*, in a double incarnation. First, it is the Diderot voice, the overseer who initiates but does not determine the results of the discussions. Second, and more important for our purposes, the reader himself, by moving back and forth between the subject matter in the conversations and the testing of these ideas in the interplay of the characters, is himself drawn into the speculation. Because he can both hear and judge the conversations, he is able to formulate the conclusions that the characters themselves fail to arrive at. Diderot the author programmed his reader's insertion into the text; the *vieux* is initiating a *nouveau* into the swarm.

Can we then make an analogy between the kind of poetic experiment proper to a literary work and a recognizable scientific practice by positing that the literary equivalent of a single closed experimental system might be a single text thought of as a closed world? As a literary equivalent of a "black box"? Clearly we cannot. Such a model, like deterministic materialism, depends on the action-reaction dichotomy: the researcher acts on a reactive object, but this reader is not outside the text, judging. He is himself reacting and being acted upon. We read not only to *know*, but also to *feel*; we learn that feeling is one kind of knowing, one way to rearrange our thoughts, to transform ourselves, to understand the process of transformation. We, as much as the characters in the text, are a part of the demonstration. It does not end with the last page, with Bordeu's hasty and cynical rejection of a sexual attachment to Mlle. de l'Espinasse. As she says, "je n'écoute que pour le plaisir de redire" (206; "I only listen for the pleasure of retelling"), but the continuation will be carried out not by her, not by Bordeu, but by the *Rêve's* readers.

The *Encyclopédie* was Diderot's most ambitous extrapolation of this model. In this spirit, the *Encyclopédie* was not d'Alembert's but Diderot's dream. The mechanism of reading outlined in the *Rêve*, its relationship to the material functioning of the world outlined both here and in the *Interprétation de la nature*, and the appropriate ways to describe this world and the natural philosopher's interactions with it were the crucial issues for Diderot in defining the encyclopedic project and its cultural meaning. It was to instantiate the memory of a people, performing the function that memory serves in an organism. Diderot intended it to promote natural organization, to control and encourage the expansion and the guidance of the swarm of philosophers that made up the French Enlightenment. To this work we must now turn.

THREE

Savants and Philosophers

T he *Encyclopédie* contains several articles and treatises about the nature, justification, purposes, and possible consequences of its own project. In discussing encyclopedism from different and irreconcilable points of view, these articles enable the reader to sense the structure and purpose of the debates characteristic of the overall work. Moreover, they also give the reader a first view of Diderot working out the relationship of his natural philosophical epistemology, sketched here in the preceding two chapters, to the project to which he dedicated so many of his productive intellectual years.

One of these articles, Diderot's "Encyclopédie," can be considered to have been a dramatic redefinition of the whole *Encyclopédie* project right at the most intense and most inventive moment of the entire enterprise. His article was a reevaluation based on his experience of the actual operation of the project as well as a polemical response to the public's criticism of the published volumes. Its greatest interest, however, lies in its relationship to the other texts dealing with the project. It both reflects upon them and in some ways distinctively answers them all, especially as they are all permeated by the fear of "revolution," defined not simply as political disturbance but as catastrophe, as cultural or geographical interruption or rupture — in other words, as a historical analog of the shock to an organized physical system that I discussed in chapter 1. For each of the other texts, the *Encyclopédie*, in different ways, is proposed as the response that can accommodate the change resulting from such shock. Most important in this sense is the "conversation" that the article "Encyclopédie" engages with d'Alembert's "Discours préliminaire." Given Diderot's construal of intellectual community and exchange, we should not be surprised that his article feeds off the "Discours" for its substance. A reader of Diderot's article needs to be familiar with the "Discours" to be able to appreciate the subjects Diderot addressed and to follow the rhetorical performance that transformed the meaning of d'Alembert's arguments.

Of course, "Encyclopédie" formed more than just a complement to the "Discours." Diderot's idiosyncratic notions of change and historicity, so central to his theory, were in direct opposition to d'Alembert's notions. The "Encyclopédie" article not only answered but also satirized the "Discours." Hence, we must make a preliminary excursion through the "Discours" really to understand what Diderot did in his own encyclopedic texts.

The "Discours préliminaire" and the Crystalline Structure of Knowledge

In the "Discours préliminaire" (1751), D'Alembert claimed to structure his discussion of the *Encyclopédie, ou dictionnaire raisonné des sciences, des arts et des métiers* around the double attribution given in the title: the *Encyclopédie* is both *encyclopedia* and *dictionary*.

L'Ouvrage dont nous donnons aujourd'hui le premier volume, a deux objets: comme *Encyclopédie,* il doit exposer autant qu'il est possible, l'ordre & l'enchaînement des connoissances humaines: comme *Dictionnaire raisonné des sciences, des Arts & des Métiers,* il doit contenir sur chaque Science & sur chaque Art, soit libéral, soit méchanique, les principes généraux qui en sont la base, & les détails les plus essentiels, qui en font le corps & la substance.[1]

The work whose first volume we are today publishing has two goals: as *Encyclopedia,* it should reveal, as much as possible, the order and interrelations of human knowledge: as *complete Dictionary of the sciences, arts, and skills,* it should contain, for each science and each art, whether liberal or mechanical, the general principles that form its basis and the most essential details that make up its body and substance.

1. *Encyclopédie, ou Dictionnaire raisonné des sciences, des arts et des métiers, par une société de gens de lettres* 35 vols. (Paris/Lyon: Briasson, David l'aîné, Le Breton, Durand, 1751-67), 1:i. The "Discours préliminaire" will henceforth be referenced directly by page number. Other articles of the *Encyclopédie* are indicated by volume and page number, except those by Diderot, which come from DPV.

D'Alembert did indeed begin his text by elaborating this encyclopedic "enchaînement" of human knowledge in the first half, but
although he purported to describe the work as a dictionary in the second half, he instead recounted in some detail a strategically polemical
history of science focused principally on the major figures of European natural philosophy. Why did d'Alembert so baldly abandon his
stated schema?

The problem lay in the definition of knowledge that d'Alembert was
both attempting to describe succinctly for his reader and in which he
himself profoundly believed. He wove together the commonplaces of
philosophy current in Paris in the early 1750s; this theory of knowledge
was the one Diderot attacked in his own article. The most typical
embodiment of this view was probably best presented in Condillac's
writings, especially the *Logique*, but also in the *Art de raisonner* and the
Traité des systèmes; indeed, d'Alembert cites the *Traité* approvingly later
on in the "Discours." One of Condillac's stated principal aims was to
reconcile Descartes and Locke, to provide a synthesis of the Cartesian
"natural" methodical reasoning with the theory of "natural" sense
data–based thought. In so doing, Condillac thought he had conflated
the naturalness of intellectual procedures with the naturalness of the
material world.[2] The resulting doctrine promoted logical analysis as a
procedure that functions similarly in both the material and the mental
worlds: their structures mirror each other. This operational homology
suggests that the two supposedly separate domains of body and mind
are linked in an essential and accessible way. The existence of this link
does not imply that the mental and material domains are continuous,
though. A mind-body distinction is maintained. In fact, unless they are
distinct, the need for analysis to provide a bridge from one domain to
the other evaporates.

2. This is a highly schematic description of a monumental epistemological construction
that required many thinkers and many decades. For a more substantial discussion the reader
might want to consult, among many other possible works, the following three. The most
ambitious is Michel Foucault's *Les Mots et les choses* (Paris: Gallimard, 1966), all of pt. I. A rather
different description (not entirely in agreement with Foucault's), aimed at showing the specifically natural scientific consequences of these theories of knowledge and language, is in my
Between the Library and the Laboratory (Baltimore: Johns Hopkins Press, 1984). The third is
M. M. Slaughter, *Universal Languages and Scientific Taxonomy in the Seventeenth Century*
(Cambridge: Cambridge University Press, 1982). However, to show my reader the philosophical structure to which Diderot's work will respond, the simplistic version in the "Discours
préliminaire" will suffice.

How does this bridging analysis work? For Condillac, the world could be construed as a bewilderingly complex countryside where nonetheless some objects call to our eye more strongly than others because they establish the functioning of the secondary objects around them.[3] It is not clear whether the selection mechanism, this "calling to the eye," resides in the world or in the mind; the suggestion in Condillac's text is that the question makes no sense because it is a joint operation. What is clear is that it is a "natural" and hence inevitable, unwilled reaction on the part of the observing mind. Natural analysis sorts out first the principal objects and their relations to each other and then the relationships of the secondary objects to their principal objects. For this picture to hold, it is necessary to assume that the world consists of discrete objects and their interrelationships. The appropriate way to describe this world is to enumerate the objects and then specify the relations of each object to the others. This same mode of analysis can just as well be applied to the wide range of phenomena that exist in the mental domain. The result of performing this analysis on mental objects would produce a work like the *Art de raisonner*; combining the analysis of mental objects and material objects would produce the *Logique*, which, through its presentations of various acts of analysis, embodies the ultimate analytical exercise, the analytical description of analysis.

In Condillac's work *analysis* is thus a multifaceted term. It refers to three things: a *procedure*, which is abstracted from a *structure* posited for the material world, and a *structure* posited for the mental universe. Which of the three is being referred to is often unclear in the context where the term is used. This is often because the various authors who rely on this type of analysis strategically blur the differences so as to make their project logically unassailable.

As I mentioned at the beginning of chapter 1, the authority of the natural philosophical program was conditional on two things: its own logical coherence and its consequent capacity to undermine the divine warrant of theological discourse. The weak point in the Condillac-d'Alembert strain of Enlightenment discourse is both revealed and supposedly resolved by the transformation of God into an epistemological function. A whole series of consequences aimed

3. Etienne Bonnot, l'abbé de Condillac, *La Logique, ou les premiers développemens de l'art de penser* (Geneva, 1785), bk. 1, chap. 2.

at this resolution derives from this use of analysis as the mind-body bridge. The first is that the "fit" posited between natural world, natural mind, and natural procedure suggests that phenomenal descriptions that conform to this structure derive from their conformation a warrant for their truth value. This warrant, however, is only assumed, it cannot be proven, as Diderot understood, and as the beginnings of both the *Interprétation* and the *Rêve de d'Alembert* underline. Attempts to sustain it tend to rely on providential teleologies: for example, God must have constructed the homology to allow human beings to perceive and avoid most efficiently the things that injure them. This prompts a related question as to where the meaning of the mind-body analysis field originates. In the mind, as it seems to for Descartes? In the material world, as it seems to for Locke? In the abstracted procedure of analysis itself, as it seems to in a first reading of Condillac? In other words, which of the spheres making up the field of analysis determines the others? A second consequence of the introduction of a god function into the issue is that it makes possible the argument that the origin of the meaning of the analytic field lies nowhere within the analytic space. The three types of analysis coexist, have always coexisted and interdetermine each other's meanings. No priority can be established among them.

Although resorting to a divine being thus plugged a logical hole in the coherence of the epistemology, Condillac's and, by extension, d'Alembert's philosophy of knowledge were not particularly concerned with a theological god or his place in the intellectual universe. The analytical architecture I have just outlined served a different purpose, similar to one of the functions of the method presented in Descartes' *Discours de la méthode*. Those who speak analytically should thereby speak naturally, and thus with authority. The claim to naturalness and the analytic warrant therefore serve to establish a group of speakers whose utterances by definition dominate or control those of interlocutors who do not belong to the group. These speakers are easily recognized as being the *philosophes*, whose subscription to the analytical theory of knowledge and the resultant program for action characterized the knowledge-oriented strain of the French Enlightenment.

D'Alembert's "Discours" depended on this theory and corresponding authority more than it explicated them. He first recast the analytical structure using three different metaphors: the universe as

clockwork (vi), as labyrinth (vii), and as the map of the world (ix).
All three were commonplaces, but he quickly moved to focus on the
last two; unlike the clockwork metaphor, the labyrinth and the map
intrinsically require an internal user—someone experiencing their
structure directly—to determine their meaning. In other words, they
synthesize within their images both the analytical structure of the
world and the analytical procedure that the philosopher uses. Like
Condillac's detour through providence, they also avoid clarifying
whether the analytic structure is actually intrinsic to the material
world or whether it is a pattern imposed only by the philosopher's
act of viewing.[4]

D'Alembert raised an interesting problem concerning the relinking
of discretely perceived (analyzed) phenomena: what is the nature of
the resulting object? Is the synthetic complex so derived itself a
thing, and does it therefore deserve its own word to name it? The
answer is at first glance surprising, but it provides the light we need
to see d'Alembert's vision of the *Encyclopédie.*

> Les idées de tout, de partie, de plus grand & de plus petit, *ne sont-elles
> pas, à proprement parler, la même idée simple & individuelle*, puisqu'on
> ne sauroit avoir l'une sans que les autres se présentent toutes en même
> tems? ... Qu'on examine une suite de propositions de Géométrie
> déduites les unes des autres, en sorte que deux propositions voisines se
> touchent immédiatement & sans aucun intervalle, on s'appercevra
> qu'elles ne sont toutes que la première proposition qui *se défigure*, pour
> ainsi dire, successivement & peu à peu dans le passage d'une con-
> séquence à la suivante, mais qui pourtant n'a point été réellement multi-
> pliée par cet enchaînement, & *n'a fait que recevoir différentes formes.* ...
> On peut donc regarder l'enchaînement de plusieurs vérités géométri-
> ques, comme des traductions plus ou moins différentes & plus ou
> moins compliquées de la même proposition. (viii; my emphasis)

---

4. Hence the problem of relativism did not arise. For the neo-Kantian problematic (interestingly elaborated in Nelson Goodman's *Ways of Worldmaking* [Indianapolis, Ind.: Hackett, 1978], for example) to apply, it is necessary for the philosopher or scientist to pose the
question of the adequation of his form of description to the structure of the world. Only
then can he question whether he can ever have access to that world and ask what a term
such as *reality* or *objectivity* can mean. For the Enlightenment analytic construct, this question can be posed only by challenging the unjustifiable warrant furnished by the homology
of its three components. If the homology is read as coincidence rather than as the sign of
truth value, it can be recast as a construction rather than as the guarantor of a mode of
direct access to perceiving the material and mental worlds.

The ideas of "whole," of "part," of "greater" and "smaller," *are they not, properly speaking, the same simple and undivided idea,* since we can't have one without all the others showing up at the same time? . . . Examine a series of geometrical propositions deduced one from the others, such that two neighboring propositions touch each other immediately and without intervening space, and you will see that they are all only the first proposition, which *changes its shape,* so to speak, successively and little by little in the passage from one consequence to the next, but which nonetheless has not been multiplied by this linking together. . . . We can therefore consider the linking together of several geometrical truths as more or less different or more or less complicated translations of the same proposition.

D'Alembert's "translation" operation resembled that in Condillac's *Langue des calculs,* which attempted to reconcile the description of empirical phenomena with mathematical certitude. As with d'Alembert here, Condillac was dealing with a mathematical problem clearly defined as a one-dimensional linear logical process, the description of pure quantity. Although this seems far removed from the clearly nonlinear multiplicity of connections of a Condillacean analytic map or labyrinth of truth statements, d'Alembert's algebraic translation as described above can indeed be viewed as an analytic track that also produces a synthetic complex. The successive translations are in effect "secondary objects" whose successive experiencing will allow the analyst to ferret out the "primary object" that each only partially indicates or reveals. The fully revealed primary object then by contrast shows the incompleteness of its predecessors with respect to itself. It constitutes them as secondary objects clustered "around" it whose meanings are dependent on it. Only in this way can we follow d'Alembert's extrapolation back out from the desert world of algebraic translation to the infinite variety and complexity of the phenomenal world.

Il en est de même des vérités physiques & des propriétés des corps dont nous appercevons la liaison. Toutes ces propriétés bien rapprochées ne nous offrent, à proprement parler, qu'une connoissance simple et unique. . . . *L'Univers, pour qui sauroit l'embrasser d'un seul point de vûe, ne serait, s'il est permis de le dire, qu'un fait unique & une grande vérité.* (viii–ix; my emphasis)[5]

5. Notice how similar in feeling d'Alembert's description is to Diderot's in the *Interprétation* that "la nature n'a peut-être jamais produit qu'un seul acte" (35; "nature has produced

It is the same with physical truths and the properties of bodies when we see their links. All these neighboring properties offer us, strictly speaking, only one single, simple, and unique piece of knowledge. . . . *The universe, for the one who is able to encompass it all from a single point of view, would only be, if we can speak this way, a single unique fact and great truth.*

The picture he presented of the homogeneity of scientific truth reduces truths related to one another to restatements of the same truth. D'Alembert did not say that it is one complex truth; rather, he seems to have believed that one single ("simple") law might eventually be found to underlie the generation of all phenomenal events. In this his position was finally antithetical to Aristotelian essentialism, grounded as that was in the particularity of empirical observation. This divergence was all the more expectable in that d'Alembert's notion of truth was shaped by mathematical experience rather than by empirical observation.

In d'Alembert's hands, therefore, instead of giving the philosopher a complex and totalizing network for capturing the differences and diversity of material phenomena, the analytic procedure reduces the world to an interlocking set of fewer and fewer principal or primary objects. Analysis becomes the privileged term; it is part of the complex as well as the tool to reduce the complexity. Using it, the enormous complex that forms the single fact of universal knowledge can, ideally, be both constructed and intellectually digested.

One cannot claim that d'Alembert's description was entirely coherent. In part, this difficulty arises, we shall see, because he used deceptive detours made possible by his metaphors to try to reconcile the problem of assuring the reliability of the world with tools deriving from highly variable perception. The three images he chose, especially the labyrinth and the *mappemonde*, present variability of per-

---

only a single act"); the picture is again one of a unified nature. But the switching of a single term, *acte* for *fait*, operates the entire conceptual shift from the fixed Newtonian architecture to the stable resonating organism-event.

The similarity of the descriptions may perhaps be one of the reasons why Diderot's notion of the *Encyclopédie* is so often confused with the description d'Alembert presented in the "Discours préliminaire"—for example, in the first half of Foucault's *Les Mots et les choses* and chap. 9 of James Creech's *Diderot: Thresholds of Representation* (Columbus: Ohio State University Press, 1986). As we shall see in the second part of this chapter, the two were quite far apart.

ception as an illusion that arises from the fact that the person within the labyrinth, or the person following from point to point on the map, is unable during the experience to get above the labyrinth or the map and see it as one organized whole. D'Alembert designated the philosopher of the all-inclusive analytically constructed and organized encyclopedia as the person to try to attain the vision of this "unique great truth" (ix), and thus defined him and prescribed his actions (xv).

Perhaps the image of a crystal structure is more appropriate than any of his own images to the actual structure that d'Alembert was manipulating. In effect, the crystal model has one component that his three lack but the second half of the "Discours" clumsily suggests: *because* "la nature est toujours la même" (xx; "nature is always the same"), science generates its own progress. What each person can achieve is a step above what is already known: Newton could discover the universal laws of celestial mechanics only because he stood on the shoulders of his predecessors. Each great thinker is a complex of Russian boxes containing all of his genial predecessors' discoveries. The encyclopedia that attempts the enormous task of speaking all knowledge would be inevitably incomplete; this would not undermine its value as long as it had been correctly constructed to include and describe properly the knowledge that existed at any date. On the contrary: this encyclopedia would form the perfect seed-crystal both to provoke new scientific discoveries (made by extension from the already existing templates) and to determine their place in the overall structure of knowledge.

This brings us to the real theme of the second half of the "Discours," which is where d'Alembert claimed that he would oppose as complementary the definitions of the *Encyclopédie* as dictionary and as encyclopedia. The distinction as concerns a presentation of knowledge becomes simple, a dictionary being only an alphabetical ordering. As such, it facilitates the fragmentation of analysis of knowledge into components (like articles). Any written text must be physically linear, but the linearity of the dictionary is trivial; it carries no logical constraint like argument or consequence. Instead, the dictionary's structure is provided by cross-references. If the analysis has been done properly, however, even the cross-references may be redundant:

Il nous reste à montrer comment nous avons tâché de concilier dans ce Dictionnaire l'ordre encyclopédique avec l'ordre alphabétique. . . .

On a tâché que l'exactitude & la fréquence des renvois ne laissât là-
dessus rien à désirer; car les renvois dans ce Dictionnaire ont cela de
particulier, qu'ils servent principalement à indiquer la liaison des
matières; . . . Souvent même nous avons omis le renvoi, parce que les
termes d'Art ou de Science sur lesquels il auroit pû tomber, se trou-
vent expliqués à leur article, que le lecteur ira chercher de lui-même.
(xviii–xix)

It remains for us to show how we have attempted to reconcile encyclopedic order with the alphabetic order in this Dictionary. We have
tried to make it so that the exactness and frequency of the cross references leave nothing to be desired, for the cross references in this
Dictionary are special in that they serve principally to indicate the
links between subject matters. Often we have even omitted a cross
reference, because the terms of the Art or Science that they would
have indicated are explained in their own article, which the reader
will know to look for for himself.

In other words, the dictionary is only the physical structure that
will efface itself before the encyclopedic ordering virtual in the cross
references. Given the all-encompassing nature of the encyclopedic
structure, then, there is really not much to say about the dictionary
itself. In fact, d'Alembert basically made no practical distinction. He
stated elsewhere in the *Encyclopédie* that a classic word- or nomen-
clature-dictionary correctly constructed would form in effect an
encyclopedia with extremely brief, nonexpository articles.[6] His theory of knowledge thus made the definition of the dictionary into

---

6. See d'Alembert's article "Dictionnaire" (4:958b–70a):

On peut distinguer trois sortes de *dictionnaire*; *dictionnaires* de langue, *dictionnaires*
historiques, et *dictionnaires* de Sciences et d'Arts: division qu'on pourroit présenter
sous un point de vûe plus général, en cette sorte; *dictionnaires* de mots, *dictionnaires*
de faits, & *dictionnaires* de choses. . . . En effet, un *dictionnaire* de langues, qui paroît
n'être qu'un *dictionnaire* de mots, doit être souvent un *dictionnaire* de choses quand
il est bien fait: c'est alors un ouvrage très philosophique. *Voyez* GRAMMAIRE. (958b)

We can distinguish three sorts of *dictionary*; language *dictionaries*, historical *dictionar-*
ies, and *dictionaries* of the Sciences and the Arts: this division could be presented from
a more general point of view in the following way: word *dictionaries*, fact *dictionaries*,
and thing *dictionaries*. . . . In effect, a language *dictionary*, which seems to be merely
a word *dictionary*, should often be a thing *dictionary* when it is well constructed: then
it forms a very philosophical work. *See* GRAMMAR.

a nonissue; d'Alembert dispensed with the question before even beginning its discussion.

The "Discours" is actually divided not the way d'Alembert describes it, as complementary portrayals of dictionary versus encyclopedic structurings of the project, but into a first section on the structure of knowledge and a second on the actual subject matters and the men who invented them, the thinkers who attained—or made it possible for others to attain—the *coup d'oeil philosophique*.

The problem is to grapple with history. What is the relationship of history, the contingent evenemential, to the uncovering of the structure and content of knowledge? One of the classic consequences of the Enlightenment's analytic descriptions of the faculties of the mind is that the procedure that the mind should follow in perceiving its own operations is assumed to be the "natural analytic" way that each mind typically does in fact analyze itself. Moreover, the hierarchy of faculties so derived determines the hierarchy of the studies of these faculties. Theoretically, the disciplines ought to develop chronologically in the same order that the mind follows, and then the observed historical development of philosophy would coincide with the encyclopedic hierarchy. Both should be reflections of the natural structure of the world. However, neither of these predictions turns out to fit the observed phenomena. Does this mean that the doctrine of natural analysis is faulty? D'Alembert's answer was that the discrepancies primarily arose from the vagaries and accidents of history that disrupt the natural development of knowledge. Revolutions indiscriminately and thus arbitrarily destroy some parts of the crystalline architecture of acquired knowledge and therefore disrupt the overall organization that holds between the parts. For d'Alembert, the analytic structure provides not only a picture of relationships but also a necessary architecture of structural support. When the structure is disrupted, the crystal grows nonsymmetrically, aberrantly, or monstrously, because any particular domain no longer has the constraining effect of all of its naturally related intellectual domains to hold it to a correct expansion. D'Alembert held that the great modern European philosophers had to rectify the past problems as well as continue to build; they had to do their best to restructure the heart of the crystal as well as to force it to grow.[7]

7. The great men all provided examples of role models: Bacon, who in a sense designated and defined Nature; Descartes, whose inventive genius developed the method; New-

In this they were helped by the academies. D'Alembert defined the academies as physical structures that mimic that of the encyclopedic order of knowledge. They served to provoke and perpetuate knowledge in the spirit of Bacon. They formed a compound institutional and historical edifice made up of great modern European thinkers that mirrored the crystalline and accretive structures of knowledge: d'Alembert's *cité scientifique* thus could become transhistorical.

Curiously enough, these philosophers were as a result thought of by d'Alembert as being unengaged with respect to their human context. Even though d'Alembert began part I of the "Discours" in a typical Enlightenment fashion with a picture of the origins of knowledge as lying in physical and moral need, a modern reader would describe the payoff as utilitarian. The philosophers may have claimed, especially in Diderot's *Prospectus* to the *Encyclopédie* and in the rewritten version of it that followed d'Alembert's "Discours," to be utilitarian, but when d'Alembert actually specified the relationship of knowledge to determining future endeavor, the only acceptable utility turned out to be tautological. It is the development of a philosophical skepticism intended to allow philosophers to sort out facts worthy of being accumulated from those not. Their work is utilitarian to the degree that it propagates and enriches itself, not because it furnishes tools for the use of mankind outside the *cité scientifique*.

Earlier, d'Alembert had generated an intellectual community whose divisions reflected the Baconian divisions of the tree of knowledge into history, philosophy, and poetry. The three branches paralleled the three mental faculties of memory, reason, and imagination; therefore the three types of thinkers were the "Erudits, Philosophes, et Beaux-Esprits" (xviii; "men of erudition, philosophers, and innovative minds"). By way of Montesquieu, the historians were eventually to be assimilated into the philosophers. The ideal philosopher would in fact be the successful synthesis of the merely accumulative

---

ton and Huyghens, who, unlike Leibniz, tempered the creative genius of speculation with the spirit of observation; Voltaire and Buffon, who taught how to write and stylize so as to maximize the transmission of knowledge; Rameau, who naturalized music; and the critical figure of Montesquieu, who extended the natural method to politics, and who thereby potentially subjected historical event—the nemesis of the analysts—to scientific description and control. From this a new normative role for philosophy arises.

and not yet analytic erudite with the philosopher. This would yield the *savant*, the one who *knows*, and whose knowing is the prerequisite to allow him to extend knowledge. He is the prototype citizen of the *cité scientifique*, the man who will participate in the writing of the encyclopedia. The encyclopedia is the archive of the content of knowledge at any moment, and, more importantly, of the state of the natural analytic crystalline structure of knowledge. This archive should both further the *savants'* work and forestall the consequences that any possible future revolution could have in depleting or disorganizing the culture's stock of knowledge.

There is a crucial figure in his discussion that d'Alembert was unable to assimilate, however: the poet, the creative inventor, the genius. Several times this figure or his talent comes up in the text, but always as the exception, the unexplainable, as that which cannot be reduced to system or method. The genius is the *écart* and as such presents both the source of innovation and the danger of disorganization: he is the man of history, of event, and not of science. The genius is also the man of passion, of controlled and constructive passion. And again, this is something that separates him from the *savant*.

Ironically, it is the genius that raised for d'Alembert the problem of the place of language within an analytic complex. For how does one transmit knowledge the most effectively, the most eloquently and persuasively? For Condillac each properly analytic perception was to have its own word to name it, and syntax, for example, should signify to the reader the link existing between perceptions named. (Condillac therefore privileged scientific taxonomies and nomenclatures and promulgated the doctrine that "une science est une langue bien faite" ["a science is a well-made language"].)[8] D'Alembert extended the discussion from virtual language to language in action. Rules for argument can be learned and can yield the dispassionate analytic discourse that characterizes remarkably well d'Alembert's own text. He called these rules grammar rather than rhetoric. His grammar reproduced the analytic logic within actual language performances; its persuasiveness comes from the analytic guarantee of the knowledge transmitted, whereas in his construal rhetoric was an accumulation of tricks with no analytic foundation. In other words, he derived a natural rhetoric and called it grammar.

8. Condillac, *Logique*, 106.

But what about eloquence? If rhetoric has been dismantled, can eloquence somehow be subsumed to this grammar?

> Les hommes en se communiquant leurs idées, cherchent aussi à se communiquer leurs passions. C'est par l'éloquence qu'ils y parviennent. Faite pour parler au sentiment, comme la Logique & la Grammaire parlent à l'esprit, elle impose silence à la raison même; & les prodiges qu'elle opère souvent entre les mains d'un seul sur toute une Nation, sont peut-être le témoignage le plus éclatant de la supériorité d'un homme sur un autre. Ce qu'il y a de singulier, c'est qu'on ait cru suppléer par des règles à un talent si rare. C'est à peu près comme si on eût voulu réduire le génie en préceptes. (x)

> When communicating their ideas, men also seek to communicate their passions. It is through eloquence that they manage to do so. Made for speaking to the feelings, as logic and grammar speak to the mind, [eloquence] silences even reason, and the feats it can be used by a single man to perform on a whole nation are perhaps the most striking testimony to the superiority of one man over another. What is singular is that anyone could think to improve such rare talent with rules. It's a little like wanting to reduce genius to precepts.

The answer, surprisingly, is no. Eloquence, like genius (of which it seems to be a signature, moreover), comes from nature, not from method, no matter how natural the logic is that founds the method. But curiously, d'Alembert never dealt with this disruptive component in his text. The exclusion reads stylistically like an oversight rather than as a deliberate attempt to eliminate a danger (although there is some suggestion of that). Even so, d'Alembert clearly has told only one side of the story, for this nature of eloquence and genius was not the nature of d'Alembert's picture of the natural sciences: this nature has no discernible precepts and therefore cannot be analyzed and taught. It is a nature of change, especially of changes of state (passion is a state), and of the transmission of changes of state. It is not a nature characterized by fixed structure but a nature that contains chance events and is not reducible to Newtonian determinism or—more important—determinability. It is to this nature that the genius belongs, and of which he is the local and human embodiment. The creative impulse disturbs the calm accretion of positive knowledge, the carefully controlled and ordered development of the crystal. The genius simply had no logical place in d'Alembert's system, and so he had to be eliminated from the project of the *Encyclopédie*.

This disruptive element had a generalized form. Pervading the "Discours" is an implicit enemy, and as was hinted in d'Alembert's discussion of Montesquieu, this enemy is history. History is not only what happens, it is the existence of happening; it is change, revolution, innovation. Hence for d'Alembert genius and poetry belonged to history and not to science. The inherent role of his *savant* was implicitly to resist the change brought about by historical events, to preserve intact the human perception of the timeless truth of crystalline knowledge. The *savant* wishes himself outside historicality and in the realm of the universal, of truth understood as the drive toward the clean singularity of the mathematical translation. The encyclopedia was d'Alembert's tool, therefore, to fight history. The only acceptable change was to be a change that is not really change: the accumulation and uncovering of what was always already there, not the creation of something truly new.

Clearly this view of the encyclopedia was antithetical to any understanding that the post-*Interprétation* Diderot could have of his part in the project. Diderot's creative force was allied to natural history; it lay at the heart of his entire conception of nature and of intellectual endeavor. We will see that the genius, the person who embodies this creative force, rather than being excluded so that the *Encyclopédie* might function, must on the contrary be hidden at the very heart of the devious and subversive machine that is the Diderotian transformation of the *Encyclopédie*.

The Dynamic Encyclopedia: Generating Waves of Invention

Diderot's article "Encyclopédie" was written "after the fact": the fact of the public discontent with the disparity between the architectural harmony of the work that d'Alembert had vaunted in the "Discours préliminaire" and the confusion and awkwardness of the unwieldy first few volumes.[9] We can regard Diderot's article partly as a strategic response to these criticisms. The first response had been the "Avertissement des Auteurs" to the third volume; it attempted to justify the d'Alembertian picture presented in the "Discours," to

9. See John Lough, *Essays on the* Encyclopédie *of Diderot and D'Alembert* (London: Oxford University Press, 1968), 279.

shore up the claim that method bestowed moral impartiality and sufficiency upon the analytic *savant*. Its tone and the effect instead projected a long howl of outrage. Having added no new argument to counter the quite incisive and penetrating attacks made from very different quarters, the essay ended on the defensive. With the article "Encyclopédie," Diderot took the offensive ostensibly to deflect the widespread attack on one of the most justifiably vaunted dimensions of the project: the cross-reference structure. Diderot's polemical tone is all the more understandable when we remember that he wrote his article "Encyclopédie" in just a few days, sick with a fever, pressed to beat the deadline of the sixth volume.[10] Such circumstances hardly lend themselves to a cold, philosophical reevaluation of the encyclopedic project, as may be borne out in the seemingly haphazard organization of the article. This "disorganization," however, hid an eloquence (in the d'Alembertian sense) that is a great deal more effective than the willfully dispassionate argument of the "Discours." The picture that Diderot drew was a seductive and dramatic one, very much in tune with the new materialist theories that were shaping themselves in his thoughts around this time, in response precisely to the other articles he had written for the *Encyclopédie*.

Diderot's answer to his critics remained implicit but underlay the entire formulation of this article. It can be summarized in the following argument: only readers capable of true philosophical insight will be able to follow the efficient functioning of the cross-reference system of the *Encyclopédie*. The work may indeed appear misshapen or deformed to everyone else, to readers of limited intellectual capacity. Critics who find the work unsatisfactory have seriously misunderstood its designs, have thereby indicted themselves as not being of the philosophical elect, and so have disqualified themselves as judges.

The strategy was clever, even outrageous. Diderot's maneuver must have angered the critics of the *Encyclopédie*. It certainly shifted the general perception of the intent of the work, and thus it raised the stakes in the ideological battle between the philosophers and the church or state apologists, who saw themselves as the targets of the subversion that functioned as theorized in the article.[11] Here, appar-

10. DPV 5:174.

11. For an overview of the institutional reactions to the first few volumes, see Lough, *Essays*, chaps. 5 ("Contemporary Books and Pamphlets on the *Encyclopédie*") and 6 ("Contemporary French Periodicals and the *Encyclopédie*").

ently carried along by his own rhetoric, Diderot moved beyond the exigencies of the political moment to speculate about the long-term effects of intellectual training on a "natural" social structure. He discarded the definition of the project with which he began the article, the d'Alembertian notion of the encyclopedic dictionary as the ordered accumulation of the total stock of human knowledge and replaced it with an entirely different image, that of the *Encyclopédie* as the "living school for philosophers."

This replacement is usefully characterized as the transformation of the d'Alembertian *dictionary* into the Diderotian *encyclopedia*. From one point of view this characterization is arbitrary, since both editors used the terms as though they were synonymous. But from another point of view, this is a natural way to mark the difference between them. It is d'Alembert who, even more than in the "Discours préliminaire," insistently presented the encyclopedia as a "belle machine de savoir ordonné" ("beautiful machine of organized knowledge") in his article "Dictionnaire."[12] Responding in the article "Encyclopédie", Diderot redefined the notion of the encyclopedia and thus gave us the other possible model, the complement to that elaborated by d'Alembert.

Diderot's presentation was subtle and often difficult to follow. There is a whole panoply of reasons for this difficulty, but I shall focus on the principal source: an ongoing demonstration of the active relationship to be established between a writer and his reader, a relationship that we noted above was grounded in Diderot's materialist theory of mind. It helps to recall that the article "Encyclopédie" followed hard upon the writing of the *Interprétation de la nature* and therefore drew directly upon the construal of natural philosophy that we saw elaborated there. The *Interprétation*'s dynamics of elastic systems constituting the interplay of identity-events in the mechanical continua from brute matter to thinking man and from thought to matter was to be put to the test in the *Encyclopédie*. The *Interprétation* described what "theory" means in a natural philosophy and then provided the theory of that theory, or rather, the natural philosophy of natural philosophy. The article "Encyclopédie" described a test-event, the attempt to realize what was only theorized in the *Interpré-*

12. D'Alembert, "Dictionnaire," in Diderot and d'Alembert, eds., *L'Encyclopédie*, 4:958b–69b. See also Georges Benrekassa, "La Pratique philosophique de Diderot dans l'article 'Encyclopédie' de l'*Encyclopédie*," *Stanford French Review* 8 (1984): 189–212.

tation: the project of the *Encyclopédie* as the site of the active production of natural philosophical interpretations.

Thus, rather than being the site of an accumulation of relatively static knowledge (as outlined in the "Discours préliminaire"), the encyclopedia must be cast in terms of the elastic interactive systems of the *Interprétation*. It was to become an open-ended conversation between the multitude of members in a *cité scientifique*. A member's act of writing articles for the *Encyclopédie* to be published was merely the pretext for the conversation that would organize the *true* encyclopedia, the living encyclopedia made up of the philosophers' dynamic exchange of ideas as they worked to adjust their articles to each others'.

Conversations

The conversation model for a work presenting knowledge was a departure from the standard formats in use at the time. Diderot's contemporaries had two structures to follow: the (basically Cartesian) linear treatise and the Condillacean analytic description. Both structures attempted to represent at once the structure of mental reality and that of the world; each therefore put forward a claim to a certain "naturalness" and corollary authority. But each relied on a different expository structure.[13] Descartes's model was of a purified linear argument, a linear treatise formed by a chain of simple ideas that led to eternal truths. Condillac's version, outlined at the beginning of this chapter, provided the most rigorous exposition of the Enlightenment update of Descartes's model. A valid written description of the Condillacean-analyzed world would have to reproduce the structure of the interlocking set of hierarchies of natural objects, so one ideal format was the one that d'Alembert described in the "Discours préliminaire": articles were linked by the cross references to form the Baconian tree of knowledge.

Given Diderot's definition of nature as dynamic rather than static, it is understandable that he would wish to replace Descartes's deductive chain of ideal, immaterial reasoning and the Condillacean pyramids of fact by a materialist literary discourse marked by multiple speeches and active words. In the article "Encyclopédie," therefore,

13. For a more detailed discussion, see my *Between the Library and the Laboratory*, chap. 3; and my "1754: From Natural Science to Scientific Discourse" in *The New History of French Literature*, ed. Denis Hollier (Cambridge, Mass.: Harvard University Press, 1989).

Diderot consciously replaced both formats for writing with a method for reading that must at first have seemed *un*natural to his contemporaries.

The written *Encyclopédie* can be interpreted structurally to manifest this idea of exchange: the play of the cross references then becomes the defining structural characteristic of the work, replacing the static "tree of knowledge" display of the "Discours préliminaire." The cross references then form a kind of written (but not frozen) conversation, juxtaposing different voices, opposing points of view without resolving the oppositions, and therefore forcing the encyclopedic reader, like the student of the *Interprétation*, to generate his own justifications for the links implied by juxtaposition, to come up with his own new ideas.

But first Diderot had to teach his reader to converse. He did this not by argument but by demonstration.

The first part of his article quickly restated d'Alembert's model. The unadvised reader follows the path indicated by the argument, which proceeds more or less to reproduce the already banalized description of the dictionary. But the argument becomes increasingly erratic and devious the farther he reads. The reader has two options: either to dismiss the bizarre passages and treat them as faulty rhetorical construction or to acknowledge his confusion and stop to reread the incomprehensible passages in order to try to force them into coherence with the rest of the text.

It is at this point that Diderot confronts his reader with a basic issue. Nature, he tells us, limits the potential of the dictionary because humans have inherent limitations: they have limited life spans, limited intellectual energy, and differing mental capacities and training. What if, in an attempt to circumvent these difficulties, the editors were to choose only the best minds and ask each to complete the work of equally gifted predecessors? A major difficulty would still remain: because nature is in continual flux, physical as well as social revolutions can take place that may rupture contact with the knowledge from cultures that have disappeared or even from the immediate cultural past. How can one avoid the cultural chaos brought about by these revolutions?

Diderot answers through what is in effect a miniarticle situated at the center of the article "Encyclopédie." Implicitly entitled "Langue," the miniarticle sets the stage for the second part of his discussion of the nature of the encyclopedic project. It says that the light to pierce the shadows can be transmitted from generation to generation only if language is perfected. Drawing indirectly on his materialist theories of change, he attempted to characterize what distinguished the dynamic of human events from other material events, concluding that the mobilizing force for human history is the medium of language. An idea is a thought—in other words, a dynamically determined event occurring in the intersecting space of material human existence and mental operation, as we saw demonstrated in the *Rêve*. Like the vibration patterns in a solid, an idea is formed out of both thought-motion and the mental-material "substance" in which it occurs so that, like the wave model I used in chapter 1, it and the word or complex of words that represents it do not exist as discrete or abstract entities outside the context of the medium of human language and interaction. Language thus is also an "elastic" system. Diderot argues that each country's language is shaped by and embodies all the previous historical events and thought-events of its people; it in turn heavily determines their future thoughts and, therefore, the shape of the possible events of the country's or people's history. It acts both to conserve past knowledge and to shape future knowledge. Inherent in language is a sort of cultural inertia that tempers too abrupt, possibly destructive intellectual or historical change. Inherent also, however, because language is in constant use, is a sort of cultural momentum that, unlike the d'Alembertian archive, acts to prevent historical stagnation.

The only fixed and stable language, the only one that can embody the Condillacean-d'Alembertian ideal of a "perfect language," is therefore a dead language. Although Diderot thus clearly disagreed with Condillac and d'Alembert as to the desirability of a perfect language in this sense, such dead languages could have their uses (197)—as the medium through which modern languages could be learned. Dead languages form a stable, dependable reference point for the simple reason that their history is over, their cultures and peoples no longer exist. A dead language like Latin, however, having become merely a code and no longer functioning as a living language, would not be able to serve the intellectual purpose that d'Alembert had envisioned in the "Discours" (xxx), which was to unify the world of scientists and their knowledge through the international and cross-cultural use of one universal language. For d'Alembert, Latin's great advantage was precisely that it is dead—its immutability guaranteed the stability of the crystal structure of knowledge. It also would, of course, eliminate the historical, the culturally evolving semantic value of terms as a source of misunderstanding between *savants* from different countries and as a source of misunderstanding between present *savants* and future ones. Diderot's warm advocacy of the use of Latin merely to learn other modern languages hid his ironic criticism of d'Alembert's proposal: one does not translate one's work into Latin so that English speakers can then read it without having to learn French. One uses Latin to learn English and then speaks to one's English interlocutors in their own language to promote innovation and creation in interaction with them, as well. If Latin were to be granted anything more than this provisional function as a code, it would have to be continually modified to incorporate the new knowledge brought about by the interactions of the *savants*, and this would make it again into a living, changing, and hence undependable source language, destroying precisely the guarantee function for which it was prized. The real innovations can take place only in the play between living languages and their speakers.[14] It is through language that man distinctively contributes to the organization of the material world. Therefore, the task of the philosopher becomes one of understanding language's ongoing links to and effects on its natural and historical context and of directly and essentially intervening in the structure and use of the living language.

Si l'on compte les hommes de génie, & qu'on les répande sur toute la durée des siècles écoulés, il est évident qu'ils seront en petit nombre dans chaque nation & pour chaque siècle, & qu'on n'en trouvera presque aucun qui n'ait perfectionné la langue. Les hommes créateurs portent ce caractère particulier. Comme ce n'est pas seulement en feuilletant les productions de leurs contemporains qu'ils rencontrent les idées qu'ils ont à employer dans leurs écrits, mais que

14. An acute example of the use of translation (although not through Latin) to force a change in another country's way of perceiving particular philosophical or scientific questions occurred later in the century in the translation of Lavoisier's "new French chemistry" texts into English. Lavoisier personally oversaw the translation so as to maximize the importation into English of chemical neologisms from the new French chemistry, which caused some consternation and comment on the part of his English interlocutors. See my "Translating the Language of Chemistry: Priestley and Lavoisier," *The Eighteenth Century* 22, no. 1 (1981): 21–31.

c'est tantôt en descendant profondément en eux-mêmes, tantôt en s'élançant au-dehors, & portant des regards plus attentifs & plus pénétrants sur les natures qui les environnent, ils sont obligés, surtout à l'origine des langues, d'inventer des signes pour rendre avec exactitude & avec force ce qu'ils y découvrent les premiers. C'est la chaleur de l'imagination & la méditation profonde qui enrichissent une langue d'expressions nouvelles. (196)

If we count the men of genius and spread them out across the duration of past centuries, it is evident that there will be few in each nation and each century and that we will find almost none having perfected language. Creative men have this particular characteristic. As it is not only in going through their contemporaries' productions that they encounter the ideas they will use in their writings, but sometimes by diving deep into themselves, sometimes leaping outward to observe most attentively and penetratingly the surrounding natural phenomena, they are obliged, above all at the beginnings of languages, to invent signs to render with accuracy and force what they are the first to discover. It is the heat of imagination and deep meditation that enrich a language with new expressions.

One talks not only for one's own understanding. Language allows human knowledge to progress through the confrontation of different bodies of knowledge, and this also provokes new ideas and produces new words and the possibilities of new types of behavior. Although ever reaching the end of such a development is impossible, Diderot tells us that the more the language is "perfected," the more "la distance des temps disparaît; les lieux se touchent; il se forme des liaisons entre tous les points habités de l'espace & de la durée, & tous les êtres vivants & pensants s'entretiennent" (189; "the distance between times disappears; places touch; links form between all the inhabited points of space and duration, and all living and thinking beings converse with one another"). One of the purposes of a "universal" language, then, is not to represent all of the knowledge acquired by all of the cultures but to force the creation of this gigantic coherent, resonant conversation. This conversation works against the disruptive potential of nature, the nature that causes revolutions. "Un idiome commun serait l'unique moyen d'établir une correspondance qui s'étendît à toutes les parties du genre humain, & qui les liguât contre la nature, à laquelle nous avons sans cesse à faire violence, soit dans le physique, soit dans le moral" (189; "A common idiom would be the single way to establish a correspondence that would stretch to all the parts of the human species and would league them against nature, to whom we must ceaselessly do violence, whether physical or moral").

This is the eloquent nature of the "Discours," the nature that disrupts. This nature also innovates, however, as Diderot had already shown in the *Interprétation*, but because it does so without regard to the institutionalized values locally holding when change occurs, its shifts are perceived as disruptive or violent. In other words, violence or disruption is dependent on point of view. Rather than repressing, dismissing, or eliminating this nature altogether by the construction of the crystal structure of knowledge, the philosopher maintains cultural continuity (not cultural fixity) by managing this nature with its own tools: "nous avons sans cesse à [lui] faire violence" ("we have ceaselessly to do it violence"). How? The Diderotian philosophers work with this nature, provoking innovating change, all the while minimizing disruption. Their tool to accomplish this is the dialectical living language, which both allows the invention of procedures to work on nature and changes its users' view of the world so that they can digest the changes. Unlike the fixed archive, this language constitutes and changes its own structure through conversation—including ideally conversations across distances of space and historical time.

Clearly, given this notion of what the underlying function of language is, the conversations that must count above all are those established between contemporary philosophers and their predecessors, or with their successors, the ever present Diderotian nephews. In other words, the *vieux* in Mlle. de l'Espinasse's monastery are not real people succeeding each other. What endures are the actions of preceding philosophers, insofar as they are embedded in the constantly changing language and its dynamic tool, the *Encyclopédie*.

So be it, but then how are the nephews to learn to establish this dialectical relationship between their own ideas, nature, and their language? In short, how are they to read? Unlike the erudite contemporary readers, who read only for brute accumulated knowledge, succeeding generations will have to start their encyclopedic reading experience with the "language" article strategically placed at the center of the article "Encyclopédie" (188). They are not to read it as real knowledge, though; they are to read it in the same way that Diderot read Denys d'Hélicarnasse concerning his theories of language—not for the content, but for the tone, the style, and especially the uncertainties.

> C'est en recueillant ainsi des mots échappés au hasard, & étrangers à la matière traitée spécialement dans un auteur où ils ne caractérisent que ses lumières, son exactitude & son indécision, qu'on parviendrait à éclaircir l'histoire des progrès de l'esprit humain dans les siècles passés. (191)

> It is by thus gathering the chance words, foreign to the subject matter treated specially in an author['s work], where they characterize only his lights, his accuracy and his indecision, that we can clarify the history of the progress of the human mind in past centuries.

Diderot thus pushed his reader to read against the grain of the explicit argument, on the bias, and above all not bound by its specific content, which would inevitably become outdated by the progress of knowledge. This progress comes not from accumulating content but from provoking an act of thinking, that of questioning definitions of words and the status of an argument. This questioning can take place only where the reader detects uncertainty or ambiguity that indicates that the speculative thought of the past writer had not yet resolved itself into positive knowledge.

Diderot claimed here to be providing his reader the key for reading the great authors of the past. Actually, he was arguing on the bias himself, to show rather than to tell the reader of the article "Encyclopédie" how to read all other texts. His own is explicitly and intentionally broken up, the argument is sometimes illogical, and there is an enormous variation in tone and style. The reader is obliged to turn back to past paragraphs to construct implicit arguments, to rearrange the ideas, to correct, to compare, and, in other words, to think out for himself answers to the questions the discussion raises. In effect, Diderot was trying to train his reader to read against his own expectations concerning acceptable rhetorical structure. He had to read as if participating in a conversation, learning to converse first with himself and the text so as to converse eventually with others.

But what does it mean to converse? Is it not again an exchange of represented facts between men of knowledge, deciding who is "right" and who is "wrong?" Do the philosophers not read their predecessors, and are they not interpreted by their successors in terms of some ideal final judgment of achieved fixed knowledge? After a very long development of the pros and cons of these and related points, Diderot introduced his famous conceit of the Italian lover's hundred portraits of his mistress, to eliminate the question once and for all.

Un Espagnol ou un Italien pressé du désir de posséder un portrait de sa maîtresse, qu'il ne pouvait montrer à aucun peintre, prit le parti qui lui restait d'en faire par écrit la description la plus étendue & la plus exacte; il commença par déterminer la juste proportion de la tête entière; il passa ensuite aux dimensions du front, des yeux, du nez, de la bouche, du menton, du cou; puis il revint sur chacune de ces parties, & il n'épargna rien pour que son discours gravât dans l'esprit du peintre la véritable image qu'il avait sous les yeux; il n'oublia ni les couleurs, ni les formes, ni rien de ce qui appartient au caractère: plus il compara son discours avec le visage de sa maîtresse, plus il le trouva ressemblant; il crut surtout que plus il chargerait sa description de petits détails, moins il laisserait de liberté au peintre; il n'oublia rien de ce qu'il pensa devoir captiver le pinceau. Lorsque sa description lui parut achevée, il en fit cent copies, qu'il envoya à cent peintres, leur enjoignant à chacun d'exécuter exactement sur la toile ce qu'ils liraient sur son papier. (204)

A Spaniard or an Italian urgently desiring to possess a portrait of his mistress, whom he could [nonetheless] not show to any painter, took the only option left open to him—to make the most extensive and exact written description of her; he began by determining the exact proportion of her whole head; he then passed to the dimensions of her forehead, her eyes, nose, mouth, chin, and neck; then he came back to each of these parts and spared nothing that would enable his discourse to engrave in the mind of the painter the true image that he had under his eyes. He neglected neither color, form, nor anything belonging to her characteristics: the more he compared his discourse with the face of his mistress, the more he found it a good likeness; he believed above all that the more he saturated his description with little details, the less freedom he would leave to the painter; he left out nothing that he thought the paintbrush could capture. When his description seemed finished to him, he made a hundred copies that he sent to a hundred painters, enjoining each to execute exactly on the canvas what they would read on his paper.

What we have here is a detailed description of the lover's perfect performance of the Condillacean analysis, carried out methodically and precisely. According to the entire theory of perception underlying the Condillacean-d'Alembertian epistemology, it therefore should have produced in language the perfect and dependable representation of the appearance of the mistress. This is language at its most representational, or at least a user of language manifesting the greatest faith in the representational power of language. However, as we rightly expect, "les peintres travaillent, & au bout d'un certain temps notre amant reçoit cent portraits, qui tous ressemblent rigoureusement à sa description, & dont aucun ne ressemble à un autre, ni à sa maîtresse" (204; "the painters worked, and at the end of a certain time, our lover received a hundred portraits, which all rigorously resembled his description and none of which resembled the others or his mistress"). The Latin lover's faith in the representational power of language has indeed been betrayed. Still, a hundred beautiful and "rigorous" portraits have been produced. What accounts for the differences between the portraits among themselves and with respect to the mistress? Diderot says, "L'application de cet apologue au cas dont il s'agit, n'est pas difficile; on me dispensera de la faire en détail" ("The application of this argument to the case under consideration is not difficult; the reader will excuse me from carrying it out in detail"), and yet the application is more subtle than it seems, for the preceding discussion was about the national variations in the pronunciation of Greek verse, which nonetheless do not prevent Swedes from appreciating the harmony of a line as much as the French or the English. Let us, then, perform the application for Diderot: the differences in each pronunciation, each rigorously conforming to the information available in the Greek letters, results from each country's differing understanding of harmonic sounds as determined by the sound of its own language. Now the sound of its own language results from precisely the type of historical shaping that determines its structure and "content." Can we say that the French are right and the Swedes wrong? Can we say that one pronunciation is closer to the Greek original than the other? Would more study or research give us finally the "right" answer or the "right" pronunciation? Clearly that was not what was at stake here. Just as with the Italian's mistress, modern appreciators of Greek can have no access to the original, to the supposed referent. But in fact, the issue was not really one concerning the impossibility of a sign's ever adequately representing an originary referent at all. For the Italian lover, indeed, there is, as James Creech would say, a nostalgia for representability. Nor will we ever be able to hear ancient Greek verse as read by ancient Greeks. But Diderot's tale mocked such pretensions, denounced such nostalgia. His issue here was to switch the focus from representation to another function, to deprogram the d'Alembertian or Condillacean reader, whose intent to denote cleanly and dependably forces him into a fetishistic relationship to an absent referent, and to allow him to see another relationship between word and world.

Let us take the anecdote from the opposite point of view, from that of the performers and not the originators. Whether the Swedes or the French are accurate in their pronunciation of Greek or not, they have heard relations of sounds that they recognize as harmonious and that they incorporate as part of their language experience to figure out new ways to speak more harmoniously in their own language. From the painters' point of view, a hundred very beautiful paintings have been produced, each one embodying the interaction between a specific painter's own material and esthetic history and a text he is reading. It is his reading experience that is expressed on the canvas (and not represented—his act of painting *is* his act of reading). The newly modified and harmonized French is not a representation of Greek harmonious speech; instead, it is an expression of its speaker's understanding of the sound of his own words as he utters them. In other words, there is something very present in the speech or in the painters' paintings;[15] the speech and paintings are not signs of something absent but are event-objects in themselves. It would not even be accurate to say that they represent themselves.

I would emphasize that Diderot here eliminated the validity of the notion of representation as a structure underlying all possible attempts at transmission of cognitive content. Even the Italian lover's description of his mistress is not a representation—he just thinks it is. The well-trained Condillacean lover has not understood that even his description, seemingly so immediate and "objective" is nothing other

15. We will return to the question of the special status of paintings in chapter 5 when discussing the notion of the *modèle idéal* in the *Salon de 1767*: the fact that painting endures, that the activity of painting leaves a very particular sort of monument that still should not be representational, is at the heart of Diderot's revamping of his esthetic theories in this *Salon*.

than his highly idiosyncratic activity of looking at her. For Diderot, content was in the experience made possible. This is why I use the term *expression* here, even though it is not quite adequate to the Diderotian phenomenon being described (the idea that one is expressing *something* can be misinterpreted to mean that the painter is expressing the mistress or the speaker Greek harmony). Diderot is instead elaborating a poetics (in the sense developed in the *Rêve*) of presence, where a textual experience generates a reading-event that creates new cognitive material, which exists only through the activity of its expression.

Although he never explicitly made the connection in this article, this reconstrual of the nature of textual activity allows us to understand Diderot's peculiar attitude toward plagiarism, a subject that seems at first not to be particularly relevant to the *Encyclopédie*.[16] Diderot and d'Alembert were indeed accused of having plagiarized Chambers's *Cyclopedia* as well as many other works to get the content of their articles. The idea of plagiarism depends, however, on the idea that there is an original being copied and therefore an original performance being parasitized. It depends on the idea that the work of art is a fixed object distinct from its reader-activator. Diderot would have replied, Is the painter's picture a plagiarism? Obviously not, and not just because it is a commissioned work or because the medium is different from the one used for the original description. Like the painter's response to the written description, a variation on a theme was not plagiarism, because in the new context, with new "expressors" and readers, it was just as likely to be a new object resulting from interaction with the old. This was, for Diderot, one of the essential characteristics of cultural contact and transmission across time; it was, in fact, as his model of language as the embodiment of the history of a culture shows, what made it possible. So for a *savant* to try to claim isolation for his own production with respect to his cultural past was either dishonest or mad (how could a work or idea be truly original—that is, derived from no cultural antecedents—and still be comprehensible?). To try to produce isolation with respect to his contemporaries or his successors' work was to deny the very point of intellectual production.

16. Diderot will eventually confront the issue of his own alleged plagiarisms with respect to his theater and especially at the end of his life in his meditations on Seneca in the *Essai sur les règnes de Claude et de Néron*, DPV, vol. 25.

In this light, the project of the *Encyclopédie* again becomes coherent: it was to *promote* the kind of interaction and commentary that origin-nostalgic Condillaceans might have called plagiarism. It was to engage the cultural ancestors through commentary on their work and analogical modern expression; it was to engage the nephews through their act of expressive reading; it was to foster the creation of new ideas through the ongoing conversations of the contemporary article writers.

With this issue the reader arrives at the heart of the article "Encyclopédie," the description of the *Encyclopédie* itself as the transcription of one giant conversation where everything is controlled by the famous system of cross references. The cross references, naturally, were overseen by the principal editor of the project, Diderot.

Diderot's cross references as outlined in the last third of this article, however, were very different from d'Alembert's. They no longer outlined the "Système figuré des connoissances humaines." If there was a Diderotian equivalent to the hierarchy of knowledge in the "Discours," it lay in an implicit ranking of philosophers, and not of domains of knowledge, even though for both Diderot and d'Alembert these hierarchies were structured through the cross references. Diderot set up first a hierarchy of four types of cross reference. This structure produced a corresponding series among the philosophers interacting with the text. A little study shows that for each category of cross reference there implicitly corresponded one category of author and two possible categories of reader. Let us deal with the authors first.

Figure 3.1 shows Diderot's ranking of philosophical ability. The writers the most involved with brute positive knowledge and the least philosophically able were the critics of the *Encyclopédie*, who in effect were Diderot's target in this article (they were right to feel singled out). Slightly less benighted were the workhorse writers like the Chevalier de Jaucourt, who could dimly perceive the value of the project even if their work was accumulative rather than critical. The content editors completed and then organized the articles written by the workhorse authors in each discipline; the cross-reference editors began the suggestive work by setting up the relations between disciplines. So far the structure of the project does not seem to depart much from that suggested by the "Discours préliminaire" for a philosophical dictionary, and certain resemblances still exist with the intel-

FIGURE 3.I   Writers

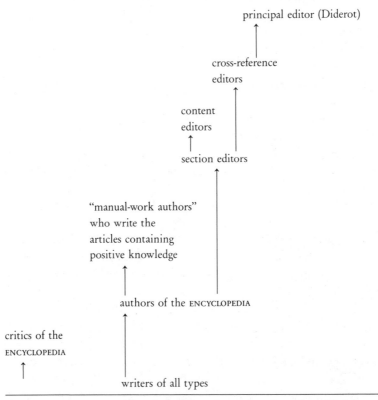

lectual community proposed in the *New Organon* by Bacon, to whom both Diderot and d'Alembert paid direct allegiance in their texts.

Diderot's real innovation shows through in the two hierarchies of readers summarized in figure 3.2. These two hierarchies develop in opposing directions, and the directions have real import. It is easy to imagine a justifiable intellectual trajectory in either direction, but for Diderot the choice of direction infallibly indicated the intellectual capacities of the reader in keeping with the implicit distinction made in the *Interprétation* between scientist and natural philosopher. Through this doubling of the hierarchy, the work resolved itself into

FIGURE 3.2   Readers of the Encyclopedia

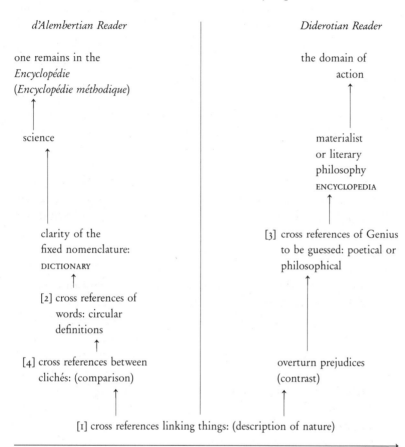

d'Alembertian Reader | *Diderotian Reader*

one remains in the
Encyclopédie
(*Encyclopédie méthodique*)

↑

science

↑

the domain of
action

↑

materialist
or literary
philosophy
ENCYCLOPEDIA

↑

clarity of the
fixed nomenclature:
DICTIONARY

↑

[2] cross references of
words: circular
definitions

↑

[4] cross references between
clichés: (comparison)

↑

[3] cross references of Genius
to be guessed: poetical or
philosophical

↑

overturn prejudices
(contrast)

↑

[1] cross references linking things: (description of nature)

————————————————————————————→
direction of increasing virtue
(philosophical intelligence)

←————————————————————————————

direction of accumulation of knowledge
(erudite stupidity)

two mutually exclusive but coextensive projects—the "dictionary" and the "encyclopedia." This division was the work of a single man, the principal editor. He had to oversee the whole project; it was his gaze that would establish the crucial cross references, but his gaze was anything but the detached and neutral overview of the Condillacean analytic observer. It would be the penetrating gaze of the Diderotian materialist, likened not to vision but to touch, in keeping with the epistemology of the *Interprétation*—a gaze that would bring things into contact, establish relationships, start off conversations. This active and intervening gaze would upset balances, raise doubts, initiate motion, and transform the beautiful but sterile machine of the dictionary into a living and changing encyclopedic organism.

Let us therefore consider in detail the cross references and the readers they produce. The first kind of cross reference, the "cross reference of things" (see fig. 3.2 [1]), furnished a static description of nature. For the d'Alembertian reader looking for a body of positive knowledge, these cross references permitted the establishing of a synthetic map of the world through comparison. But for the Diderotian reader, the effect was to lead him into a practice of making contrasts. He was to see differences, question his own acceptance of definitions, redefine concepts for himself. He was to learn to recognize and to regulate his own faculty of judgment, to distinguish and to rank.

The second sort of cross reference, the cross reference of words (see fig. 3.2 [2]), enabled the d'Alembertian erudite to clarify through circular denotative definitions the internal structure of scientific nomenclature. In other words, it established a dictionary. This is perfectly understandable, for a nomenclature was commonly thought of at the time as being fixed, established, rigid. But for the Diderotian reader, working not in the realm of nomenclature but inside the living, evolving, and analogical language, these cross references served a very different purpose. The implication of the notion of a synonym is that words only statistically denote: every word has a main meaning surrounded by a cloud of connotations. In this structure we can perceive the "event-ness" of the idea that constituted a word's meaning. From a series of synonyms, each slightly displacing the main meaning with respect to the others but all linked by connotations, the Diderotian reader could see the nuances, the suggestiveness of language, the plasticity of the terminology covering any one intellectual subject.

We now arrive at the third type of cross reference, the crucial type that constituted what Diderot called the cross references of genius but, on the basis of the definition of the word culled from the *Rêve*, might also be called the poetic cross references (see fig. 3.2 [3]). Diderot made it clear that these cross references could not be explicitly designated in advance by the editor. The reader himself has to intuit from his ongoing contact with the body of ideas or things under discussion where analogies between them might lie, to see in reverie the poetic rapports. This was the encyclopedic equivalent of the experimenter's *tâtonnement* and constituted more than just an act of speculation. This reader creates new ideas or things out of the material of the disparate articles. He creates the epistemological equivalent of Bordeu's mixing of species: new combinations, beings that have never existed, by analogy with some that do. We are here clearly no longer in the domain of the dictionary, but have found the motor of the Diderotian encyclopedia. These poetic cross references lead to "revolutions" in the sciences, make inventions possible, help bring lost ancient arts to light. Diderot cautioned, however, that with a reader of limited intelligence or an erudite scholar of limited judgment, this sort of intuition unfortunately risked producing what we saw with Mlle. de l'Espinasse and Dr. Bordeu: literally monsters, what Diderot here called "conjectures chimériques." After all, the chimera was an impossible animal created by the monstrous mingling of animal categories. Happily for the scientists, the rigid structure established in the nomenclature by the cross references of words effectively eliminated this danger. Inside this nomenclature, a perfectly denotative semantic field, it is precisely the poetic, the analogic, that was eliminated. Consequently, this elimination kept the reader from making the analogies that would allow him to see the world differently, to displace questions, to judge the world of knowledge from the point of view of a changing external world. The d'Alembertian scholar would remain locked in the domain of science, occupied with the accumulation and the correction of knowledge and able to perceive only the content of the *Encyclopédie*.

From these d'Alembertian readers, apolitical and detached, came the workhorse authors mentioned before. Blinded by their preoccupation with positive knowledge, they were insensible to the revolutions and upheavals of the end of the eighteenth century and the beginning of the nineteenth. These readers, and the resulting authors of the *Encyclopédie*, really did exist, and they lived through the events of their time taken up with the revision of the first encyclopedia, turning out the enormous, the monstrous *Encyclopédie méthodique*, which would not be finished until well into the nineteenth century. Theirs was truly the *travail de la bêtise*: d'Alembert the *savant* become Bouvard and Pécuchet.

The reader produced by antithetical training, however, the Diderotian reader, was intended to follow a wholly opposite evolution. With sufficient genius to perceive the existence of and then to profit from the judgment training made possible by the cross references, he would become not an erudite scholar, not a *savant*, but the natural philosopher of the *Interprétation*. Because his judgment would serve to regulate his intuition, the philosopher would know how to converse poetically and creatively with nature. His *conjectures* would appear *chimériques* only to the uninitiated, in the way that the *bizarreries* in *Pensée* XXXI resolved themselves into fruitful and meaningful hypotheses as the natural philosopher learned to sense and listen to the dynamic structure of nature.

Seen in this way, the encyclopedia became a very different project— it would store knowledge, but its primary purpose would be to provoke speculation by both its authors and its readers (and between its authors and its readers) and thereby lead to the creation of new knowledge and new forms of knowledge. The importance of the written encyclopedia for Diderot would be clear, therefore, only when it was placed back within the flow of time. The encyclopedia would serve as the memory of a people, created to prevent the cultural devastation brought about by natural or political catastrophes. The encyclopedia was to be a tool to maintain organization in the face of change. Yet it was not to maintain organization, even its own, as a static or unchanging structure. For Diderot, memory was not merely a form of fixed archive. As another manifestation of the solid wave model, it was a generative structure working to maintain a continuous "identity" across time even though its contents inevitably had to change. The memory of a people, its encyclopedia, would help to maximize organization by attempting to guide change, would provide the *vieux* for the future generations. This is the context in which the essential meaning of one of the most famous quotations from "Encyclopédie" can be understood: "Si ces renvois de confirmation & de réfutation sont prévus de loin, & préparés avec adresse, ils donneront à une *encyclopédie* le caractère que doit avoir un bon dictionnaire; ce caractère est de changer la façon commune de penser" (222; "If these cross references of confirmation and refutation are planned with foresight and prepared with skill they will furnish the *encyclopedia* with what should be the characteristic of a good dictionary; this characteristic is to change the common mode of thinking").

Diderot's *Encyclopédie* was not intended primarily to tell a people what to think; it was intended to introduce its readers into the conversation stored in the cross references so as to teach them how to think and how to feel out nature. Reading it would be a training experience that would quite literally shape the judgment of the future philosophers and so help them to speculate deftly and efficiently, thereby passing from being readers to being philosophical authors themselves as they elaborated upon, rather than extended, the work of their predecessors.

Style and the Genius

But what would it mean to elaborate upon this work? Did Diderot mean that his philosophical readers, like the d'Alembertian scientist, were to enlarge the corpus of written knowledge? Clearly not. Since for Diderot nature was in continual flux, the d'Alembertian accumulation of knowledge could never be anything but an illusory and tragic ideal, entrapped in historical time. Diderot provided, toward the end of his text, the delirious description of a world invaded by and crushed beneath the weight of books published by those who *tout bêtement* accumulated knowledge. Such knowledge, by its very volume, would soon become inaccessible. The ideal *Encyclopédie* should, instead, *dis*accumulate: it should reduce, to the strict, efficient, strategically chosen minimum, the stuff of past positive knowledge. Moreover, this fixed knowledge was really only the pretext to unleash the philosophical speculation embedded in the cross references. From this one can understand his last curious reflection: the philosophical inventors, those who would know how to use the encyclopedia to maximum benefit, "liront peu & s'abandonneront à des recherches qui seront nouvelles" (235; "they will read little and abandon themselves to research that will be new").

In such a context the act of writing would clearly play an unexpected role. For the natural philosopher, it would not merely encode information of a fixed sort. His writing would have to be the vehicle for ideas and procedures that could shape and challenge the mind of the reader. Just as scientific nomenclature was opposed to the resonating field of connotations in the cross references, so would Diderot's notion of the nature of philosophical writing be quite different from the Cartesian model's linear linking of clear and distinct ideas written in a self-effacing style so as to let the eternal crystalline structure of the material or logical world manifest itself directly to the reader's perception. Diderot's philosopher was not just to present knowledge, he was to interpret knowledge to his reader. Reducing to the minimum the reader's awareness of the philosopher's involvement could not be a desired goal, for such writing would generate an untrue and misleading picture of the world. The question of style in such a context could not be considered either trivial or as relating to the merely aesthetic as decorative. It had to become a philosophical issue; it was to be the factor determining whether writing was effective or not, whether it could *toucher, attacher,* and thus *instruire.* So we are not surprised to find that the article "Encyclopédie" ends with a long passage on style: "Ces considérations sur l'esprit & la matière d'un dictionnaire encyclopédique nous conduisent naturellement à parler du style qui est propre à ce genre d'ouvrage" (254; "These considerations about the spirit and substance of a good encyclopedic dictionary lead us naturally to speak of the style that is proper to this sort of a work").

It is important to emphasize immediately that for Diderot style did not reflect the individuality of the author—it was linked to the work. Style as mere decoration to demonstrate the virtuosity of an author would be a perversion of his role as interpreter of, or interface with, the world. Such style would veil the truth, obstruct the reading experience, and therefore deform the mind of the reader. The proper style for the philosopher, Diderot wrote, quoting Petronius, is not pretty, but "natural."

> Il serait à souhaiter, quand il s'agit de style, qu'on pût imiter Pétrone, qui a donné en même temps l'exemple & le précepte, lorsque ayant à peindre les qualités d'un beau discours, il a dit, *grandis, & ut ita dicam pudica oratio neque maculosa est neque turgida, sed naturali pulchritudine exsurgit.* (257)[17]

> It would be desirable, when dealing with style, to imitate Petronius, who provided at once both the example and the precept when, having to depict the qualities of a fine discourse, he said, "Great and—dare I say it—chaste eloquence admits neither cosmetic decoration nor turgidity; rather it rises up in its natural beauty."

17. Petronius, *Satiricon* II.

This natural beauty meant, for Diderot, a direct style intended to touch and shape the mind of the reader. To do so, the style had to reveal with clarity both its message about the world and the essential relationship of its own dynamic structure to the dynamic of the material world. Further, this style had to be embedded in an equally natural rhetoric, which did not mean for the natural philosopher what it meant for the scientist.[18] Utter impersonal simplicity of construction and of argument could only correlate with the belief in the eternal architectures of truth, with a world in which motion displaces but does not change. D'Alembert's style, derived from the analytic procedures and determined by grammar (as he defined it) was therefore logically sound, but as a result purely mechanical. The natural philosopher's style, on the other hand, not only must not exclude the theme of change from the text but must explicitly include it both thematically and structurally. As the problematic of the living statue in the *Rêve* demonstrated, Diderot believed that the power of language to represent was not statable in terms of a simple opposition between the sign and its fixed referent. He had two reasons: 1) the world of words is not separate from the world of things, and 2) words and things—as well as their interrelationships—continually change and these changes have to be rendered perceptible. Therefore the representation of change by direct designation or description in the text could be neither sufficient nor effective. The most important thing for the text to transmit was the *sensation* of the process of organizing and transforming thought. Linear logical argument does not organize. It represents organization. It does not transform. It eliminates transformation. The philosopher's natural rhetoric, what d'Alembert called *eloquence,* does not inform; it persuades. It changes minds; it transforms the understanding of ideas and situations.

The function of the sophisticated and multifaceted rhetoric in the *Encyclopédie* was to make the reader aware of the process of persuasion, to force him to realize when changes in his own thoughts and attitudes (intellectual affinities) were taking place. The philosophical reader should therefore be drawn by the *Encyclopédie*'s style, by its rhetorical structure and operation—that is, by its poetics (in the sense used in the *Rêve*)—to perceive both the dynamic shape of the world

18. For an extended discussion of scientific nomenclature and the resulting rhetorical constraints in an almost contemporary example, see my *Between the Library and the Laboratory,* chap. 7.

and the way the reader's own actions are integral parts in it. For style defined this way, complexity not only was perfectly acceptable but could actually be required to transmit the experience of the complexity and the particular dynamics of a subject matter. Complexity poses a problem only when it is arbitrary (think of the debate in the *Encyclopédie*'s grammar articles about inversion in French style).

In other words, the writing format that the natural philosopher should adopt was one that was conceptually open-ended, that would force inventive speculation and thought by its very operation and structure, that would bare the authorial function in operation and require an active and independent reader. This is certainly a characterization that any modern reader would recognize as well qualifying what we consider to be distinctive to literature. The natural philosopher was not to write closed, definitive, logical accounts of the fixed knowledge of the world. He was not a scientist, and he did not engage in scientific writing. On the contrary, he wrote an extended and engaged literature whose forms were more varied (and had to be, by the very nature of the inventiveness being promulgated) than those that we recognize now. He wrote to invent, to challenge, to bring about change, and to create more natural philosophers.

Who can write like this? Who can think like this? The work Diderot was evoking here sounds suspiciously like that of the dangerous men of eloquence of the "Discours," the unassimilable who create *écarts*, who disrupt the harmony and symmetry of the slow but continual accumulation of ordered knowledge. In other words, these men possess at least some form or quantity of genius. For d'Alembert, by definition, they constituted precisely the *écarts*: the accidents, the divergences from the norm, whose work could be admired and appreciated but, being essentially idiosyncratic, was irrelevant to those attempting to construct an overall analytic description of nature.

But in a different context, a different definition holds: the definition of genius must be adjusted to take into account the different theory of knowledge and the natural philosophy underpinning it. The genius for Diderot was the one most likely to cause change, not because he was the least in harmony with nature, but because he was the most in harmony with nature. The genius of "Encyclopédie," therefore, is the same genius that we met in the *Interprétation*, who sees through to the dynamic principles of nature. Just as for d'Alembert the *savant* in his self-effacing ordering was the voice of one kind of nature—the fixed Newtonian determined nature—so for Diderot the philosophical genius, by giving voice to new ideas or, as editor of the encyclopedia, distilling the essence of the articles in further editions or generating clever cross references, embodied the innovative change that was at the heart of Diderotian materialism.

Understanding nature better than anyone else, the philosopher works dialectically with it to adjust the language to the changes that he sees have already taken place and to nudge nature and people toward changes that he feels should take place and away from ones that perhaps might be avoided. As was clear in the *Interprétation*, Diderot saw humanity not as a category to set in opposition to nature; culture and nature are not opposing terms. On the contrary, man is one of the active forces within nature, a nature that includes him and his productions. In the *Entretiens sur le fils naturel*, there is a famous description of the man of genius absorbed in enthusiastic contemplation of the natural world.

> Le lendemain je me rendis au pied de la colline. L'endroit était solitaire et sauvage. On avait en perspective quelques hameaux répandus dans la plaine; au delà une chaîne de montagnes inégales et déchirées qui terminaient en partie l'horizon. On était à l'ombre des chênes, et l'on entendait le bruit sourd d'une eau souterraine qui coulait aux environs. (DPV 10:98)

> The next day I took myself to the foot of the hill. The site was solitary and wild. The perspective was of several hamlets scattered over the plain; beyond lay a chain of uneven and ragged mountains that ended part of the horizon. I was in the shadow of oak trees, and the muted sound of a subterranean stream running in the area could be heard.

At first we seem to be in a Rousseauist wild nature, in which man is merely tolerated or overwhelmed with complementary feelings of its power and his difference from it. But in fact, the passage goes on to show that man is an integral part of this nature.

> C'était la saison où la terre est couverte des biens qu'elle accorde au travail et à la sueur des hommes. Dorval était arrivé le premier. J'approchai de lui sans qu'il m'aperçut. Il s'était abandonné au spec-

tacle de la nature. Il avait la poitrine élevée. Il respirait avec force. Ses yeux attentifs se portaient sur tous les objets. Je suivais sur son visage les impressions diverses qu'il en éprouvait; et je commençais à partager son transport, lorsque je m'écriai, presque sans le vouloir, "Il est sous le charme." (98)

It was the season when the earth is covered with the fruits she yields to the work and sweat of men. Dorval had arrived first. I approached without his seeing me. He had abandoned himself to the spectacle of nature. His chest was expanded. He was breathing hard. His attentive eyes fastened on all the objects. I followed on his face the diverse impressions he was experiencing; and I was beginning to share his transport when I cried, almost involuntarily, "He is under the spell."

Dorval sees a natural world that includes him and his work, as well as the nonhuman and noncultural. Moreover, the longer he looks, the more his admiring gaze (see also Diderot's *Encyclopédie* article "Admiration," DPV 5:277) shows him not only so-called natural objects but also objects created by men and objects still to be created. He sees both what materially exists and the traces of past actions and events in the world around him; his vision of this world transmits to him the ability to act himself. He is the ultimate natural philosopher from the *Interprétation*.

Dorval tells Diderot how his vision works to provide communication with the material world.

L'enthousiasme naît d'un objet de la nature. Si l'esprit l'a vu sous des aspects frappants et divers, il en est occupé, agité, tourmenté. L'imagination s'échauffe. La passion s'émeut. On est successivement étonné, attendri, indigné, courroucé. Sans l'enthousiasme, ou l'idée véritable ne se présente point; ou, si par hasard on la rencontre, on ne peut la poursuivre...Le poète sent le moment de l'enthousiasme. C'est après qu'il a médité. Il s'annonce en lui par un frémissement qui part de sa poitrine, et qui passe d'une manière délicieuse et rapide jusqu'aux extrémités de son corps. Bientôt ce n'est plus un frémissement. C'est une chaleur forte et permanente qui l'embrase, qui le fait haleter, qui le consume, qui le tue; mais qui donne l'âme, la vie à tout ce qu'il touche. Si cette chaleur s'accroissait encore, les spectres se multiplieraient devant lui. Sa passion s'élèverait presque au degré de la fureur. Il ne connaîtrait de soulagement qu'à verser au-dehors un torrent d'idées qui se pressent, se heurtent, et se chassent. (99)

Enthusiasm arises from an object of nature. If the mind has seen it under striking and diverse aspects, it is occupied, agitated, tormented by it. The imagination heats up. Passion is aroused. One is successively astonished, touched, indignant, angered. Without enthusiasm, either the true idea doesn't present itself, or if by chance one does encounter it, one can't follow up on it...The poet senses the moment of enthusiasm. It's afterwards that he meditates. It announces itself through a shivering that comes from the chest and passes in a delicious and rapid manner out to the extremities of his body. Soon it is no longer a shivering. It becomes a strong and permanent heat that ignites him, that makes him pant, that consumes him, that kills him; but that gives soul, life to everything it touches. If this heat grew further, the specters would multiply before him. His passion would develop almost into furor. He would get relief only by pouring out a torrent of ideas that press in on him, bump into each other, chase each other out.

In other words, Diderot's genius is not merely a transcriber of what he sees. He is driven by his contact with the world to intervene in it actively; his intervention is inevitable and necessary because, as the remarkably eloquent physical descriptions (they are not metaphors!) insist, he is materially continuous with it.[19] In this sense, Diderot saw the genius as nature's tool to accomplish positive transformation, a transformation that occurs through poetic creation. One consequence of Diderot's contention that the nature of genius is to be in harmony with nature allows us to complete our understanding of Diderot's notion of plagiarism. If the genial philosopher's speech, like Dorval's, is a result of the state of the material world when he speaks, then the originality of his writing cannot be questioned, for his eloquence is not a manifestation of his singular identity; it is a mark of his power to interact with nature. Unlike Condillac's observer, who appears to be used by nature to analyze itself, Diderot's genial philosopher is one of the active principles of nature: he changes the coordination of the part of the world he is exceptionally talented to perceive, including changing the rules of coordination (Shakespeare, Descartes) or adapting them from one domain to another (Voltaire, Rameau, Newton). Yet as for the analytic observer, it is hard to distinguish meaningfully between the philosopher and

19. Diderot's articles "Chaleur" and "Génération" in the *Encyclopédie* complement this passage very well.

nature, so what do we mean by the "originality" of such innovation? *Original* has come to mean that one person's creation originates only with him, but Diderot's own production both theorized and demonstrated that when we characterize a work as original—whether it is fictional prose, physical theories, or Rameau's nephew's "antisocial" behavior—we are most often acknowledging that the work has changed the way we perceive a given event. Such originality is a function of degree and of the author-reader-world context. The more something changes our perceptions, the more original we perceive it to be; moreover, change the context, and the same work does not do the same thing. Chambers's articles rewritten within the *Encyclopédie* do not operate on the reader the way they did in Chambers's *Cyclopedia*. They have been "reauthored" by Diderot and d'Alembert. The question of plagiarism simply becomes inappropriate. Diderot plagiarizing Goldoni or Seneca was adjusting the dramatic, literary, or political creations of his predecessors to the changed geographical and cultural location of the Parisian Enlightenment as only he could then see and shape them.

Originality is recognized by the sense of "rightness" one gets when experiencing the shift of perception. A reader's pleasure at encountering originality comes in part from no longer having to strain to try to make an out-of-date description of the world still seem adequate. Indeed, a sense of rightness distinguishes the original from the bizarre. For the Diderotian philosopher the key to the meaning of the term *originality* lies in this sense of rightness. The bizarre just shatters the perception of a coordinated world without replacing it with a new coordination. A well-trained natural philosopher (his genius maximized and focused) can perceive the present coordination of nature (including his predecessors' works) and both describe and bring about new configurations. His work is one of the organizing events in an ongoing natural history; perhaps a particularly effective and striking one given his very direct relationship to nature, but still an event. Does an event like Dorval's torrent of words "belong" to him? Can it be understood apart from the larger context it addresses and changes? Is the Diderot character's presentation of Dorval's behavior and words—in other words, his writing of the text of the *Entretiens sur le fils naturel*—a plagiarism of Dorval? Generalizing, Diderot clearly holds that later natural philosophers would be just as entitled to consider literary works as material for their own elaboration or revision as d'Alembert's scientists do the theories and discoveries of their predecessors.

Dorval seems to have represented for Diderot the total genius whose judgment was always not only correct but also instrumental in creating new forms of rightness. In the article "Encyclopédie," Diderot was not as generous to the partial genius—the one whose vision encompasses only a part of nature, for example, music (Rameau the uncle), literature (Shakespeare), physics (Descartes and Newton). The products of a partial genius were not to be accepted unquestioningly.

J'ai pensé quelquefois qu'il serait heureux pour un peuple qu'il ne se rencontrât point chez lui un homme extraordinaire, sous lequel un art naissant fît ses premiers progrès trop grands & trop rapides, & qui en interrompît le mouvement insensible & naturel. Les ouvrages de cet homme seront nécessairement des composés monstrueux, parce que le génie & le bon goût sont deux qualités très différentes. La nature donne l'un en un moment: l'autre est le produit des siècles. Ces monstres deviendront des modèles nationaux; ils décideront le goût d'un peuple. Les bons esprits qui succéderont, trouveront en leur faveur une prévention qu'ils n'oseront heurter; & la notion du beau s'obscurcira. (DPV 5:234)

I have sometimes thought that it would be lucky for a people never to encounter an extraordinary man under whom a nascent art's progress would be too great and too rapid and who would interrupt its insensible and natural movement. The works of this man will necessarily be monstrous composites, because genius and good taste are two very different qualities. Nature furnishes one in a moment; the other is the product of centuries. These monsters will become national models; they will decide the taste of a people. The clear heads who follow them will find a prejudice in favor [of those monsters] that they will not dare challenge; and the notion of the beautiful will be obscured.

This *écart* is not of kind but of degree. It has two dimensions: speed of understanding (and hence ability to assimilate change) and the extent of comprehensiveness. The partial genius is both highly specialized and much quicker at "sniffing out" or intuiting appropriate changes in his field. His monstrosity is therefore a problem of synchronization: he must extend his vision and slow down to his audience's speed. The partial genius must be constrained by his cultural environment, and the encyclopedia, of course, would do this. It would train the partial genius to temper his particular talent by permanently listening to the voice of his general cultural context and by showing him how to evaluate the products of his own imagination with a carefully controlled critical judgment—that is, to be his own most demanding audience. It would turn the monster into a natural philosopher.

Could a "total" genius exist? In the *Interprétation* it was the natural philosopher who saw straight through to the "single act of nature," the one in whose mind everything coordinated. In the *Entretiens sur le fils naturel,* it was Dorval. If a place for one existed in the *Encyclopédie,* it was only in the role of the general editor, the editor who established the multifunctional network of cross references.[20] The general editor needed the genius's ability to achieve an almost total overview of the project so that his interventions would be less likely to cause cultural imbalance or distortions in the process of synchronizing the content and functioning of the encyclopedia with that of the rest of nature. *The greater the genius, the less likely he was to cause disruption rather than cultural revolution.* A complementary function would then be to moderate the cultural input of the lesser geniuses by drawing them into the training procedure indicated by the hierarchy of readers in figure 3.2. Moreover, the greater the natural philosopher, the more likely it would be that he could induce his pupils (or readers in this case) to learn to synthesize genius with good taste. In large measure he could do so by inducing in them mental coordination, enabling them to assimilate both faster and more harmoniously. What would have appeared bizarre (to use the *Interprétation*'s terminology) or monstrous (to use the "Encyclopédie" and the *Rêve*'s terminology) to them before their training would then more often and more quickly be seen as original.

Clearly Diderot's philosophers, unlike Rousseau's, were to be anything but critical revolutionaries.[21] They would challenge only to

20. Diderot himself, obviously, was the person implicitly indicated. Highly amusing from this perspective is Diderot's article "Editeur" (DPV 7:114-16), an ironic disclaimer of all responsibility for the content of the *Encyclopédie.* In it Diderot said nothing about the actual positive contributions made by its editors, but the final cross reference is to the article "Eloge"! The actual analysis of the editor is found, of course, in the article "Encyclopédie," which is not cross-referenced in "Editeur."

21. This is perhaps the answer to the question that Georges Benrekassa asks himself in "Pratique philosophique."

reestablish functional order in the face of the meaningless disorder sometimes produced by nature or by catastrophe. The change they would incite would be gradual, even if sometimes dramatic, and motivated by an attempt to adhere to the overreaching and reciprocal organization of world by culture and vice versa. Only they could create a local continuity that would endure across time or space, a continuity whose stability would derive from neither abstract truth architectures nor political or social structures, all denounced vehemently by Diderot (for example, 181) as equally ephemeral and transitory. They would carry out his imperative that needed cultural, social, and political changes were to be brought about in the smoothest ways possible.

I should point out here that Diderot did not believe that happiness was necessarily an indication of the good. The notion of virtue that he had derived from his early work on Shaftesbury was profoundly redefined in the context of his materialism. He held that nature favors complexity-producing organization – in other words, dynamic organization that complexifies itself. Further, this inherent drive within the organization manifests itself in ways that include not only intelligence but also the sentiment of virtue operating within human beings. In the article "Encyclopédie," Diderot drew on this drive as one of the forces to be used to create the *Encyclopédie*.[22] The multiplicity of people necessary to its creation would be called to work together by a sort of natural affinity.

> J'ajoute, *des hommes liés par l'intérêt général du genre humain & par un sentiment de bienveillance réciproque*, parce que ces motifs étant les plus honnêtes qui puissent animer des âmes bien nées,[23] ce sont aussi les plus durables. On s'applaudit intérieurement de ce que l'on fait; on s'échauffe; on entreprend pour son collègue & pour son ami, ce qu'on ne tenterait par aucune autre considération. (180)

> I add, *men bound together by the general interest of the human race and by a sentiment of reciprocal good will*, because, these motives being the most honest that can animate well-born souls, they are

22. In opposition to the drive of self-interest, which d'Alembert saw as the motivating force for the creation of knowledge in the "Discours," and which Rousseau denounced as the origin of culture in the *Discours sur l'inégalité*.

23. This is not the place to go into it, but in accordance with his materialism, Diderot here means "well-organized materially" as a result of contact with historically previous good organizations, like that of one's parents' bodies or one's teachers' minds.

also the most durable. One applauds oneself silently for what one does; one gets excited; one undertakes for a colleague or friend what one would not attempt for any other consideration.

Virtue would fuel the encyclopedists' work, but of course, it could not be a virtue relying on a fixed moral order. The incipient meaning of virtuous behavior in this context could only resemble the careful steering of complexification toward a social structure moving increasingly into harmony with the continually changing material nature. Therefore, ethical precepts would have to change as the world changed.[24]

The *Encyclopédie* was to be one medium for maintaining both this "natural culture" and the only stability that it is useful to create, that of the attentive and regulated inventive minds that understand the functioning of nature and the stakes of change. The encyclopedia as event would produce a sort of supermind of interlocking philosophers. This supermind would resemble the group mind that thinks the second half of the *Rêve de d'Alembert* but differs in that the judgment training intrinsic to the *Encyclopédie* would cause the work of each philosopher to temper as well as provoke the work of the others. Potentially, then, the *Encyclopédie* would operate in a gradual and careful way so as to minimize cultural losses while stimulating cultural advance.

As we shall see in chapter 4, Diderot directly opposed Rousseau in this view. While he did not deny, in the *Supplément au voyage de Bougainville*, that what might be seen as a precultural condition may have been relatively happy, he did indeed deny that the primitive culture of his fictional Tahiti was the site of privileged virtue. For him the source of real virtue lay in adapting one's place and time to the

24. Diderot himself attempted to provide a network of articles to initiate the tasks both of developing a greater understanding of virtue and of transmitting it to the readers and authors. During the years up until 1755 or so, he wrote his "history of philosophy" articles, which both spread throughout the body of the *Encyclopédie* the basic components of his materialist view of the world and attempted to provoke a conversation about the nature of virtue. (See esp. "Ame," "Ames des bêtes," "Animal," "Art," "Admiration," "Beau," "Cabinet d'histoire naturelle," "Célibat," "Chaos," "Citoyen," "Conservation," "Droit naturel," "Eclairé," "Eclectisme," "Homme," "Intolérance," and "Naître." Most articles discussing a particular philosophical school ["Epicuréisme," "Leibnitzianisme," and "Pyrrhonienne," for example] or the ideas of a particular people ["Arabes," "Egyptiens," "Juifs"] were also by Diderot.

changes that occur while continuing to promote beneficial changes.

Therefore, and contrary to what Rousseau argued, Diderot, working on the *Encyclopédie*, saw the arts and sciences not as the source of corruption and perversion but as the only way to avoid them. This is perhaps the context in which to understand a passage that comes from the very beginning of the article "Encyclopédie" and has caused a number of misreadings of Diderot as either revolutionary or positivist:

> Le moment le plus glorieux pour un ouvrage de cette nature, ce serait celui qui succèderait immédiatement à quelque grande *révolution* qui aurait suspendu les progrès des sciences, interrompu les travaux des arts, & replongé dans les ténèbres une portion de notre hémisphère. Quelle reconnaissance la génération qui viendrait après ce temps de trouble ne porterait-elle pas aux hommes qui les auraient redoutés de loin, & qui en auraient prévenu le ravage, en mettant à l'abri les connaissances des siècles passés? (188)

> The most glorious moment for a work of this nature would be the one that would immediately follow some great *revolution* that would have suspended the progress of the sciences, interrupted the labors of the arts, and plunged a portion of our hemisphere into shadow again. What gratitude the generation that came after this time of disorder would feel for the men who feared it from afar and who prevented its ravages by sheltering the knowledge of past centuries!

Just as had d'Alembert, Diderot confronted the notion of cultural discontinuity. But as was also clear in the d'Alembertian text, *révolution* at this time still meant a dramatic change, not necessarily (or even primarily) a political revolution in the modern sense. Translated to take into account the materialism we have been considering, it meant a violent disruption in the previously functional elastic system of the material and cultural world. This term could thus describe an earthquake, a political upheaval, or a great change in the scope of knowledge (such as the discovery of the New World). It could even encompass, on a small scale, the consequences that Shakespeare's plays had for the aesthetics of theater in England. Whatever form it took, revolution unnecessarily eliminated forms of knowledge and organization that could still have been beneficially worked into any new structure by sufficiently supple observers of the dynamic.

Of course, these observers, Diderot's natural philosophers, were not merely erudite *savants* working in a shielded *cité scientifique* to create the archive of knowledge to survive disasters, and the *Encyclopédie* was not merely an archive or stock of positive knowledge. The observers were cultural midwives who spanned discontinuity with active mental bridges. The cross references added to the archive provided a way of reactivating the voices of the past, of recreating the conversation-events that provided both inspiration for innovation and the judgment training to control it. The *Encyclopédie* was indeed subversive, as it has always been characterized. However, Diderot's philosophers were preparing not a *machine de guerre*, as the *Encyclopédie* has so often been called, but, in the well-trained transhistorical group mind generated by the cross-reference structure, an organically permanent *machine de transformation*. The change that Diderot's natural philosopher was duty-bound to bring about would for us be characterized as an evolution rather than as a revolution. This was the Diderotian program for the Enlightenment, and the tool he constructed to bring it about was the *Encyclopédie*.

Part II

Diderot's Humanism

The Economics of a Virtuous Esthetics

FOUR

Dismantling a Utopian Economics

The full applicability of Diderot's early dynamic materialism became evident only when he transferred his focus from the world of intellectual endeavor, however broadly defined, to the broader sphere of human behavior and interaction. Then Diderot finally took up the challenge he had posed himself at the end of the *Rêve de d'Alembert* to redefine *la poétique* in its full material terms. His initial move was to extend his dynamic mechanophysical model of material creation to account for human sexual reproduction. This extension allowed him to elaborate a model of all social functioning—and the place of a specifically human dynamic—that would epitomize his materialist picture and provide its final justification.

The penultimate unfolding of his social theory occurred in the beautiful but recalcitrant *Supplément au voyage de Bougainville*. The poignant picture of the Tahitian "natural culture," of villagers destroyed by Bougainville's sailors' syphilis and their equivalent contamination by European mores and religion seems at first glance to be a classic Enlightenment—even Rousseauist—denunciation of the corrupting effect of increasing civilization.[1] But against the backdrop of his materialism, Diderot's story takes on a different cast, a much more ambiguous one, and replaces the primitive innocence of Rousseau's noble savages with the shifting and disabused morality of

1. There has always been controversy surrounding the interrelationship of Rousseau's and Diderot's ideas on this question, even as early as the publication of the *Discours sur l'inégalité*. For a good discussion of both contemporaneous and traditional modern points of view, see Herbert Dieckmann's classic introduction to his critical edition of Denis Diderot, *Supplément au voyage de Bougainville* (Geneva and Lille: Droz and Giard, 1955), esp. lxxiii–xciv. All citations of the *Supplément* are to DPV, vol. 12.

Rameau's nephew. Against expectation, the final picture is anything but sinister. Diderot's salon philosophers, by abandoning utopian visions, whether negative or positive, accede (seemingly paradoxically) to a position superseding the fatalistic determinism associated with materialism.

As we might expect, the text does not deliver directly its nonetheless explicit message. The *Supplément au voyage de Bougainville* is, as its title already hints, a complex. It consists of several interlocking dialogues framing an antecedent work by another author and, in addition, Diderot's fictional supplement to it—also in the form of dialogues. As ever, the rhetorical structure provides the grid through which the speeches of the characters must be read to make their Diderotian consequences visible. No speech can be taken out of its carefully worked-out position in the overall architecture of the work and maintain its interpretive value. To construct the explicit and fairly unequivocal message, the reader must call upon a multifaceted set of reading techniques instilled into him by Diderot to complement his own choices of rhetorical structure. Again, however—as with the *Interprétation de la nature* or the *Rêve de d'Alembert* and as the Diderotian construal of the *Encyclopédie* was intended to demonstrate and put into operation—Diderot did not intend this type of rhetorical determination to constrain or manipulate his reader but to extend the author's range of tools to communicate with his reader and to foster the reader's perceptivity and judgment. He was not liberating his reader from the message in the sense of making any interpretation of the text valid; rather, he was aiding the construction of more complex messages.[2] In this way, Diderot enabled the cognitive transmission of a conceptual entity that, as his recourse to the model of touch and vibration in the *Interprétation* had long before suggested, would otherwise be incommunicable.

---

2. That he had a fairly straightforward message to transmit, that not all interpretations of his text are valid, that "not anything goes," does not mean that Diderot used rhetoric as a tool for involuntary persuasion. Recently there has come to be an almost automatic equation of discernment of complex and functional rhetorical structure to a text with revelation of manipulation—almost abuse—of the reader. This is of course an old, even ageless, construal of rhetoric and one that was quite common in Diderot's time too. It is only one construal, however, and not one that Diderot aimed his texts toward. In this sense I diverge from the Derridean and de Manian currents of Diderot criticism.

The Economics of Morality

The subtitle of the *Supplément*, "Sur l'Inconvénient d'attacher des idées morales à certaines actions physiques qui n'en comportent pas," suggests that this text will continue the libertine tradition of the end of the seventeenth century drawn from a certain reading of Descartes's and Newton's work. It manifested itself not only in the appearance of Helvétius' and La Mettrie's soulless man-machines but also in the amoralism of certain pornographers and satirists. The reader immediately knows that sex is the central subject and expects a materialist polemic against sexually constraining morality as an illusion, an invention inconsistent with the mechanical determinism of the world. Such arguments sought to justify the unlimited satisfaction of passions and desires regardless of the wellbeing of other members of a social group.[3] We shall see that, as usual, Diderot disappointed his reader's expectations while using them to sensitize him to an entirely different message.

As I mentioned earlier, the order in which the reader encounters the various scenes is crucial. Each scene provides the ethical framework in which to situate and therefore to interpret correctly the text that follows it. Following the textual order, however, is an inefficient way to display the results of this reading experience. Explicating the functioning of the text from the focal point out works better, but it requires keeping in mind the basic structure of the text. A framing dialogue between two European philosophers in a French garden begins the text, links two embedded dialogues, and wraps up the discussion at the end. The first embedded dialogue presents the Tahitian patriarch's speech (his violent, bitter farewell to Bougainville's sailors). The second, the best-known part of the *Supplément*, presents the dialogue that had taken place several weeks earlier between a European monk and a Tahitian father and natural philosopher, together with the interpolated story of an ethically astute prostitute from the American colonies. The monk's dialogue, because it is often treated as though it were the only part of the text worth explicating, is routinely read out of its structural position. As a result, I believe, its message is taken to be the inverse of what it turns out to be when

3. For example, see the complementary arguments of Sade in the *Philosophie dans le boudoir* and Rousseau's implicit attack on this position contained in *La Nouvelle Héloise*.

reread in the light of the preceding and enveloping texts. When it is replaced in its position, we can see not only how Diderot thought out the issues he was addressing but also how his rhetorical structure provided his reader, at the same time, a dramatic criticism of the positions of his contemporaries on the same questions.

The *Supplément* begins with A and B, who seem to be two Parisian salon philosophers, walking in the garden of a country house. Their discussion at first concerns the weather—their emotional response to it and its effect on their conversation and behavior, and the mechanophysical causes behind its development. Although the text does not say so, they appear to be two well-trained materialists who see not a disjunction but a strong relationship between the climatic events they undergo and their mental—hence moral—states.

A and B then embark on a similar but much more extensive comparison by discussing the "meaning" of Bougainville's voyage around the world (not the account of it that he had just published, but the actual voyage) and strategically characterize him in national terms.

> Bougainville a le goût des amusements de la société; il aime les femmes, les spectacles, les repas délicats; il se prête au tourbillon du monde d'aussi bonne grâce qu'aux inconstances de l'élément sur lequel il a été ballotté. Il est aimable et gai: c'est un véritable Français lesté, d'un bord, d'un traité de calcul différentiel et intégral, et de l'autre, d'un voyage autour du globe. (580)

> Bougainville has a taste for the amusements of society; he likes women, spectacles, delicate meals; he gives in to the world's whirlwind with just as good grace as to the uncertainties of the element on which he has been tossed around. He is friendly and gay: a true Frenchman balanced on one side by a treatise of differential and integral calculus and on the other by a voyage around the world.

So within the context of the susceptibility of reasoning man to his particular meteorological environment—climatically hence geographically specific—we find the notion of national character opposed to the idea of a universally valid morality. This relationship, all its possible variants, and its social consequences are in fact the overriding subject of the work. With this in mind, let us turn immediately to the dialogue between a monk traveling in the crew of Bougainville and Orou, the Tahitian "natural" philosopher. The dialogue is the transcription with commentary of their discussions over a period of several days when the Tahitians had welcomed the Europeans, dividing the crew up among their various huts, offering them unlimited sexual access to the various members of the community, and avidly questioning the Europeans about worlds and ways of thinking they had never suspected existed. The cultural differences toward sexual behavior are the immediate cause of the dialogue between Orou and the monk: Orou, the perfect host, encourages the monk to sleep with one of "his women," although he suggests that it might be gracious of him to accept his youngest daughter, who has never been able to get pregnant. The monk refuses, of course, in the name of religion, of his vows, of good morals and honesty. Orou is shocked.

Je ne sais ce que c'est que la chose que tu appelles religion; mais je ne puis qu'en penser mal, puisqu'elle t'empêche de goûter un plaisir innocent, auquel nature, la souveraine maîtresse, nous invite tous; de donner l'existence à un de tes semblables; de rendre un service que le père, la mère et les enfants te demandent; de t'acquitter envers un hôte qui t'a fait un bon accueil, et d'enrichir une nation, en l'accroissant d'un sujet de plus. Je ne sais ce que c'est que la chose que tu appelles état; mais ton premier devoir est d'être homme et d'être reconnaissant. (600–601)

I don't know what this thing is that you call religion; but I can only think ill of it, since it prevents you from tasting an innocent pleasure to which nature, the sovereign mistress, invites us all; to give existence to one of your own kind; to render a service that the father, mother, and children all ask of you; to reward a host who has welcomed you, and to enrich a nation by increasing it by one more subject. I don't know what this thing is that you call state, but your first duty is to be a man and to be grateful.

In the name of the most European of obligations, that of hospitality and courtesy, Orou upbraids the monk, "Sois généreux!" The entire construct of the moral condemnation of desire and sexuality is here inverted: religion is that which prevents the spontaneous courtesy of sexual relations. Here we are right in the middle of an apology for free love, or so it seems; here we are voyeuristically enjoying along with the monk the torture of four naked bodies entwining themselves around him. We quickly see, though, that the titillation, the temptation, lies not in the sexual act itself or even in the act of seduction (the youngest daughter's pleading is a natural and ultimately effective form of seduction; the monk yields in spite of his intention to remain celibate). The titillation for the monk, at least, lies in his attempt to resist. When he stops fighting nature, he returns to a form of innocence from which his religion had only separated him even while claiming to preserve it for him. (This text in many places and quite explicitly can be read as an inversion of the story of Adam and Eve.) In fact, Orou criticizes the European concept of a God who gives fixed laws that, according to him, produce both the idea and the fact of crime. Going on to speak of marriage as frozen sexual choice, he says,

> Rien, en effet, te paraît-il plus insensé qu'un précepte qui proscrit le changement qui est en nous; qui commande une constance qui n'y peut être, et qui viole la nature et la liberté du mâle et de la femelle ... qu'un serment d'immutabilité de deux êtres de chair, à la face d'un ciel qui n'est pas un instant le même, sous des antres qui menacent ruine; au bas d'une roche qui tombe en poudre; au pied d'un arbre qui se gerce; sur une pierre qui s'ébranle? (605)

> Does anything, in effect, seem more senseless to you than a precept forbidding the change that is in us; requiring a constancy that cannot be there; violating the nature and the liberty of the male and the female ... than a vow of immutability from two beings of flesh, under a sky that is not for one instant the same, in a cave threatened with ruin; beneath a rock crumbling to dust; at the foot of a tree that is splitting; on a stone that wobbles?

Orou, after leading the monk to admit that nothing is more commonplace than the sexual behavior forbidden in Europe, explains that it is mandated in Tahiti because it is natural. "Veux-tu savoir, en tout temps et en tout lieu, ce qui est bon et mauvais? Attache-toi à la nature des choses et des actions" (607; "Do you want to know, for all times and all places, what is good and bad? Cleave to the natures of things and actions"). He argues that a society which accepts that the world continually changes (in our terms, accepts a Diderotian materialism) and bases its morality accordingly, avoids the European illogic and resulting moral (and sometimes physical) suffering. Orou essentially reduces the issue to the Europeans' confusion of things that do not feel change, and can therefore be owned, with things that do feel change and can therefore have a sense of self. Things with a sense of self cannot be owned.

Ne vois-tu pas qu'on a confondu, dans ton pays, la chose qui n'a ni sensibilité, ni pensée, ni désir, ni volonté; qu'on quitte, qu'on prend, qu'on garde, qu'on échange sans qu'elle souffre et sans qu'elle se plaigne, avec la chose qui ne s'échange point, qui ne s'acquiert point; qui a liberté, volonté, désir; qui peut se donner ou se refuser pour un moment; se donner ou se refuser pour toujours; qui se plaint et qui souffre; et qui ne saurait devenir un effet de commerce, sans qu'on oublie son caractère, et qu'on fasse violence à la nature? Contraires [sic] à la loi générale des êtres. (604-5)

Don't you see that in your country you have confused the thing that has no sensibility, thought, desire, or will, that one leaves, takes, keeps, exchanges without its suffering or complaining, with that which is not exchanged, who is not acquired, who has freedom, will, desire, who can give herself or deny you forever, who complains and suffers, and who cannot become an object of commerce without your denying her character and doing violence to her nature? Contrary to the general law of beings.

Infidelity, the prime example under discussion, is therefore not a crime; it is an inevitable result of natural change. The crime is to try to force people into acknowledging unnatural states of fixity, such as fidelity, so as to gain power over them by punishing them, making them feel guilty, for actions they could not avoid without being untrue to their natures. Moreover, one must consider people as property—as things that can belong permanently to another human being—to make the idea of fidelity coherent. The Tahitians, at first glance the perfect Rousseauist noble savages, claim not to recognize any form of property, and especially not the ownership of people that underlies the European moral codes.

Here I depart from the traditional readings of this dialogue, which focus on the naïvely eloquent (eloquent because naïve) critique of European religious and moral institutions. "OROU: Oh! le vilain pays! Si tout y est ordonné comme ce que tu m'en dis, vous êtes plus barbares que nous" (626; "OROU: Oh! vile country! If everything is organized there as you tell me, you are more barbaric than we"). In

this, Diderot to a remarkable extent repeated the materialist plati-
tudes of his philosophical contemporaries. (He even had A at the end
of the dialogue find Orou "un peu modelé à l'européenne" [627; "a little modeled on the European"].) Instead of building on these words,
however, let us focus on the actual structure and functioning of
Diderot's version of the Tahitian social order. To do this, we return
to the beginning of the philosophical discussion between Orou and
the monk. We remember that it was sparked by the monk's refusal to
sleep with Orou's daughter. This refusal is read by the Tahitians not
as a moral issue but as an economic issue. "Sois généreux," Orou's
admonition to the monk, has of course in this text its contemporary
meaning of "have nobility of soul"; it also here has the modern economic meaning of "share or give of some of your property."
Although we at first think that what Orou means is that the monk
is to be generous with his kindness or courtesy, in fact, he is to be generous with his body and his body's ability to create: Thia wants a
baby, *"qui fasse une partie de ma dot*, lorsque je passerai de la cabane
de mon père dans une autre" (602; my emphasis; "who will be part
of my dowry when I move from my father's hut into another").
Orou had just said, "Elles m'appartiennent, et je te les offre: elles sont
à elles, et elles se donnent à toi" ("They belong to me, and I offer
them to you; they belong to themselves, and they give themselves to
you"). People are indeed property even in Tahiti, but in a curious
sense, as we already see. Out of the issue of sexuality comes not the
notion of desire and its unlimited satisfaction, but a peculiar concept
of property that is the pole around which the rest of the dialogue
will effectively turn.[4] Diderot has his Tahitians develop, out of a first-
order version of his materialism, a "natural economics" that will
serve as the foundation of a social and moral order.

L'AUMONIER Et lorsque vous vous y [in a marriage] trouvez mal?

OROU Nous nous séparons.

L'AUMONIER Que deviennent vos enfants?

OROU O étranger! ta dernière question achève de me déceler la profonde misère de ton pays. Sache, mon ami, qu'ici la naissance d'un

4. In this I reverse the reading of Dieckmann, intro. to *Supplément,* lxxxi–lxxxiv: I hold
that Diderot did not see the notion of property arising from the notion of sexuality but
rather saw it structuring the concept of sexuality in a distinctive way.

enfant est toujours un bonheur, et sa mort un sujet de regrets et de larmes. Un enfant est un *bien précieux,* parce qu'il doit devenir un homme; aussi, en avons-nous un tout autre soin que de nos plantes et de nos animaux. Un enfant qui naît, occasionne la joie domestique et publique: c'est un *accroissement de fortune* pour la cabane, et de force pour la nation. . . . En passant de la cabane de son mari dans celle de ses parents, une femme emmène avec elle ses enfants qu'elle avait apportés en dot: on partage ceux qui sont nés pendant la cohabitation commune. . . .

L'AUMONIER Mais des enfants sont longtemps à charge avant que de rendre service.

OROU Nous destinons à leur entretien et à la subsistance des vieillards, une sixième partie de tous les fruits du pays; ce tribut les suit partout. Ainsi tu vois que *plus la famille du Tahitien est nombreuse, plus elle est riche.* (609-10; my emphasis)

THE ALMONER And when you're unhappy [in a marriage]?

OROU We separate.

THE ALMONER What happens to your children?

OROU Oh, foreigner! your last question finally reveals the profound wretchedness of your country. Know, my friend, that here the birth of a child is always a happiness and his death a subject for regret and tears. A child is a precious commodity, because he must become a man; so, we take care of him much more than our plants and animals. The birth of a child brings domestic and public joy; it's an increase in the fortune of the hut and the strength of the nation. . . . when moving from her husband's hut back to her parents', a woman takes with her the children she had brought as dowry: the children born during cohabitation are shared. . . .

THE ALMONER But children are a burden for a long time before being of service.

OROU We earmark one sixth of all the harvest of the country to their upkeep and to the support of the old; this tribute follows them wherever they go. Thus you see that *the more numerous a Tahitian family is, the richer it is.*

Children thus are treasured not as persons but as the source of material riches. Although Orou does not say so, clearly the family with a great number of children can be considered rich only if the allowance each child receives is greater than what he can use and therefore provides an excess for his parents' use. Children are, then, the sign of wealth, of success. Children may be owned, but adults may not; children are defined as adults when they are fit to start producing healthy children (and therefore additional sources of riches to increase their parents' wealth until they leave home). Given that adults cannot be owned, no fixed family structure exists, either of marriage or of paternity, to specify which parent takes a child. The substitute is a complex system used to determine who owns which children. It in effect replaces any moral system. Solomon's logic would be highly inadequate in Tahiti.

In such a one-dimensional economic order, the way to create wealth is to create children. The way to create children is to maximize sexual contact. Therefore, as Orou eventually explains, the monk's generosity would be a form of tribute (624). In other words, he would be providing Orou's daughter a "free" child in exchange, presumably, for his consumption of a portion of the household's food resources. He would pay his way in the only currency the country recognizes: sexual production.

Is this the motivation behind all Tahitian sexuality? If so, what happens to the notion of desire and its relationship to sexual exchange? "Plus nos filles ont d'enfants, plus elles sont recherchées; plus nos garçons sont vigoureux et beaux, plus ils sont riches" (610; "The more children our daughters have, the more sought-after they are; the more vigorous and handsome our boys are, the richer they are"). *The point of sex is to create children to increase wealth, not to satisfy desire.* Indeed, as eventually becomes subtly evident, desire is a culturally determined concept. What makes a person sexually desirable in this particular country is his or her apparent ability to engender children.[5]

B [deciphering the monk's marginal annotations where he comments upon the] différence des idées de la beauté dans une contrée où l'on rapporte les formes au plaisir d'un moment, et chez un peuple où elles sont appréciées d'après une utilité plus constante. Là

---

5. Diderot believed in the hotly disputed idea of the "double semence": that women as well as men had a form of semen necessary to the creation of a child, rather than just being vessels sheltering the homunculus gathered from the males. His seeming advocacy here of equality between men and women is thus fitting in an economic system whose only form of production is procreation.

[in France], pour être belle, on exige un teint éclatant, un grand front, de grands yeux, des traits fins et délicats, une taille légère, une petite bouche, de petites mains, un petit pied...Ici, presque aucun de ces éléments n'entre en calcul. La femme sur laquelle les regards s'attachent et que le désir poursuit, est celle qui promet beaucoup d'enfants . . . et qui les promet actifs, intelligents, courageux, sains et robustes. Il n'y a presque rien de commun entre la Vénus d'Athènes et celle de Tahiti; l'une est Vénus galante, l'autre est Vénus féconde. (613)

B [deciphering the monk's marginal annotations where he comments upon the] difference in the ideas of beauty held by a country where forms indicate the pleasures of a moment and those of a people where they are appreciated according to a more constant utility. There [in France], to be beautiful, one must have a glowing complexion, wide forehead, large eyes, fine and delicate features, a tiny waist, tiny mouth, little hands, little feet...Here almost none of these elements enters in. The woman who attracts all eyes and whom everyone desires, is the one who promises many children, . . . children who are active, strong, intelligent, courageous, healthy, and robust. The Venus of Athens and Tahiti have almost nothing in common; one is a Venus of loose morals, the other a Venus who is fertile.

In other words, desire is provoked by a sign, not by direct physical contact or appearance. This sign designates a source not of sexual performance or pleasure but of wealth. As we have seen before, however, the notion of sign in a Diderotian context requires careful examination. Here, as in the *Encyclopédie* and, as we shall see in the next chapter, in the *Salon de 1767*, it is not a simple representation but an exemplification in a form that resembles Nelson Goodman's definition of the term.[6] For Orou continues, "Une Tahitienne disait un jour avec mépris à une autre femme du pays: 'Tu es belle, mais tu fais de laids enfants; je suis laide, mais je fais de beaux enfants, et c'est moi que les hommes préfèrent'" (613–14; "One Tahitian woman said scorn-

6. "The so-called intrinsic stylistic features of a work are never merely possessed but are among those possessed properties that are manifested, shown forth, *exemplified*—just as color and texture and weave, but not shape or size, are exemplified by the tailor's swatch he uses as a sample" (Nelson Goodman, *Ways of Worldmaking* [Indianapolis: Hackett,1978], 31–32). Given the great weight that the notion of "style" carried in Diderot's theory of intellectual production (cf. chap. 3), and that the Tahitians' only form of cultural production is the creation of children, the analogy holds here.

fully one day to another: 'You are beautiful, but you make ugly children; I am ugly, but I make beautiful children, and it is I whom the men prefer'"). The child's sign function is to exemplify, because he designates his mother's economic desirability metonymically: he functions as a sign because he is the physical product of her sexual success. Desirability defined as primarily economic. In a work about sexuality, it is striking that pleasure is never valorized. Nor is love a motivating force in this system, even love for one's children. Everything returns to the question of wealth.

> L'AUMONIER ... la tendresse maritale, l'amour paternel, ces deux sentiments si puissants et si doux, s'ils ne sont pas étrangers ici, y doivent être assez faibles.

> OROU Nous y avons suppléé par un autre, qui est tout autrement général, énergique et durable, l'intérêt. ... Sois sûr que partout où l'homme sera attaché à la conservation de son semblable comme à son lit, à sa santé, à son repos, à sa cabane, à ses fruits, à ses champs, il fera pour lui tout ce qu'il est possible de faire. (622–23)

> THE ALMONER Conjugal tenderness, paternal love—these two such powerful and sweet feelings, if they are not foreign here, at least must be fairly weak.

> OROU We have replaced them with another, otherwise general, energetic, and lasting, that of interest. ... Be assured that wherever man is attached to the conservation of his own kind the way he is to his bed, his health, his leisure, his hut, his produce, his fields, he will do everything possible for [his own kind].

The underlying notion of this entire dialogue is Orou's firm belief that all forms of desire are variants of one natural impulse: a drive to satisfy self-interest. A lust for property and physical lust are equivalent; the anxiety to preserve one's nonliving property is the same as the anxiety felt to protect children. This was not a cynical or ironic observation on Diderot's part. He was trying to theorize an epistemological genesis: the natural impulse of lusting-toward any thing or experience creates the concept of property as object (*lusting toward* here picks up his earlier use of the notions of attraction and affinity). Diderot thus derived the notion of property from his definition of nature. In that definition, nature is continuous with a notion of property (and therefore with "culture"), not antithetical to it.[7] From the drive to amass wealth, Orou derives a coherent notion of utility, and from utility, a lucid morality. From this same concept of morality, he then derives social rank and status: they are the index of fecundity, because fecundity guarantees wealth.

This clear one-to-one deterministic relationship among wealth, fecundity, social status, and morality has several interesting consequences, the most unexpected of which is an apology for incest. As is predictable, though, this incest is not the titillating transgression so beloved of Enlightenment pornographers and libertines. Given that sexual favors signify social respect for, or recognition of, a person's "rank" or demonstrated procreative capacities, a father's kindest gesture for a daughter seemingly too ugly to make her way into the sexual exchange circuits is to provide her with a beautiful child, which immediately marks her as desirable, which immediately causes her to be perceived as beautiful.[8] Similarly, a son's most respectful gesture toward his mother can be to recognize her rank by sleeping with her (620) and therefore, one must suppose, showing his appreciation for the beauty she had already given to him by increasing it for the child he is fathering. Incest is the procedure that allows us to see that this system provides, out of the notion of property, a natural form of genealogical hierarchy. For if a generalizable standard of physical appearance is overshadowed as a demonstration of desirability by the indication of an ability to produce good children, this quality can be judged in a child only by looking at its resemblance to its parents. Parents designate children as desirable, children their parents.

The resulting sexual aristocracy on this island is determined by reproductive performance. It safeguards the well-being and the interdependence of every member of the social order. Both a "natural" morality and a "natural" social order derive from reducing sex to the natural function of the production of children, because in Tahiti children are the carriers of excess wealth. They are the carriers of the

7. Thus he obviously directly contradicts Rousseau's position in the *Discours sur l'origine de l'inégalité*, where, derived from an opposed definition of nature, the notion of property once abstracted drives the wedge between man and nature by forming the epistemological foundation of culture. I will return to this issue later.

8. Note that there is nonetheless a slippage between first-order desirability or physical attractiveness and second-order or economically mediated desirability. This slippage, invisible to the Tahitians, will, as we shall see, incapacitate the Tahitians' economic system with the arrival of the Europeans.

excess, but the parents' "visible genealogy"–their resemblance to their own parents and to their children–is the sign of it.

Of course, the system can be turned around: sex is fun, even for Orou, who attempts all along to downplay as seemingly gratuitous the non-profit-oriented side of the issue. But good genealogy does get a Tahitian more than average access to sexual partners–in other words, more sexual enjoyment. The more children he has, the more desirable he looks as a source of children. The more access he gets, the more access he earns. His cumulative profit in this system is not only more food but also more sexual enjoyment. Moreover, in this culture the excess food, the riches, can buy only one commodity: leisure time from raising food, what the old man calls *le repos* (592). So, the more actual wealth one has in this system, the more time one has for sex. Wealth doubly brings access to sexual enjoyment. This means that the economic sign structure is actually double: children are the sign of excess food (property), which is the sign of access to sexual pleasure. Yet children also demonstrate sexual success, the sign of excess property. So children, property, and sex function equally as the sign and the referent of each other.

The enrichment process is clearly self-accelerating. Even in this supposedly free and egalitarian society, the rich get richer–in both property and sexual enjoyment. I will return to the peculiarity of the Tahitians' form of luxury when I discuss the old man's speech. First, though, we need to consider the constant albeit almost imperceptible hierarchization operated by the enrichment process. The society sorts itself into fewer and fewer families ruled by sexual patriarchs. Inequalities of rank obviously appear, but so do those of gender: for old men, age guarantees that the sheer number of children they have had will designate them as desirable sex partners, whereas the old women, now sterile, are forbidden access to the sexual exchanges because their enjoyment would be nonproductive, no matter how many children they might have furnished their society in the past (621). If they transgress this prohibition, a certainly natural desire by Tahitian or any other society's standards, the old women are imprisoned or sold into slavery–they become property. In addition, women who have sexual relations during their menstrual periods are locked up in their families' huts whereas the men who sleep with them are merely reprimanded. Orou acts as though the growing inequalities, predictable outgrowths of a social order structured as theirs is on self-interest, do not exist. The longer he talks, the more the abusive side of Tahitian culture reveals itself. Yet Orou seems not to notice the consequences of what he is saying, not to hear the incoherences in statements like "elles m'appartiennent et je te les offre: elles sont à elles, et elles se donnent à toi" (601; "They belong to me, and I offer them to you; they belong to themselves, and they give themselves to you"). The first half of his statement speaks the truth, while the second half presents the self-image that his society believes in and that masks its true functioning.

The Tahitians view their society as being in equilibrium with nature—or better, they feel that they have realized an ideal, the creation of a fixed social structure that accommodates the changeability of the natural world. Notice that their culture does have a directional development of a sort. It must have been more egalitarian years before; it becomes relentlessly more hierarchized as the years go by, according to the principle of a single-parameter meritocracy. The Tahitians, however, do not perceive this vector. They do not see that their own culture is being shaped by forces that it itself creates but that they cannot deal with because the forces escape their perception. Their perception is set by the closed tautology of this natural economic-social-moral exchange system. As we shall see, this vector makes the Tahitian culture vulnerable to precisely the natural change it seeks to accommodate or to incorporate in the most efficient way. Tahitians feel that the social structure the most in harmony with and the most adequate to express human participation in the continual change of the physical world is their own. They seem not to recognize that they see their social organization as fixed; in other words, they have institutionalized it unknowingly. This is because their focus is on the changeability of nature, and their culture is minimized and hence hardly visible. Minimized, however, does not make it any the less institutionalized and fixed, or any the less capable of being bypassed by a world that changes out from under it. The Tahitians' perception of their culture as naturally fixed—an oxymoron in terms of their own theory of nature—keeps them from seeing the changes actually taking place and makes them incapable of dealing with either those changes or, most importantly, changes that come from outside their environment.

The patriarchs of this society, the tacit rulers who result from Tahiti's slow hierarchization, are the richest Tahitians of all, justifiably so according to the natural economics I have just elaborated. They are also the holders and the wielders of a seemingly natural authority based on their procreative prowess. We are eager to meet one and find to our surprise that we already have: he is the *vieillard,* the old man whose bitter speech to Bougainville's departing sailors predicts the end of his own culture and precedes in textual order the dialogue between Orou and the monk. It is in the light of his speech that we see the source of the weakness of the natural morality propounded by Orou and so highly appreciated by the monk.

> C'est un vieillard qui parle. Il était père d'une famille nombreuse. A l'arrivée des Européens, il laissa tomber des regards de dédain sur eux, sans marquer ni étonnement, ni frayeur, ni curiosité. Ils l'abordèrent; il leur tourna le dos et se retira dans sa cabane. Son silence et son souci ne décelaient que trop sa pensée: il gémissait en lui-même sur les beaux jours de son pays éclipsés. (589)

> It is an old man who speaks. He was the father of a large family. On the arrival of the Europeans, he cast disdainful looks on them without manifesting either astonishment, fear, or curiosity. They addressed him; he turned his back on them and retired to his hut. His silence and worry revealed only too clearly his thoughts: he groaned inwardly over the good days of his country, gone forever.

The old man is one of the few privileged patriarchs. He supposedly incarnates in the greatest concentration the qualities distinguished and valorized in Tahiti. He should by definition, therefore, welcome the challenge of inevitable change that Orou, as we saw above, qualifies as the primordial natural law for the Tahitians (605). He should be the one to lead his people to find the most productive and least damaging adaptation to the arrival of the Europeans. Nonetheless, as should be predictable for a culture that so clearly functions according to an ideological model masking the development of power structures, the old man rejects change out of hand. He does not even wait until the departure of the Europeans to mourn the effects of syphilis and religion that by then have manifested themselves only too dramatically. *At the very moment of their arrival, before he even knew what changes would take place,* the old man turned his back (literally) on Bougainville and his sailors and retreated from participation in the shock of the confrontation of two cultures. In other words, he abdicated the authority he had earned; he turned his back less on the Europeans than on his duty, the performance of which supposedly justified and produced his elevated rank. Why?

His parting speech, where for the first and only time he breaks silence, is both an action and a refusal to act.

> Pleurez, malheureux Tahitiens! pleurez; mais que ce soit de l'arrivée, et non du départ de ces hommes ambitieux et méchants: un jour, vous les connaîtrez mieux. . . . Un jour vous servirez sous eux, aussi corrompus, aussi vils, aussi malheureux qu'eux. Mais je me console; je touche à la fin de ma carrière; et la calamité que je vous annonce, je ne la verrai point. O Tahitiens! ô mes amis! vous auriez un moyen d'échapper à un funeste avenir; mais j'aimerais mieux mourir que de vous en donner le conseil. Qu'ils s'éloignent, et qu'ils vivent. (589–90)

> Weep, wretched Tahitians! weep; but may it be for the arrival, not the departure, of these ambitious and mischievous men: one day you will know them better. . . . One day you will serve them, as corrupt, vile, and wretched as they. But I console myself; I am reaching the end of my run; and I will not live to see the calamity that I announce. Oh, Tahitians! Oh, my friends! You could have a way to escape from a doomed future; but I would rather die than counsel you to do it. Let them go away, and let them live.

His age, which normally imposes greater responsibility, is here referred to as a pretext for not confronting the situation. He indicates to his people that the "answer" to their problem is to kill all the Europeans to keep them from returning and enslaving the Tahitians, and yet at the same time he forbids the action. He seems able to perceive the only possible adequate response but unable to make the gesture necessary to save his culture. Soon, as we expect, the parallels between syphilis, religion, and the European notion of property are established; each sort of exploitation and abuse reflects and supports the others. The result will be the physical death of the infected children and the cultural death of a people. And what a people: innocent, strong, and healthy even to the advanced age of the old man. "Tes jeunes compagnons ont eu peine à me suivre; et j'ai quatre-vingt-dix ans passés" (592; "Your young companions have a hard time following me, and I am over ninety years old"). Why would such a culture have to acquiesce, have to die? If they are so strong, both physically and morally, why should they be vulnerable to the invasion of the Europeans? Why does the old man refuse to use his strength to adapt the change to his people's advantage? Unlike the other primitive peoples discussed by A and B at the beginning of the text, the old man appears at first to be representative of Tahiti's *excess* of civilization. Although he suggests that the Tahitians will be quite capable of killing their own syphilis-infected children, he both incites his people to kill the Europeans and claims that they are not capable of it. The "usages d'une cruauté nécessaire et bizarre" that allow other cultures to survive and that "met[tent] les philosophes à la torture" (583; the "practices of a necessary and bizarre cruelty . . . [that] torture the philosophers") seem out of the Tahitians' reach because of their natural respect for other human beings. In other words, the old man presents both to the Europeans and to his own people the picture of an inevitable tragedy à la Rousseau, straight out of the *Discours sur l'origine de l'inégalité*: the naturalness of their original morality begets the Tahitians' moral success, and yet this same naturalness causes their vulnerability, their inevitable destruction at the hands of the corrupt Europeans. However, after exhorting his people in effect to acquiesce in their own destruction, the old man turns on Bougainville. His eloquent diatribe then demonstrates, in spite of the Rousseauistic echoes in his denunciation of the very notion of civilization, what the real roots of his tragic predictions are, and they turn out, as we shall see, not to be what he claims.

It is both interesting and timely to point out here that Orou speaks Spanish (this is what allows the old man to have his speech translated so that the departing Europeans can understand him), so clearly there has already been a previous contact with Europeans—and a contact, presumably, that did not destroy Tahiti. Whatever shock it brought about in the dynamic object that was the previous Tahiti was somehow accommodated. Further, no memory remains, individual or cultural, of that previous contact. Apparently, whatever Tahiti accommodated then *it no longer can assimilate.*

"Ici tout est à tous; et tu nous as prêché je ne sais quelle distinction du *tien* et du *mien*" (590; "Here everything belongs to everyone; and you have preached to us some incomprehensible distinction between *yours* and *mine*"), the old man accuses the Europeans. But what does such a statement really mean in this context? The answer, quite simple at first glance, is that the distinction between *yours* and *mine* does not, as we might think, refer merely to the pigs and the beads that the natives steal and that Bougainville's sailors and monks kill them to recover, thus supposedly introducing them to the rules governing the ownership of inanimate things. The text directly following the above quotation demonstrates that it is the sexual meaning of the notions of "yours" and "mine" that is in question. Sexual swapping with the Europeans does not work the same way as with other Tahitians.

> Nos filles et nos femmes nous sont communes; tu as partagé ce privilège avec nous; et tu es venu allumer en elles des fureurs inconnues. Elles sont devenues folles dans tes bras; tu es devenu féroce entre les leurs. Elles ont commencé à se haïr; vous vous êtes égorgés pour elles. (590)

> Our daughters and our wives we hold in common; you have shared this privilege with us; and you have lit in them unknown furors. They have gone mad in your arms; you have become savage in theirs. They have begun to hate each other; you have slaughtered each other for them.

Thus the Tahitian women learn to be possessive of a particular European man and to resist exchange, and the European men do violence to prevent their own exchange of these women. No answer is given in the old man's speech as to why the Europeans should be so strangely sexually disturbing to the Tahitians that the result of contact with them would be a form of mad proprietary frenzy. The old man passes right over this issue, he seems not to see its implications. He seems, moreover, to be blind to the fact that in a culture totally based on an economy of voluntary sexual exchange, the most powerful disruptive force will of necessity be that which upsets the equilibrium that maximizes the functioning of economic self-interest by eliminating sexual desire. Again, although the old man blames the monk's indoctrinating for it, the young people have learned the associated concept of shame less from what must have been a meaningless religious harangue than from the experience of a new form of desire. This new form of desire makes their previous sexual comportments seem economically, rather than morally, inadequate to deal with new passions and therefore with new physical and social forces.

This interpretation of the old man's accusations becomes clear only with Orou's definition of the Tahitian Venus much later in the dialogues. In a culture where desire is created by and strictly limited to the recognition of productivity, the notion of sexual desire as being provoked by something other than the strict notion of wealth-producing fecundity upsets the entire system of exchange and especially the forces regulating this exchange. The result is the creation of a multiparametered, open-ended, sexuality. Physical attractiveness is no longer determined by economic criteria. Whatever the source of the European notions of physical beauty and sexual desire, they are not in accord with those regulating Tahiti. Hence, the women no longer understand the experience of sexual enjoyment in terms of a culturally totalizing economic system. They no longer understand participation in a sexual act as the creation of wealth, or wealth as only the sign of sexuality. This ground-state system has come unhinged, and sex from now on also exists outside the cultural context of Tahiti, whence "les fureurs inconnues"–quite literally previously unknown and strategically unknowable forms of sexual desire.

The advent of this change breaks apart the fixity that the Tahitians had been able to hide from themselves; it reveals both the arbitrariness and the vulnerable point of their institutions. The culture that to the Europeans had at first appeared to be founded on free love now shows itself to be ruled by just as constrained a definition of desire and of acceptable sexual interchange as existed in Europe. The Tahitians' love is anything but free, in either meaning of the word. The Europeans do not see this at first, because the Tahitians' rules are orthogonal to their own. Both sets of rules are determined by a cultural economics, but neither understands the other's notion of economic value. The Tahitians, ironically, are all the more bound by their rules because they do not see them–they are completely internalized, so that the Tahitians really believe that their choices of sexual partners are unmediated. Thus arises the power of the "fureurs inconnus" to disrupt: to modify their rules, they would have had to be able to externalize and thus recognize them as rules.

The problem of internalization leads to the second reason for the old man's abdication of responsibility, which is in fact probably the cause of the first reason, his culture's inability to be cruel.

Laisse-nous nos moeurs; elles sont plus sages et plus honnêtes que les tiennes; nous ne voulons point troquer ce que tu appelles notre ignorance, contre tes inutiles lumières. Tout ce qui nous est nécessaire et bon, nous le possédons. Sommes-nous dignes de mépris, parce que nous n'avons pas su nous faire des besoins superflus? Lorsque nous avons faim, nous avons de quoi manger; lorsque nous avons froid, nous avons de quoi nous vêtir. Tu es entré dans nos cabanes, qu'y manque-t-il, à ton avis? Poursuis jusqu'où tu voudras ce que tu appelles commodités de la vie; mais permets à des êtres sensés de s'arrêter, lorsqu'ils n'auraient à obtenir, de la continuité de leurs pénibles efforts, que des biens imaginaires. Si tu nous persuades de franchir l'étroite limite du besoin, quand finirons-nous de travailler? Quand jouirons-nous? Nous avons rendu la somme de nos fatigues annuelles et journalières la moindre qu'il était possible, parce que rien ne nous paraît préférable au repos. Va dans ta contrée t'agiter, te tourmenter tant que tu voudras; laisse-nous reposer: ne nous entête ni de tes besoins factices, ni de tes vertus chimériques. (592)

Leave us our morals; they are wiser and more honest than yours; we have no wish to barter what you call our ignorance for your useless enlightenment. All that is necessary and good for us we possess. Are we worthy of disdain because we haven't managed to create superfluous needs for ourselves? When we are hungry, we have things to eat; when we are cold, things to clothe ourselves. You entered our huts: what are they lacking, in your opinion? Pursue where you will what you call the commodities of life; but allow sensible beings to stop when they have nothing to gain from continuing their painful efforts but imaginary goods. If you persuade us to go beyond the narrow limits of need, when will we finish working? When will we enjoy life? We have made the sum total of our yearly and annual fatigue as small as possible, because nothing seems preferable to leisure. Go back to your own country to busy yourselves, torment yourselves as much as you wish; let us rest: don't harangue us with your factitious needs and chimerical virtues.

The old man's culture, which prides itself on its strength and its health, is then here described by B, before Diderot's reader reaches the Orou dialogue, as a profoundly indolent culture. Having not yet read and digested the dialogue between Orou and the monk, Diderot's reader has no way of understanding the functioning of the Tahitian social order. Of course, any concept like *le repos* can have meaning only within its specific social context. Working from a European context, the reader may follow B and view the Tahitians as lazy and inferior *sauvages*. But the old man's speech makes clear that the

Tahitians' "indolence" is a willed state. The ground-state nature of their civilization—their limiting their endeavors to the satisfaction of need and their refusal to complexify their understanding of need in order to include the purely enjoyable (the esthetic)—is something that the Tahitians must ceaselessly strive to maintain. They have chosen to adapt their culture to a particular geographical and climatic setting that makes their culture not only possible but also seem the most reasonable construct. As B will enviously admit, "la passion de l'amour, réduite à un simple appétit physique, n'y produisait aucun de nos désordres" (627; "the passion of love, reduced to a simple physical appetite, doesn't produce there any of our disorders"), its warm climate, rich soil, geographical isolation, and the fact that Tahiti is an island make it a place in which needs are quickly and relatively painlessly met. For what is a need? In the simplest form, it is what the physical body requires to survive—food, warmth (shelter), water. In a slightly less simple version, we must add successful sexual reproduction, for the survival of the individual has no meaning without the survival of the species. The Tahitians' social organization guarantees the satisfaction of all these needs, and their physical setting makes this guarantee trivially realizable. Their social organization results from the organization of their physical environment; the material determinism again operates in a predictable way.

But the Tahitians take great pains to do no more than satisfy need. Their will to indolence is really a will to an economic efficiency made practicable by their climatic setting—an economic efficiency that also parallels the simplicity of their climatic setting. As long as absolutely nothing changes.

To preserve this economic efficiency, "besoins factices" and "vertus chimériques" must be prevented at all cost. They would disrupt the tenuous equilibrium that the Tahitians feel they have established between themselves and their environment. The sense of "vertu chimérique" is clear: the religious and moral scruples brought by the European monks are not endemic or appropriate to the social organization of Tahiti as we have described it, the natural outgrowth of its physical setting. Virtue would be clearly and quickly counterproductive (although for all the wrong reasons, it may end up being the only possible survival mechanism as syphilis ravages the population).

The idea of the "besoin factice," however, is more problematic, for the situation is not as simple as the old man's speech would make it seem. Need and the resulting work required to satisfy it are notions normally set in opposition to the notion of *jouir*. As the old man himself explicitly shows, the opposition holds for Tahiti, too. *Le repos* is the Tahitian site of *jouissance*. Repose, as we remember from Orou and the monk's discussion, is the only form of luxury that exists in Tahiti. We normally think that where needs are quickly met, the leisure time will almost automatically be spent developing "besoins factices" or luxuries—the esthetic comes in the door out of which the daily drudgery has been banished. However, in this country with a surplus of leisure time, in which leisure time is the most prized form of profit, there is an explicit denial of the esthetic and there is no complexification of culture. The reason is simple: luxury is fundamentally an economic concept determined by the characteristic parameters of each economic system. For each parameter a form of unequal access to benefit or profit exists and determines a corresponding class of luxury. Tahiti, with a culture of a single economic parameter, therefore has only one form of luxury. While others work to satisfy need, the rich do not: they enjoy themselves. Their profit, though, is both an end in itself as a form of enjoyment and the only means to earn further riches. In other words, the Tahitians' indolence is not a form of laziness (of nonproductiveness), but is economically productive, exactly like their constrained definition of desire. The genius of the Tahitian economic system is that it is self-reinforcing: the profits are not withdrawn from the system by being used. On the contrary, their very enjoyment is the only possible form of reinvestment of capital into the system. Enjoyment of luxury for the individual is translated into satisfaction of the entire society's needs. The concept of open-ended or selfish enjoyment is diverted and dismantled. However, the reverse consequence is that in order for the system to keep on functioning, no other parameters can be introduced, no other forms of luxury can be desired. *Le repos* is the only luxury that can exist without threatening the fragile because one-dimensional economic-social system, because, like their curious definition of desire, it is the only definition of luxury that can be reconceptualized into need.[9] The result of the incursion of the Europeans, therefore, is less that it introduces a transcultural notion of sin or corruption than

9. Diderot is here reversing Rousseau's definition of luxury in the *Discours* (today's luxury becomes tomorrow's need, whence moral corruption). Cf. Diderot's allusion to Rousseau's definition in the article "Encyclopédie" (DPV 7:176).

that it takes the notions of desire and luxury, notions that for the Tahitians must remain synonymous, and complexifies society by separating them. As B acutely perceives, "la passion de l'amour, réduite à un simple appétit physique, n'y produisait aucun de nos désordres" (627). Passion and desire must be reduced, maintained at the level of need instead of being allowed to exceed need, for the system to keep operating. For this simplicity to be maintained, nothing can be allowed to change, no contact with the outside can be permitted, and no recognition of the Tahitians' own slow economic-cultural evolution can be acknowledged. No possible adequate response to any form of change exists that can preserve the Tahitian system of sexual exchange.

Tahiti's blindness not only allows but even forces it to develop slowly into something quite other than what it thinks it is; the distance between the laudable ideals it espouses and the actual functioning of its invisible hierarchy is immediately apparent to outsiders but will never become apparent to the Tahitians, because they have willingly given up the means to regain their vision. The old man's speech is the best example of this. Every accusation that he hurls against the Europeans is true, but the larger, looming, silent accusation is made only in the reader's mind: the Tahitians are just as responsible for their own destruction as the Europeans are. The old man is tragically unable to see that his own culture's adoption of minimum sufficiency leaves his people with no tools to adapt to or accommodate cultural change. This is because change for the Tahitians is perceived as change—and therefore as something it is their "natural" duty to welcome and adapt to—only when it originates in the domain of the non-human material dynamic, but not when it comes from the human. For Diderot this betrays the fact that the Tahitians work with the same conceptually false opposition as the overinstitutionalized Europeans that Orou denounces; they accept a nature-culture opposition. But for Diderot the physical and the human realm are inseparably part and parcel of the overall natural world. He even structures the old man's speech to show that the speaker does not see the inescapable relatedness of nature and culture, but the reader must.

L'idée de crime et le péril de la maladie sont entrés avec toi parmi nous. Nos jouissances, autrefois si douces, sont accompagnées de remords et d'effroi. Cet homme noir, qui est près de toi, qui

m'écoute, a parlé à nos garçons; je ne sais ce qu'il a dit à nos filles; mais
nos garçons hésitent; mais nos filles rougissent. . . . Vois cette enceinte
hérissée de flèches; ces armes qui n'avaient menacé que nos ennemis,
vois-les tournées contre nos propres enfants: vois les malheureuses
compagnes de vos plaisirs; . . . c'est là qu'elles sont condamnées à périr
ou par nos mains, ou par le mal que tu leur as donné. (593–95)

The idea of crime and the peril of disease came to us along with you.
Our pleasures, once upon a time so sweet, are accompanied by
remorse and fright. This [man in black] next to you who listens to
me has spoken to our boys; I don't know what he has told our girls;
but our boys hesitate, our girls blush. . . . See this enclosure topped
with spikes; these arms that had threatened only our enemies—see
that now they are turned against our own children; see the wretched
companions of your pleasures; . . . that is where they are condemned to die either by our hands or from the disease that you have
given them.

The most profound change that will happen to the Tahitians is not
their projected subjugation by the returning Europeans, bitterly pre-
dicted by the old man as the inevitable consequence of their visit. It
results instead from the twin afflictions of religious scruples about
sex and the threat of syphilis that strike down the system of economic sexuality that structures their society. When free sexual
exchange is eliminated, the principle of Tahitian culture disappears.
Only then can the Tahitians be subjugated; only then will they
become "aussi corrompus, aussi vils, aussi malheureux que [les
Européens]" (590; "as corrupt, vile and wretched as [the Euro-
peans]"). Tahiti does not see its own failures, because it has institutionalized—precisely the sociocultural process that it most abhors in
the Europeans—the *fixed image of its own naturalness*. This fixed
image blinds it to its own abandonment of adaptive interaction with
the natural changing world. The Tahitians live in their real world but
perceive it only through the utopian vision of it that they have
constructed.

Diderot leads his readers, however, to see both what the Tahitians'
culture is and why their failure is self-inflicted. He does so by presenting their refusal to adapt (the old man's speech) before their creed of
adaptation (Orou's speech). Readers are never allowed, therefore, to
participate in the utopian dream that Orou's seductive innocence con-

structs. Orou's speech is not so much to the monk as to the Diderotian reader who, having been provided with historical hindsight,
already knows that the Tahitian's is an impossible dream, impossible
because only an unchanging world can immortalize this culture ideologically so devoted to the transient. What we understand while
listening to this noble savage's dream is that it is also clearly undesir-
able—a judgment that Rousseau could not make, because he intentionally institutionalized nostalgia for the primitive to find a way to
turn his back on change. Because the placement of these two dialogues is in antichronological order, Diderot's reader is never permitted to idealize a primitive culture. He has to face its faults before
ever being allowed to perceive its virtues. He must always hear the
Tahitians' words through the spectacle of their own failure, and as a
result, their culture gains a peculiar status: Diderot uses it to criticize
one form of European culture (the complex of the church-monarchy
institutions) while at the same time showing us that Tahiti cannot
serve as a model culture and, further, that there cannot be such a
thing as a model culture.

The *Supplément* is, therefore, an antiutopian text. It is not a negative utopia, but a text constructed against the very utopian impulse
itself defined as a nostalgia for fixity and universality, whether natural or cultural. Necessarily belied by the dynamic of the material
world, a utopia is not a model to aim for, therefore, but a philosophical trap to be avoided. It leads to alienation from the dynamically
material world and hence to cultural atrophy and oblivion.[10]

Tahiti's insufficiency helps us converge on the image of what only
a philosophically (in Diderot's sense of the term) responsive European culture will be able to accomplish. The *Supplément* has already
performed, therefore, a double elimination before, in effect, ever
beginning to construct its own alternative view of a workable society. It has eliminated the primitive naturalistic utopia after using it to
denounce the hierarchical European society, since each is inadequate

10. From this position I would argue against Jacques Proust's construal of Diderot as
being, because of his materialism, an *avant la lettre* Marxist historical materialist (in his otherwise definitive reading of the *Rêve de d'Alembert*, in Denis Diderot, *Le Neveu de Rameau,
Le Rêve de d'Alembert*, ed. Roland Desné and Jean Varloot (Paris: Messidor/Editions
Sociales, 1972; reprint 1984). I disagree with Proust not because Diderot is not materialist,
obviously, but because he already, long before Marx wrote his utopian economic and social
program, had demonstrated the incompatibility of a truly uncompromising materialism
with a utopian vision.

to a dynamic materialist view of the world. In so doing, Diderot has eliminated both the notion of society as purely cultural and the opposing notion of society as purely natural. By showing that Tahiti dooms itself by thinking itself to be purely in the domain of the natural, Diderot sets it up as the reverse of hierarchical Europe. While we may have thought (and most interpretations of this text do indeed conclude) that Tahiti is therefore the alternative to Europe, we see that on the contrary, the Tahitians' reverse symmetry means that they share the same fault: each assumes that nature and culture (or civilization, to use a more Diderotian vocabulary) are in opposition. Accordingly, they are equally insufficient for the philosopher. From his very earliest work on, Diderot's materialism always denied the possibility or even the meaningfulness of a nature-culture opposition.

Does the text, then, propose a third position, a social model that reincorporates culture into nature, that reconciles political and social reflection with dynamic materialism? This is the most important function performed by the seemingly decorative, often disregarded framing dialogue between A and B.

The Mechanics of Social Change

Recall that the text began, after its invocation of dynamic change in the shifting moods of men and weather, with the description of Bougainville, whose voyage around the world was the event that provoked the encounters and exchanges I have just discussed. This Frenchman with his jaded and idiosyncratic eye provides A and B with a text that allows access to a multiplicity of geographies and corresponding social practices. After what seems to be a quick reiteration of Rousseau's derivation of social hierarchy from the notion of property in the *Discours sur l'origine de l'inégalité* (584), the discussion leads to the first evocation of the problem of confrontation between existing cultures. Here the point is not simply to compare cultures; it is to introduce a form of shock into cultures and bring about cultural "vibration." We see Tahiti not as an ideal state against which to judge the Europeans but as a closed although coherent culture brought into contact with another. Tahiti is Diderot's cultural thought-experiment. It is a culture undergoing shock itself, and its members are also undergoing shock.

A Avez-vous vu le Tahitien que Bougainville avait pris sur son bord, et transporté dans ce pays-ci?

B Je l'ai vu; il s'appelait Aotourou. . . . Il s'ennuyait parmi nous. L'alphabet tahitien n'ayant ni *b*, ni *c*, ni *d*, ni *f*, ni *g*, ni *q*, ni *x*, ni *y*, ni *z*, il ne put jamais apprendre à parler notre langue, qui offrait *à ses organes inflexibles trop d'articulations étrangères et de sons nouveaux*. Il ne cessait de soupirer après son pays, et je n'en suis pas étonné. Le voyage de Bougainville est le seul qui m'ait donné du goût pour une autre contrée que la mienne; jusqu'à cette lecture, j'avais pensé qu'on n'était nulle part aussi bien que chez soi; résultat que je croyais le même pour chaque habitant de la terre; *effet naturel de l'attrait du sol*; attrait qui tient aux commodités dont on jouit, et qu'on n'a pas la même certitude de retrouver ailleurs. . . . Bougainville a renvoyé Aotourou, après avoir pourvu aux frais et à la sûreté de son retour.

A O Aotourou! que tu seras content de revoir ton père, ta mère, tes frères, tes soeurs, tes compatriotes, que leur diras-tu de nous?

B Peu de choses, qu'ils ne croiront pas.

A Pourquoi peu de choses?

B *Parce qu'il en a peu conçues, et qu'il ne trouvera dans sa langue aucun terme correspondant à celles dont il a quelques idées*. (585–86; my emphasis)

A Have you seen the Tahitian that Bougainville took on board and brought to this country?

B I saw him; he's called Aotourou. . . . he was unhappy with us. The Tahitian alphabet having neither *b*, *c*, *d*, *f*, *g*, *q*, *x*, *y*, nor *z*, he was never able to learn to speak our language, which required from *his inflexible organs too many foreign articulations and new sounds*. He never ceased longing for his country, and I'm not surprised. Bougainville's voyage is the only one that has given me a taste for a country other than my own; until reading about it I had thought that one was nowhere as well off as at home; as a result I thought it would be the same for every inhabitant of the earth—the *natural effect of the attraction of the soil*, attraction that results from the favorable conditions that one enjoys and is not certain of finding elsewhere. . . . Bougainville sent Aotourou back, after having provided for his expenses and the safety of his return.

A Oh, Aotourou! How happy you will be to see your father, your mother, your brothers and sisters, your compatriots again; what will you tell them about us?

B Little, and that they won't believe.

A Why little?

B *Because he conceptualized little, and he will find in his own language no terms corresponding to those of which he did get an idea.*

This passage is the paradigmatic moment in the *Supplément*. Many of the themes and especially the conclusions that are demonstrated through the "empirical" interpretive experience of reading dialogues between characters from different cultures are first sketched out here. However, as we can now see, they are sketched in a form that disguises their real meaning; the reader who encounters this passage "on the way into" the text is most likely to extract from it at first only the commonplace Enlightenment or Rousseauist polemic in which the noble savage is corrupted by contact with members of a more civilized culture. Reread, however, in the context of the dialogue between Orou and the monk, which itself has to be reread in the context of the old man's self-indicting speech, and we see that what at first seems a utopian praise of the innocent Tahitian culture is in fact the opposite.

A Et pourquoi ne le croiront-ils pas?

B Parce qu'en comparant leurs moeurs aux nôtres, ils aimeront mieux prendre Aotourou pour un menteur, que de nous croire si fous.

A En vérité?

B Je n'en doute pas: la vie sauvage est si simple, et nos sociétés sont des machines si compliquées! Le Tahitien touche à l'origine du monde, et l'Européen touche à sa vieillesse. L'intervalle qui le sépare de nous est plus grand que la distance de l'enfant qui naît à l'homme décrépit. Il n'entend rien à nos usages, à nos lois, ou il n'y voit que des entraves déguisées sous cent formes diverses, entraves qui ne peuvent qu'exciter l'indignation et le mépris d'un être en qui le sentiment de la liberté est le plus profond des sentiments. (587)

A And why won't they believe him?

B Because when comparing their mores to ours, they will prefer to take Aotourou for a liar rather than believe us so mad.

A In truth?

B I have no doubt of it: the savage life is so simple, and our societies are such complicated machines! The Tahitian touches the origin of the world, and the European its old age. The interval that separates us is greater than the distance between the newborn and the decrepit man. He understands nothing of our practices, our laws, or he only perceives them as obstacles disguised under a hundred diverse forms—obstacles that can only excite the indignation and scorn of a being for whom the feeling of liberty is the most profound of sentiments.

We now know how to read this passage; we know that its full meaning is better indicated by the reasons given in the preceding quotation than in the resonances that this passage has with the Enlightenment commonplaces. Aotourou cannot adapt, not because he is morally superior and is a martyr to his innocence, but because he is physically and therefore mentally incapable of cultural adaptation.

The test case of Tahiti is the Diderotian mental experiment to show what happens when an internally complex social group fails rather than what it looks like when it succeeds. In the first part of the dialogue between A and B, we see the future of Tahiti already exemplified in Aotourou's failure to adapt. He has learned some of the European notions; he has learned some European speech and ways of behaving. Yet he can learn only so much, for his physical organization is an adaptation to and therefore accumulatively a function of the Tahitian environment. When Aotourou returns, the culture of Tahiti itself will prefer not to believe his claims about what Europe is like not because, as a first reading ironically suggests, no sane person would behave like the Europeans, but because Tahiti's culture has no tools to understand what he is saying. The Diderotian definition of sanity is context dependent: it means fitting within the ever evolving structure of social comportment. What is sanity in Europe is insanity in Tahiti *and vice versa*, as the monk's decision to be a man in Tahiti and a monk in Europe really demonstrates. Appropriate social comportment is determined by the constant interaction of physical site and the cultural machine. Now, if we keep in mind that complexity is a positive value for Diderot when it results from *génial* adaptation to an ever changing physical environment—whether for the singular thinking individual, for the small group mind of Bordeu, d'Alembert, and de l'Espinasse, or for the more ambitious open-ended group mind of the *Encyclopédie*—then we see that the Tahitian simplicity is a danger sign, a warning of vulnerability. B is not complimenting the Tahitians when he says, "La vie sauvage est si simple, et nos sociétés sont des machines si compliquées!" Even the monk implicitly acknowledges the inability of the Tahitians to complexify sufficiently to understand European motivations, no matter how much clearer and more lucid their vision of essential notions may appear. Several times, near the end of his dialogue with Orou, he makes statements like "Cela serait trop long et trop difficile à t'expliquer" (626; "It would be too long and too difficult to explain to you"). He speaks in good faith. He chooses not to explain, not because he would make Europe appear too foolish, but because Orou's culture has embedded within its language neither the intellectual complexity nor the historical experience to allow the Tahitians to understand motivations so differently derived.

Diderot's most striking demonstration of the interrelatedness of physical and cultural processes of adaptation comes at the beginning of the long passage above: Aotourou literally cannot form the sounds that would allow him to speak the more complex speech of the Europeans. As we know from the "Encyclopédie" argument, speech is the bridge between the world of the physical and the world of the mental; his insufficiency of speech betrays an equivalent incapacity to conceptualize. Aotourou's physical simplicity is a mirror of what we will eventually perceive to be the cultural simplicity of Tahiti. Diderot's innovation here is to go from the characterization of an individual to the characterization of an entire culture made up of similarly organized individuals.[11] Both types of simplicity arise from the same processes of adaptation. Even more, as is clear to the reader of *Le Rêve de d'Alembert* or *La Religieuse*, the parallel organizations are

11. The distinction is still important, though, because the counterexample for the case of the individual exists in Diderot's early materialist writings: the case of the blind mathematician Saunderson in the *Lettre sur les aveugles*. He may have been blind, but he was born into and complexified by contact with his already complex culture. Aotourou is not a Saunderson analogue, because the culture that shaped him not only is simple but also drives toward simplicity. Even contact with the Europeans can complexify one man just so much, just as being blind can simplify one man only so much.

not just parallel reactions to a common stimulus. They are causally related to each other. The more complex the body, the more complex the thoughts it can have, and the more complex a culture a group of such bodies can produce. In turn, the more it will complexify the physical world in which it is embedded (think of the view of Nature that Dorval has before his eyes in the *Entretien sur le Fils naturel* in chapter 3). In fact, we finally have here the first hint of the definition of culture Diderot is generating: a culture is not a particular structure but an entire group's ability to function as one complex physical and cultural organism to absorb and accommodate physicocultural shocks—in other words, to guarantee supple mutual complexification most efficiently.

The discussion of Aotourou's plight is the passage that leads into the old man's speech, which, as we have seen, set the stage (ultimately) for the dialogue between Orou and the monk. The picture of an individual's failure sets into relief a culture's failure and forces us to see the tragedy underlying what looks like success in Orou's eloquent presentation. The "Suite du dialogue entre A et B," which closes the text, picks up a double thread: at the simplest level it merely continues the primordial, anti-Adamic Tahitian dialogue. At a more strategic level it picks up the original dialogue between A and B precisely where it left off.

> B Ici le bon aumônier se plaint de la brièveté de son séjour dans Ta-hiti, et de la difficulté de mieux connaître les usages d'un peuple assez sage pour s'être arrêté de lui-même à *la médiocrité*, ou assez heureux pour habiter un climat dont la fertilité lui assurait un long engourdissement, assez actif pour s'être mis à l'abri des besoins absolus de la vie, et assez indolent pour que son innocence, son repos et sa félicité n'eussent rien à redouter d'un progrès trop rapide de ses lumières. (627, my emphasis)

> B Here the good almoner complains of the brevity of his stay in Tahiti, and of the difficulty of knowing better the practices of a people wise enough to halt at *mediocrity* or happy enough to inhabit a climate whose fertility assures them of a long torpor, active enough to take care of the absolute necessities of life and indolent enough that their innocence, leisure and felicity have nothing to fear from a too rapid development of their enlightenment.

This is hardly the picture one would present of a culture that one wished to imitate, of a culture that could productively be substituted for the complex machine of European civilization. Although we the Enlightenment philosophers first read the terms such as *engourdissement* or *indolence* with self-satisfied irony, we can appreciate the bucolic noble savage even if those blinded by the prejudices of our institutions cannot. Then, however, we are struck by the "s'être arrêté de lui-même à la médiocrité, *ou* assez heureux pour habiter un climat dont la fertilité lui assurait un long engourdissement" ("wise enough to halt at mediocrity *or* happy enough to inhabit a climate whose fertility assures them of a long torpor"). The *or* here recursively undermines the apparent cultural control of the Tahitians: their physical environment is as responsible as they are for their happy simplicity.

"Un progrès trop rapide de ses lumières" is the real issue here. It seems a strange thing for a philosopher to fear, but apparently any culture has a cultural shock threshhold above which it becomes estranged from its environment; any more tears apart its social organization. The Tahitians are the extreme test case because, as well as being "young," their culture is willed to the simplicity associated with cultural youth. They do indeed embody the mediocre, in its old sense of traditional wisdom tied to its bucolic Rousseauist environment. The incursion of the Europeans is the shock of the opposite extreme: they are hypercomplex and seeking confrontation, "lestés d'un bord d'un traité de calcul différentiel et intégral et de l'autre d'un voyage autour du globe" (580; "balanced on one side by a treatise on differential and integral calculus and on the other by a voyage around the globe"). European civilization, damned already in this text for its institutional faults, nonetheless, from the same environmental and cultural history of adaptation that created its vices, continually produces some individuals like Bougainville who seek out the new, who catalyze cultural change by their very presence. We will return to the reason and its consequences in a few paragraphs. For now, it is sufficient to see that we are prevented from falling into a nostalgia for the innocence of childhood: the ambiguity of the connotations of "childhood" and "innocence" that we could still turn either for or against a utopian vision at the end of the first section of the framing dialogue has been eliminated. The nostalgia now is a nostalgia for *real* mediocrity—a mediocrity redefined by the failure of Aotourou and the choice of the old man not to adapt. Since the monk, in spite of great temptation, does not "jeter ses vêtements dans le vaisseau et passer le reste de ses jours parmi [les Tahitiens]," A asks, "Malgré cet éloge," meaning the very existence of such a temptation, "quelles conséquences utiles à tirer des moeurs et des usages bizarres d'un peuple non civilisé?" (628; "throw his clothes into the boat and spend the rest of his days among [the Tahitians]. . . . In spite of this praise, what useful consequences can be drawn from the morals and bizarre practices of a noncivilized people?"). The discussion therefore immediately turns to the subject we expected from the beginning: the comparison between the culture of Tahiti and the culture of Europe, especially concerning the validity of particular ethical systems determining sexual behavior and religious institutions. The Tahitians will die because of their mediocrity. They are conceptually indigent because of their physiological indigence, which results from the unstimulating effects of their climate—although they seem to have been blessed with a paradisiacal environment, it is precisely this environment that keeps them from having the capacity to accomplish what their own clear-minded perceptions dictate. They cannot change with the world as it changes. So, as the old man's speech shows without understanding, they sign their own death warrant. They are not the model to adopt, they are the state to which only the culturally sick or dying, like the old man, would wish to return.

Does Diderot provide a positive alternative? Indirectly, of course. Although it is often argued that the *Supplément* raises questions that it does not answer,[12] I think that the text does give the beginning of an answer. It does so in the only form it can, given that the very notion of generalized moral or cultural prescriptions was what was under attack. The curious second half of the dialogue between A and B points to the essential difference between Tahiti and Europe as being the difference in climate. This seems both trivial and a throwback to standard Enlightenment topoi—as found in the works of

---

12. An orthogonal complement to my reading, and one that starts from this premise, is provided in Dieckmann's reading of the *Supplément*, although he remains at the level of the classical discussion (that is, that this is a text about love and sex, not about culture and the nature of Enlightenment philosophy). He finds a tension between the wish for a stable model (at the level of a perfect and honest man-woman relationship) and the instability of experience that can undermine the best intentions. He finds that no single answer can be provided, just a sensitivity to the issues. I hope that his reading can be incorporated into the more general view I am trying to present here.

both Montesquieu and Rousseau, for example.[13] However, Diderot as usual means something quite different from the contemporary usage.

A and B discuss over several pages the European variants of the Tahitian truths. B demonstrates with insistent logic the perversity of European sexual mores. In fact, through studying the structure of this perversity, he reveals the perversity of all exploitative institutions in Europe. The judgments implied by comparison in the dialogue between Orou and the monk are here made coldly explicit. "Combien nous sommes loin de la nature et du bonheur!" (636; "How far we are from nature and happiness!"). The lot of man is happy only in Tahiti (doomed Tahiti). It is tolerable in Venice, where civilization is at a minimum, but has become openly brutal servitude that imprisons the body though it cannot enslave the mind. All Europe is unhappy, in servitude, is repressed in the name of illusory virtues. So does one move to Tahiti? No.

Let us remember that the perverse cultural institutions now in place in France may be distinguished from the people within them. Take the curious suppleness of Bougainville himself, his remarkable intellectual and social adaptability and eagerness. To the description of him from the beginning of the work corresponds a passage from the closing frame: "B. Je vois qu'aussitôt que quelques causes physiques, telles par exemple que la nécessité de vaincre l'ingratitude du sol, ont mis en jeu la sagacité de l'homme, cet élan le conduit bien au delà du but, et que le terme du besoin passé, on est porté dans l'océan sans bornes des fantaisies d'où l'on ne se tire plus" (628; "B: I see that as soon as some physical causes, for example the necessity of conquering the harshness of the soil, have brought into play the wisdom of man, this effort leads him far beyond his goal, and that, once the need is overcome, we are carried into the limitless ocean of inescapable fantasies from which we never escape"). At first we might read this passage as an explanation of why European culture is flawed. This impetus that carries the Europeans to produce, to create, to achieve always beyond their goal is in fact the reason they cannot will themselves to adequate effort with satisfaction, to eliminate the source of *jouissance*, to deflect self-interest into social good. It is this

13. Cf. Rousseau, *Origine des langues*; Montesquieu, *Considérations sur les causes de la grandeur des romains et de leur décadence* and *Essai sur les causes qui peuvent affecter les esprits et les caractères*. Montesquieu linked his observations to the well-established tradition of travel literature and hippocratic literature as well.

excess that produces the notion of luxury, of the aesthetic, of the
fureurs inconnus. And so, this *élan* is the source, even the defining
characteristic of European culture; from it are derived not only the
Europeans' evils but also their principles for survival. This *élan* is
what makes history—development—rather than utopia unavoidable.
Diderot shows us that the geographical condition of Europe is point
by point opposed to Tahiti. Europe is not an island. It does not have
a beneficent climate. Survival requires an unending struggle against
both a hostile environment and invasion by other peoples. Europe
is an open environment. Tahiti is closed, in terms both of climate
and of men. The Europeans can never hide from themselves the historical, the developmental. They do not even have the option of
choosing the Tahitians' cultural suicide (although this may be one
ironic way of interpreting the curious *éloge* of Venetian despotism).
They may have fallen into horrible or exploitative cultural institutions by not always maintaining a sense of how dynamically material their world is, by allowing what were once necessary responses
to fossilize into arbitrary ahistorical rules. Still, because theirs is a
culture of struggle and thus *élan*, and because their geographical environment will remain difficult, they will adapt, no matter how much
their institutions obstruct change. *Bougainville's very existence, the
fact of his voyage, proves this.* Tahiti may die, but the very drives that
cause the Europeans to venture into contact with and thus kill
the Tahitian culture will allow the Europeans to survive. They do
hear new truths or rediscover old truths from Orou, but they do
not therefore feel shame at the old man's words and resolve to go
home to "Tahiti-ize" Europe.[14] The less obvious but longer-range
answer seems to be that what may allow the Europeans to survive is

14. I must point out that the strategic value of the interpolation of the good-hearted
American prostitute's story into the very middle of Orou's dialogue can be understood as
forcing the parallel between Orou's social valorization of unlimited reproduction and a
European ideology of marriage. The prostitute standing before the court judging her in
effect redemonstrates to her judges that marriage was intended to enclose and protect children born to a couple in order to make them more useful to society, not to exclude and bar
from society perfectly useful children born outside it. By making marriage function primarily as an exclusionary device, the Europeans have perverted its natural function. The
American colonies are a halfway station between Tahiti and the old Europe—the colonists,
to survive in the rough colonies, have had to listen to the voices of nature and can, because
their institutions are less rigid, adapt more quickly. Diderot will attempt to produce a European version of this modern antiutopian arcadia in the *Salon de 1767*.

what we might ironically call their *moeurs sauvages*: their need actively to adapt to their mercilessly changing world, to meet its dynamism with their own rather than passively allowing it to structure them, just as other "savages" used infanticide or castration rituals to protect their cultures in hostile environments in the earliest pages of the text.

Diderot omits Bougainville's response to the old man's speech. It is irrelevant, anyway. His voyage itself is the best response that he can make, and he has always already traveled before even meeting the old man's tirade. He had gone to meet the world, and the old man's tirade is just a part of what he will absorb, transform, take back, and change Europe with. Bougainville emblematizes for Diderot the good side of an always double Europe: woven into the archaic and rigid Europe of the exploiting institutions has always been the creative if unpredictable world of the striving producers. Like the *Encyclopédie*'s successive editions, the highly visible rigid outer shell of fixed structure coexists with, only to be sloughed off by, a perpetually self-transforming invisible inner organism. Bougainville, like so many other Diderotian geniuses, is *lesté* toward the mind by a profound contact with the world—and this propensity is produced by his culture. He is perhaps unusual, but not an anomaly. He may be rare, but he does not contradict his culture's deepest motivating forces. His voyage will, like the discourse of any good Diderotian philosopher or encyclopedist, provoke sympathetic vibrations at home: the monk (who has moved from shell to inside) will clearly teach a different morality; A and B will have a conversation leading them to "deconstruct" their institutions, thus enabling them to proceed to effective action of their own. The Enlightenment philosopher of Europe is, in the end, a more truly natural philosopher than even Orou.

A   Que ferons-nous donc? Reviendrons-nous à la nature? Nous soumettrons nous aux loix?

B   Nous parlerons contre les loix insensées jusqu'à ce qu'on les réforme, et en attendant nous nous y soumettrons. Celui qui de son autorité privée enfreint une mauvaise loi autorise tout autre à enfreindre les bonnes. Il y a moins d'inconvénient à être fou avec des fous, qu'à être sage tout seul. . . . Imitons le bon Aumonier. Moine en France, sauvage dans Otaiti.

A Prendre le froc du pays où l'on va et garder celui du pays où l'on est.

B Et surtout être honnête et sincère jusqu'au scrupule avec des êtres fragiles qui ne peuvent faire notre bonheur sans renoncer aux avantages les plus précieux de nos sociétés. Et ce brouillard épais, qu'est-il devenu? (643)

A What should we do, then? Go back to nature? Submit ourselves to the laws?

B We will speak out against senseless laws until they are reformed, and meanwhile we will obey them. The person who on his own private authority breaks a bad law authorizes everyone else to break the good ones. It is less troublesome to be mad with the madmen than to be wise all alone . . . Let us imitate the good almoner. Monk in France, savage in Tahiti.

A Take the habit of the country one goes to and wear the one of the country where one is.

B And above all, be honest and sincere, with the utmost scrupulousness, with the fragile beings who can only make our happiness by renouncing the most precious advantages of our societies. And this thick fog, what has become of it?

This text has often been accused of advocating conformism, even of advocating a relativism that allows one to rationalize any existing moral system. Yet clearly Diderot, while rejecting Tahiti as an answer, does not justify the existing abusive European institutions. I think that the conformist misreading stems from one simple error: equating Bougainville with the monarchy or the monk with the church. Neither equation is valid. The philosopher's duty is to provoke continual change, but not so much change that the culture cannot absorb the shock. Again we see, as in the article "Encyclopédie," that Diderot is no revolutionary in the modern sense. That does not mean, as modern readers sometimes accuse him of saying and as Rousseau certainly felt, that if you are not a revolutionary you must be a conformist. For Diderot, the most effective but still the hardest (and perhaps most thankless) action is to judge what law is senseless according to the context, to perceive the counterproductive motivations behind particular interpersonal behavior patterns, and continually to push from within for change in one's own behavior and in public institutions. It is not a retreat from responsible moral action but the contrary. Diderot's philosopher still has to make real moral judgments, even if they are context dependent. A revolution would be a moral retreat, for revolutions either destroy culture altogether or just substitute one fixed system for another. Therefore they do not attack the real causes of the ills they are trying to reform: when their reforms become inadequate because the culture has evolved away from them, they just institute another abusive system. A virtue in Tahiti may indeed prove to be a vice in the particular time and place occupied by a Parisian. What was a virtue in Tahiti before the arrival of the Europeans may become of necessity a vice after they leave if the culture is to survive the invasion of syphilis. Behavior that would have been termed vicious by the Tahitians may gain a new status as a virtue, only to be overturned in its turn when the conditions making it reasonable have changed. The duty of the philosopher is not to sit by passively and allow Venices to develop all over Europe but to strive continually to see and bring about change and to judge its consequences for his future behavior.

The answer, as always in Diderot, is neither to write a treatise on moral logic nor to set down a code of explicit moral prescriptions. Tahitian institutions should not be exported to Europe any more than Catholicism should be imposed on the Tahitians. Nonetheless, principles for active and responsible moral action can be deduced by the experience of reading a work like the *Supplément* in which the unacceptable and damaging easy solutions are dismantled. Diderot would have the reader of the *Supplément* gain a sense of the nature of his own place within a social and physical environment to help him identify essential weak points that he can move to reform.

Diderot himself suspects here that one of the greatest flaws in European social functioning derives from a misadaptation of sexuality. As sexuality links man's physical, mental, and social functioning, the greatest ills are produced when its mechanisms are distorted. This was therefore the most appropriate and suggestive subject for him to use as an example in the *Supplément*, and he returns to it to end appropriately on the open-ended, nondeterministic light note that throws the responsibility for judgment back on his reader.

A [Le brouillard] est tombé.

B Et nous serons encore libres cet après-dîner de sortir ou de rester?

A Cela dépendra, je crois, un peu plus des femmes que de nous.

B Toujours les femmes; on ne saurait faire un pas sans les rencontrer à travers son chemin.

A Si nous leur lisions l'entretien de l'Aumonier et d'Orou.

B A votre avis qu'en diraient-elles?

A Je n'en sais rien.

B Et qu'en penseraient-elles?

A Peut-être le contraire de ce qu'elles en diraient. (643–44)

A The fog has lifted.

B And we'll be free again after dinner to go out or stay in?

A That will depend a bit more, I think, on the women than on us.

B Always the women; one can't take a step without finding them in one's path.

A What if we read them the conversation between the Almoner and Orou?

B In your opinion, what would they say?

A I have no idea.

B And what would they think of it?

A Probably the opposite of what they would say.

As I think should by now be fairly clear, the *Supplément* is not a pessimistic or fatalistic work in spite of Diderot's savage determination to avoid easy solutions and the consequent harshness of tone. His refusal to propound a program does not protect Diderot from belonging to an Enlightenment project that can still, from a modern standpoint, be denounced with real acuity as naively optimistic.[15] To nuance this judgment, however, we need one more component. The *Supplément* deals with moral consequences of actions and shocks

---

15. See the very interesting issue of *Critique* (no. 456, May 1985) on these questions, esp. Vincent Descombes, "Les mots de la tribu"; and Louis Dumont, "Identités collectives et idéologie universaliste: Leur Interaction de fait."

from outside a particular cultural context and only suggests principles for actions and reactions occurring within. What does such action look like within a French context? The most revealing place to look for Diderot's elaboration is not in his short stories that continue to deal directly with desire and sexuality but in the two texts that seem to complement the *Supplément* explicitly, that deal with the peculiarly European, even Parisian, versions of luxury as the meeting place of the economic, the moral, and the aesthetic: the *Salon de 1767* and the *Neveu de Rameau*.

Toward an Empirical Esthetics

The *Salon de 1767* addresses in less depth but from a wider perspective many of the issues that would be raised a few years later in the *Supplément au voyage de Bougainville* and in the work with which I shall end the second half of this book, the *Neveu de Rameau*. In these three texts, Diderot attempted to isolate the specific mechanisms in his materialist theory that could explain human culture. The result was a conceptual space projected by the interaction and interdefinition of economics, esthetics, and ethics. Each text polarized one aspect: the *Supplément* focused on economics, the *Salon de 1767* on esthetics, and the *Neveu de Rameau* on ethics. The *Salon de 1767*, although written—or at least finished—before the *Supplément*, nonetheless operates, I believe, as the hinge-text between the two others.[1] In it Diderot recounted his empirical investigation, in the real-life European setting of the Academy of Art's Salon, of the trilateral relationship between money, art, and morality. He used economic concepts to valorize various types of esthetic activities and even suggested the revalorization of the notion of "value" that would be crucial to the *Neveu de Rameau*.

Like Diderot's preceding *Salons*, the *Salon de 1767* appeared in the *Correspondance littéraire* and was ostensibly a careful description, for

---

1. The dating of Diderot's late works always poses a tricky problem, and not just because so few of them were published when he wrote them (or published at all). The major difficulty is of a different order: it can in fact be misleading to try to date the late texts, because they were nearly all written and substantively rewritten over periods of sometimes as long as ten to fifteen years (except for the *Salons*, obviously). The critical apparatus to DPV, which provides the most up-to-date overview of the presumed chronology of Diderot's works, demonstrates this amply. I feel, therefore, that it is justifiable to treat these three works as though they were, for our *conceptual* purposes, effectively contemporary.

the exiled *philosophes* and their foreign royal patrons, of the paintings in the French Academy of Art biennial exhibition. In its Salons at the Louvre, the Royal Academy presented for public view and discussion both its own works and also those of outside painters whose works were judged sufficiently accomplished to be recognized by the Academy. The Salons did not function as museums or cultural monuments, however; the side effect of the Salons was predictably to create and direct a powerful art market. Up through the *Salon de 1765*, Diderot had primarily focused on describing the paintings and his reactions to them—in other words, on treating them as noneconomic esthetic objects. In this *Salon*, he dramatically switched emphasis. He did not abandon his description of the paintings, of course. On the contrary, he used his reflections on the nature of the economic forces ruling the art market to develop a new mode of reacting to, describing, and evaluating paintings, one that was much more in harmony with his materialist dynamics.

Wealth

The "Préambule" explicitly posed the question of the relationship of money to esthetic creation. Diderot wrote a long and impassioned diatribe against the moneyed amateurs, men without training or taste whose visits to the Salons awakened in them a desire to own paintings and to be recognized as arbiters of taste. The Salons both provoked this desire and, by being an art marketplace, allowed the amateurs' purchases to determine the development of the esthetics of art. Diderot's argument is that unfortunately the amateurs, having no faith in their own taste, buy according to what has been bought by others, and a stock market mentality takes over.

C'est là [at the Salon] que cette si belle chienne d'Oudri, qui décore à droite notre synagogue [the house of the Baron d'Holbach] attendoit le baron notre ami. Jusqu'à lui, personne ne l'avoit regardée; personne n'en avoit senti le mérite; et l'artiste étoit désolé. Mais, mon ami, ne nous refusons pas au récit des procédés honnêtes. Cela vaut encore mieux que la critique ou l'éloge d'un tableau. Le baron voit cette chienne, l'achète; et à l'instant voilà tous ces dédaigneux amateurs furieux et jaloux. On vient; on l'obsède; on lui propose deux fois le prix de son tableau. Le baron va trouver l'artiste, et lui

Chienne avec ses petits, by Oudry. Lithograph by Tabariès de Gransaigne (Photo: Bibliothèque nationale).

demande la permission de céder sa chienne à son [Oudry's] profit. Non, monsieur, non, lui dit l'artiste. Je suis trop heureux que mon meilleur ouvrage appartienne à un homme qui en connoisse le prix. Je ne consens à rien. Je n'accepterai rien; et ma chienne vous restera.[2]

It is there [at the Salon] that Oudry's so very pretty [painting of a] dog, which decorates our synagogue [the Baron d'Holbach's house] on the right was waiting for our friend the baron. Until him, no one had looked at it; no one had sensed its merit; and the artist was desolate. But, my friend, let us not deprive ourselves of telling about honest goings-on. That is worth more than the criticism or praise of a painting. The baron sees the dog, buys it; in an instant all the disdainful connoisseurs are furious and jealous. They show up; they nag him; they offer him twice the price of his painting. The baron seeks out the artist and asks his permission to give up his dog and give [Oudry] the profit. No, monsieur, no, the artist tells him. I am

2. Denis Diderot, *Salons,* ed. Jean Seznec and Jean Adhémar (Oxford: Clarendon Press, 1963), 3:54–55. All citations are to this edition: citations of the *Salon de 1767* are by page number to vol. 3; other *Salons* are cited by volume and page number.

only too happy that my best work belongs to a man who knows its price. I consent to nothing. I will accept nothing; and my dog will stay with you.

Money gives people without talent power over those with talent. Yet the (very rich) Baron d'Holbach, ever recurring in Diderot's correspondence and his works as the model of the man of talent, the genial force of nature, has intervened to set things right. In other words, although this early in the text Diderot has not explicitly made the distinction, clearly not all amateurs are exploitative fools. There are two schools of amateurs, the false ones and the real ones.

[The false amateurs] décrient et ruinent le peintre et le statuaire, s'il a de la hauteur et qu'il dédaigne leur protection ou leur conseil qui le gênent, le troublent dans son attelier, par l'importunité de leur présence, l'ineptie de leurs conseils; qui le découragent, qui l'éteignent, et qui le tiennent tant qu'ils peuvent dans l'alternative cruelle de sacrifier ou son génie, ou son élévation, ou sa fortune. J'en ai entendu, moi qui vous parle, un de ces hommes, le dos appuyé contre la cheminée de l'artiste, le condamner impudemment, lui et tous ses semblables, au travail et à l'indigence; et croire par la plus malhonnête compassion réparer les propos les plus malhonnêtes, en promettant l'aumône aux enfants de l'artiste qui l'écoutoit. *Je me tus et je me reprocherai toute ma vie mon silence et ma patience.* (55)

[The false amateurs] criticize and ruin the painter and the sculptor, if he has dignity and disdains their protection or advice, which bother him; [they] disturb him in his studio by the importunity of their presence and the ineptitude of their advice; [these amateurs] who discourage him, extinguish him, and who, as long as they can, keep him faced with the cruel alternative of sacrificing either his genius, his self-respect, or his fortune. I myself, I who am speaking to you, have heard one of these men who, leaning against the mantle of the artist, impudently condemned him and those like him to labor and indigence and believed that, with his most dishonest compassion, he could make up for the most dishonest remarks by promising charity to the children of the artist who was listening to him. *I held my peace, and I will reproach myself for the rest of my life for my silence and my patience.*

Diderot said nothing. He, the archetypical good amateur, did not fulfill his function, which was here clearly to counterbalance the mercenary stupidity of the bad amateur. If only in negative terms, the duality of the category is clear, a duality that provides the motivating structure of the whole *Salon de 1767*. One group tears down, the other builds. One leads to decadence, the other to renewal and innovation. Diderot's penance for not speaking then was to write the long reflections to his patrons here in the *Salon*; his answer to the cynical exploiter was to develop his theory of the *modèle idéal*.

Before confronting this notion, the key concept in his esthetic theory, we need to turn to the section of the *Salon*, much farther along, where he tried to come to terms with what made La Grenée's mannered paintings so repulsive, that is, with what constituted the essence of bad taste. To do this, Diderot first had to discuss at length the meaning of economic luxury. As we shall see, the duality structuring the *Salon de 1767* springs from the same source that created both the old and the new Europe evoked in the *Supplément au voyage de Bougainville*: that source is the creation of economic excess.

DIDEROT [Les philosophes] ont vu que les beaux-arts devaient leur naissance à la richesse. Ils ont vu que la même cause qui les produisait, les fortifiait, les conduisait à la perfection, finissait par les dégrader, les abâtardir et les détruire; et ils se sont divisés en différents partis! Ceux-ci nous ont étalé les beaux-arts engendrés, perfectionnés, surprenans; et en ont fait la défense du luxe, que ceux-là ont attaqué par les beaux-arts abâtardis, dégradés, appauvris, avilis. . . .

GRIMM Les agresseurs et les défenseurs se sont portés des coups si égaux, qu'on ne sait de quel côté l'avantage est resté.

DIDEROT C'est qu'ils n'ont connu qu'une sorte de luxe.

GRIMM Ah! c'est de la politique que vous voulez faire.

DIDEROT Et pourquoi non? . . . Maudit soit à jamais le premier qui rendit les charges vénales. (118–19)

DIDEROT [The philosophers] saw that the fine arts owed their birth to riches. They saw that the same cause that produced them, strengthened them, and led them to perfection, ended up degrading, bastardizing, and destroying them; and they divided into two camps! One group showed us the fine arts engendered, perfected, surprising;

they carried out a defense of luxury, while the other group counter-attacked with the vision of the fine arts bastardized, degraded, impoverished, made vile. . .

GRIMM The aggressors and defenders were so equally matched that no one knows who won.

DIDEROT This is because they were aware only of one kind of luxury.

GRIMM Ah! You want to get into politics!

DIDEROT And why not? . . . Accursed forever be the one who first commercialized public offices.

By making public offices obtainable through purchase and not through merit alone, the state destroyed the possibility of any viable foundation for the esthetic function. For Diderot, public offices (especially the seats on the Tax Farm) were supposed to be the positions in which public service was the most concentrated and efficient. Public officials who had demonstrated their exceptional aptitude for maximizing productivity would be named to semimanagerial offices so that they could use their talents on a broad scale and benefit many people, enrich the entire state and not just themselves. Wealth, then, in such an ideal state would result from merit and would be the sign showing the sovereign whom to name to the offices. Tenancy in the offices would work to enrich the officeholders further in proportion to their success in enriching the entire country. Then the trickle-down effect of wealth would manifest itself: these men of natural genius and thus natural and active taste would recognize parallel merit in products of other fields—Diderot's emblem for this was the case of the Baron d'Holbach's purchase of Oudry's painting. The men of merit would naturally enjoy being in the presence of meritorious objects and in buying to increase the density of such objects around them, they would patronize the development of the arts and sciences. (Diderot did not explain the mechanism here, but I will return to this question when discussing his interaction with the paintings of Joseph Vernet.)

For Diderot these objects constitute genuine luxury. Genuine luxury can arise only from the "excess" economic products characteristic of Europe: as he argued at the end of the *Supplément*, Europe's rich but harsh climate catalyzes the development of potential genius by making the struggle for agricultural survival difficult but immensely rewarding for the men of genius. When, in the *Salon de 1767*, Diderot used his materialism to describe the economic forces resulting from this geographical predisposition, the argument was basically the following: Agricultural production is the paradigm of economic value.[3] When men produce more than enough food (say) to satisfy their basic needs, the excess can be traded for goods not needed, or enjoyed in its own right. This surplus Diderot defines as good luxury, or *wealth*. Why would one produce more than needed? Diderot's argument inverted the standard relationship of luxury to pleasure. Let us continue with the example of the successful farmer. In terms of the model Diderot developed in the *Pensées sur l'interprétation de la nature*, we could say that the farmer's success is determined by how well coordinated his and nature's elastic systems are with respect to each other. The more he works, the more harmonic his relationship to nature will become. This sensation of increasing coordination is Diderot's definition of esthetic pleasure. The more efficient the farmer's production becomes, the more pleasure it gives him, and therefore he will reinvest more of his work and wealth and produce even more wealth. The important thing to notice, however, is that this wealth is the *result* of pleasure, not the *source* of it. This wealth is doubly the sign of the harmony with nature that produces it, for it both designates its producer's success (for Diderot, his merit) and manifests in its own organization a high level of harmony with nature (to Diderot, it shows taste).

The feeling for the esthetic, the ability to judge and gain pleasure from beauty, in Diderot's terms the harmony of an object or activity with respect to the organization of nature, is therefore the basis of proper economic activity and patronage. True wealth exceeds the possession of money per se, for its money is just the sign of the merit that produced it. Complementarily, excess wealth, the good form of luxury, is at the heart of all successful esthetic activity. This was precisely the luxury that made the old man of Tahiti so suspicious but made possible and was indeed embodied by Bougainville's very voyage around the world. In the *Salon de 1767*, Diderot turns the old

3. Diderot's argument that agriculture was the source of cultural vitality was essentially derived from Quesnay's physiocratic arguments; see the articles Quesnay wrote for the *Encyclopédie* in the collection of his writings published in 1767 by Dupont de Nemours as *La Physiocratie*.

man's condemnation into the highest praise. "Les peintres, les poètes, les sculpteurs, les musiciens et la foule des arts adjacents naissent de la terre, ce sont aussi les enfants de la bonne Cérès; et je vous réponds que partout où ils tireront leur origine de cette sorte de luxe ils fleuriront et fleuriront à jamais" (119; "The painters, poets, sculptors, musicians, and the horde of related arts arise from the earth; they are the children of good Ceres; and I answer you that wherever they derive their origin from this kind of luxury, they will flower, and flower forever").

Money acquired other than through harmonious interaction with nature, however, no longer signifies merit. Pleasure then comes not from production that results in wealth but only from possessing money and flaunting it through the objects it can buy. This money characterizes bad luxury because it is nonproductive. For Diderot this money is merely riches, and the men who use it, mere venal speculators.

In this light we can understand the Diderot-"Grimm" diatribe against the sale of public offices. When public offices become venal, money itself, not the merit for which money was supposed to be only the sign, becomes sufficient to provide access to these positions of great financial potential. When people of undemonstrated or untried talent come to possess large amounts of money (through either inheritance or speculation, presumably, although Diderot does not explain), money ceases being wealth and becomes mere riches, for it no longer indicates the owner's ability to provoke excess production. Riches can buy things but cannot produce things. Money as an end in itself replaces the merit it is nonetheless still thought to represent. Riches may even destroy the mechanism that brought about the development of merit: when a man of potential talent has a great deal of money, he need not struggle to survive, so he may never develop the harmonious interaction with nature necessary to teach him how to *subodorer* new inventions, new procedures, new ideas. He, and others, will confuse the possession of riches with the production of wealth. Money's value as sign will then replace its value as tool. Merit no longer uses money to produce merit. Instead, money produces money, at the expense of the nation: rather than encouraging production by investing their own talents and money into the state, the venal officeholders merely tax the fruits of other peoples' production. They thus make it even harder for those people to continue producing. The Tax Farm drains the riches without providing corresponding investment; the venal officeholders are not the sources of future production but parasites on past wealth.

When the sign of merit replaces actual merit, signs of all sorts begin to replace referents of all sorts.

> DIDEROT L'argent, avec lequel on put se procurer tout, devint la mesure commune de tout. Il fallut avoir de l'argent, et quoi encore? de l'argent. Quand on en manqua, il fallut en imposer par les apparences et faire croire qu'on en avait.

> GRIMM Et il naquit une ostentation insultante dans les uns, et une espèce d'hypocrisie épidémique de fortune dans les autres.

> DIDEROT *C'est à dire une autre sorte de luxe*; et c'est celui-là qui dégrade et anéantit les beaux-arts, parce que les beaux-arts, leur progrès et leur durée demandent une opulence réelle, et que ce luxe-ci n'est que le masque fatal d'une misère presque générale, qu'il accélère et qu'il aggrave. (120)

> DIDEROT Money, with which one can procure anything, became the common measure of everything. One had to have money, and what else? Money. When it was lacking, one had to fool people with appearances and pretend to have it.

> GRIMM And there thus arose insulting ostentation on the part of some and a kind of epidemic hypocrisy of fortune on the part of the others.

> DIDEROT *In other words, another kind of luxury*; and it is this kind that degrades and annihilates the fine arts, because they, their progress, and their endurance require real opulence, whereas this luxury is nothing but the doomed mask of a nearly general wretchedness that it accelerates and aggravates.

As a result, the whole country and its industries, its agriculture, its real wealth, and its arts and sciences, split into dual manifestations of the same original entities, just as the duality of real wealth and mere riches splits men of merit from men of no merit. The consequences are especially clear in the domain of the production of esthetic objects: those whose money is not founded on talent, on a hard-won harmony with nature, do not have the mental coordination necessary to make good decisions about what to buy and thus what to patronize.

DIDEROT C'est alors que les grands artistes ne naissent point ou sont obligés de s'avilir, sous peine de mourir de faim. C'est alors qu'il y a cent tableaux de chevalet pour une grande composition, mille portraits pour un morceau d'histoire; que les artistes médiocres pullulent et que la nation en regorge.

GRIMM Que les Belle, les Bellengé, les Voiriot, les Brenet, sont assis à côté des Chardin, des Vien et des Vernet. . . . Et bénis soient les Belle, les Bellengé, les Voiriot, les Brenet, les mauvais poètes, les mauvais peintres, les mauvais statuaires, les brocanteurs, les bijoutiers et les filles de joie.

DIDEROT Fort bien, mon ami, parce que ce sont ces gens-là qui nous vengent. C'est la vermine qui ronge et détruit nos vampires, et qui nous reverse goutte à goutte le sang dont ils nous ont épuisés. (121)

DIDEROT This is when the great artists either are not born or are obliged to lower themselves if they don't want to die of hunger. This is when there are a hundred cheap quick studies for every great composition, a thousand portraits for every history painting; when the mediocre artists swarm and the nation is choked with them.

GRIMM When the Belles, the Bellengés, the Voiriots, the Brenets, are seated by the Chardins, the Viens, and the Vernets. . . . And blessed be the Belles and Bellengés, the Voiriots, the Brenets, the bad poets, the bad painters, the tinkerers, jewelers, and ladies of the night.

DIDEROT Well said, my friend, for these people avenge us. This vermin gnaws at and destroys our vampires and pours back, drop by drop, the blood they drained out of us.

In this passage full of resonances with the *Neveu de Rameau*, Diderot provided the counterpart to the inevitable decadence caused by the inheritance of undeserved riches. In a curious way the disease provides its own cure. To complement the men unable to admire (in Diderot's sense) come the men who fawn. While the men of merit foster and sustain other men of merit to their mutual benefit, as d'Holbach does with Oudry, the vampires create and perpetuate parasites, who unconsciously but systematically strip them of their money. Oudry sought money not for its own sake, but for its role as the sign of the recognition of his genius by another man of merit, the Baron d'Holbach. The price paid for his painting was only a symbol of the recognition of his effort and a means to continue that effort, hence his refusal to give up the painting to an undeserving buyer even at twice the price.

The parasites, however, do not produce art. For them, *éclat* replaces taste, and as their false painting replaces true painting, the dichotomy continues to rend the culture. In the article "Les deux Académies," which he appended to the *Salon*, Diderot suggested that this opposition and the venality that produced it extended even into the Royal Academy of Art, where patronage and money rather than merit could also determine who was accepted into the Academy's school (339–45). Venality split the Academy into two coexistent but mutually antagonistic academies (like matter and antimatter). The dichotomy was everywhere present for Diderot in the Salon of 1767; false paintings hung side by side with true paintings exposed the state of French culture for all to see on the very walls of the Louvre.

This interpretation was provoked by a very particular experience. Diderot had just been describing for Grimm the paintings of La Grenée, paintings that he acknowledged were technically proficient but nonetheless not beautiful. They do not work as art. At first glance they are pleasing, but the more Diderot looked at them, the more they became ugly, even ridiculous. ("Mercure, Hersé and Aglaure," especially, demonstrates a faulty composition, with distorted heads, deformed torsos, and disjointed legs hanging out in space.)

> La peinture est-elle l'art de parler aux yeux seulement? ou celui de s'addresser au coeur et à l'esprit, de charmer l'un, d'émouvoir l'autre, par l'entremise des yeux. O mon ami, la plate chose que des vers bien faits! la plate chose que la musique bien faite! la plate chose qu'un morceau de peinture bien fait, bien peint. Concluez...concluez que La Grenée n'est pas le peintre, mais bien maître La Grenée. (117)

> Is painting the art of speaking only to the eyes? Or that of addressing the heart and the mind, of charming one and moving the other by means of the eyes. Oh, my friend, what a dull thing are well-made verses! What a dull thing is a well-made painting, well painted. Conclude...conclude that La Grenée is not the painter but only master La Grenée.

"Maître La Grenée": Diderot's appellation placed La Grenée solidly on the negative side of the opposition between riches and wealth. This venal painter pandered to the corrupt taste of his purchasers, and his paintings in turn further corrupted their taste and that of others like them. Rather than creating real art, he merely decorated, producing works that only allude to real painting. They are simulacra of paintings, not true paintings. They operate that way because they stand in a symbolic relation to money: they represent their purchaser's money, not the objects figured on their surfaces, which are merely stand-ins for a real artist's creation. They are prized only as parts of a mutually reinforcing collection of objects all having the same effect: the gilded carriages, demimondaine women, catered dinners, ostentatious houses, and especially purchased titles and offices, all manifesting the purchaser's possession of money. What one buys with one's money should manifest taste and thus merit. If one's money can buy a public office rather than its being awarded according to merit, then money no longer designates merit. It designates nothing but itself, it is only a simulacrum of merit.

For the venal artists and patrons, all is simulacrum; there *is* nothing but sign, nothing but representation as long as "l'argent, avec lequel on put se procurer tout, devint la mesure commune de tout" ("money, with which one could procure anything, became the common measure of everything") while gold was still anachronistically defined by "son caractère représentatif de tout mérite" (120 and 125; "its quality of representing all merit"). The ironic result is that the rich men in buying bad paintings are attempting to acquire the referent—merit—for which they already display the sign, but they find that they cannot. The harder they try to acquire the referent according to the only system they understand—the parasitic acquisition and spending of money—the more real merit evades them. Tragically, they never realize that not only their belongings but also they themselves are only simulacra, because, as we shall see with the Bertin-Hus household in the *Neveu de Rameau*, they come to believe that only their shadow world of signs exists. For Diderot, their fascination with signs, the index of their corruption, blinds them to the existence of the material world where real objects, not just signs, are created through production. Only through interaction with this world could they accede to the value they are seeking, but their very mode of understanding objects prevents this. Let us make a small detour to explain why.

Remember the mistake that the D'Alembert voice made early in the *Rêve de d'Alembert*: when the Diderot voice asked if it were possible to turn Falconet's statue of a man into a thinking, reasoning being, d'Alembert immediately said no. He posed his understanding of the question in representational terms: he recast Diderot's question into one of how to turn the simulacrum of a man into a man, how to turn a sign into its referent or, rather, how to make the statue both the sign and its referent at the same time. Diderot's mocking answer was to *eliminate* the sign nature of the statue by seeing it not as a simulacrum of a man, not as what it had been made to represent, but for what it was materially—a stone to be ground into powder and incorporated through the food cycle into the matter of a thinking man. The statue does not come alive to be the clone of the real person it represents, it does not duplicate an already existing organization; it becomes an integral part of a new organized body. D'Alembert was blinded to the only possible answer to Diderot's question because he never thought to unpack the notion of the work of art as portrait.

Daniel Brewer has produced a relevant analysis of the notion of the portrait Diderot propounded in the *Salon de 1767*.[4] Recast in terms of my construal of Diderot's notion of the function of the art object, Brewer's argument would be that portraiture is a problematic genre because, to be successful, a portrait would have to be both a sign and a work of art. For Diderot, as we shall see when discussing the paintings of Joseph Vernet, these two notions are fundamentally opposed. A portrait would have both to represent an existing external person and to evoke for the observer the activity characterizing that person. The question then arises (and Diderot's discussion of Vernet will provide the answer), Can there even be such a thing as a successful portrait? In the *Salon de 1767*, Diderot discusses the very particular case of his own portraits. Describing the one that Michel Van Loo had painted of him (see frontispiece), Diderot said:

> Mais que diront mes petits-enfants, lorsqu'ils viendront à comparer mes tristes ouvrages avec ce riant, mignon, efféminé, vieux coquet-là? Mes enfants, je vous préviens que ce n'est pas moi. J'avois en une journée cent physionomies diverses, selon la chose dont j'étois

4. Daniel Brewer, "Portraying Diderot," in Jack Undank and Herbert Josephs, eds., *Diderot: Digression and Dispersion* (Lexington, Ky: French Forum, 1984), 44–59.

affecté. . . . *J'ai un masque qui trompe l'artiste*, soit qu'il y ait trop de choses fondues ensemble, soit que les impressions de mon âme se succédant très-rapidement et se peignant toutes sur mon visage, l'oeil du peintre ne me retrouvant pas le même d'un instant à l'autre, sa tâche devienne beaucoup plus difficile qu'il ne la croyait. (67; my emphasis)

But what will my grandchildren say when they happen to compare my pitiful works with this laughing, cute, effeminate old flirt? My children, I warn you in advance that this is not I. In a day I showed a hundred different physiognomies, according to what affected me. . . . *I have a mask that fools the artist*, because too many things are blended together in it, or because—since the sensations of my soul follow one another so rapidly and paint themselves all on my face, and the painter's eye does not find me the same from one moment to another—his task becomes much more difficult than he thought.

For Diderot, the "real person," as we can guess from all of his earlier works, could never be reduced to a physical object whose external appearance could be captured once and for all. It is revealing that he used the word *mask* here; his use ironically reverses the accepted relationship between the face and its mask and so points up the opposition he is establishing. A mask is not a successful portrait. It can never be anything but the simulacrum of a portrayal, for a successful portrayal would capture the event of experiencing Diderot's activities, would somehow transmit what it was like to be with Diderot rather than what he looked like. A mask is frozen and therefore takes all the life out of the appearance of the person; a mask representing a real person's face can only be in effect a death mask. As we will see later, this was almost exactly the way Diderot understood denotative words to work as signs: they remove the "accent," the always singular affect that gives an expression life. Throughout the *Salon*, he uses the word *portrait* in the negative sense of the death mask of a thing, a simulacrum, a copy of its mere appearance.

In the d'Alembert-Diderot exchange in the *Rêve*, d'Alembert confused the mask (the portrait) with the person by thinking that fixed appearance rather than activity characterizes a person. His mistake placed him with the venal amateurs, but not because Diderot would think he shared their self-serving greed. D'Alembert's philosophical

errors were indeed consonant with the corrupt morality of the par-
venu, but only because he shared with them an underlying *conceptual* perversion. Very schematically adapting my argument from part
I, I would say that both the venal amateurs and d'Alembert thought
that the worlds of mind and body were distinct and complementary:
mind acts, body only reacts. Therefore the defining characteristic of
a body is that it is fixed, so there is no essential reason why the mask
should not be the ideal sign for a face. To the fixed object can surely
be assigned a fixed sign; the representational relation is reliable. As
the real d'Alembert so clearly argued in the "Discours préliminaire"
to the *Encyclopédie* and Condillac in the *Traité des sensations*, representational language therefore derives its universal authority precisely
from its nonpoetic nature, from its reliance on masks. The venal amateurs took this one step farther. Merit is not a quality, but an activity,
the materially poetic—that is, productive—interaction with nature.
The venal amateurs were like d'Alembert in not seeing that such activity should have spawned their money. Their riches resulted from
someone else's (long-past) activity, in which they had not participated. That activity was thus invisible to them, and they only saw
the resulting productions as being fixed, permanent, reliable sources
of money. They understood their money only through death masks.
Analogously, their notion of a work of art (beyond being a mere purchased object) was also that of a death mask: blind to the poetic function, they could recognize in art only well-established conventional
subjects, conventional treatments, the reproduction of fixed, because
no longer evolving, styles.

This is what Diderot meant by the *maniéré*—the eternal recombi-
nation of elements of dead art forms that produced no poetic
creation—and this is why he saw it as the incarnation of the corrupted taste resulting from unfounded luxury. For Diderot, obviously, for whom any mask could only hide the ever changing
dynamic nature of the object, d'Alembert with his representational
language and the venal amateurs with their simulacra of paintings
had thrown the baby out with the bathwater.[5]

Typically, Diderot's first way to counter this position and its consequences for both French painting and ethical behavior was to shift

5. At the end of the *Salon*, Diderot also appended a short discussion of the meaning of
the *maniéré* (335-39) that generalizes the treatment of the subject in his discussion of the
paintings of La Grenée and especially Baudouin.

emphasis away from the logic of the argument. Otherwise he would, after all, be agreeing to fight the representationalists on their own ground, which would mean that he accepted the authority of their notion of demonstration over his own. Instead, he showed us the negative effects that looking at La Grenée's paintings had had on him. Diderot's reaction to these paintings had already begun to show up as boredom and ill humor and a heightened awareness of physical fatigue. Like Dorval in the *Entretiens sur le fils naturel*, after having been all stirred up by an act of observing either nature or a work of art, "[on] ne connaîtrait de soulagement qu'à verser au-dehors un torrent d'idées qui se pressent, se heurtent, et se chassent" (DPV 10:99; "he would get relief only by pouring out a torrent of ideas that press in on him, bump into each other, chase each other out"), so he fled to an empty gallery and spilled forth his mood by writing the dialogue with Grimm in which he developed his theory of the duality of luxury analyzed above. His response was a poetic one worthy of the natural philosopher of the *Interprétation de la nature*. Because of the corrupt nature of the object that provoked it, however, Diderot's response was flawed by pessimism, by fatalism.

> Tout porte en soi un germe secret de destruction. L'agriculture, cette bienfaisante agriculture, engendre le commerce, l'industrie et la richesse. La richesse engendre la population. L'extrême population divise les fortunes. Les fortunes divisées restreignent les sciences et les arts à l'utile . . . partout où vous verrez une poignée de terre recueillie dans la plaine, portée dans un panier d'osier, [pour] aller couvrir la pointe nue d'un rocher, et l'espérance d'un épi l'arrêter là par une claie, soyez sûr que vous verrez peu de grands édifices, peu de statues, que vous trouverez peu d'Orphées. . . . Et que m'importe ces monumens fastueux? Est-ce là le bonheur? la vertu, la sagesse, les moeurs, l'amour des enfans pour les pères, l'amour des pères pour les enfans, la tendresse du souverain pour ses sujets, celle des sujets pour le souverain, les bonnes loix, la bonne éducation, l'aisance générale; voilà, voilà ce que j'ambitionne. (125)[6]

6. Diderot here picks up his never ending battle with Rousseau. The image of luxury that Rousseau adopted (today's luxury becomes tomorrow's necessity, whence the perversion of man from the state of nature) is homologous with the position outlined in this quotation. This is to a great extent the definition of luxury that makes possible Rousseau's attack on the arts in his *Discours sur les sciences et les arts*.

Everything carries in itself the secret seed of its own destruction. Agriculture, benevolent agriculture, engenders commerce, industry, and riches. Riches engender population. Extreme population divides fortunes. The division of fortunes restricts the sciences and arts to the useful. . . . wherever you see a handful of earth gathered up in a plain, carried in a wicker basket to cover the naked point of a rock, and in the hope for an ear of grain anchor the soil there, rest assured that you will find few edifices, few statues, that you will find few Orpheuses . . . And what do I care about these splendid monuments? Are they happiness? Virtue, wisdom, morals, the love of children for their fathers, of fathers for their children, the tenderness of a sovereign for his subjects, of subjects for their sovereign, good laws, good education, general comfort; this, this is what I seek.

So was the answer a return to Tahiti? Had Diderot recuperated after all the antiesthetic poetry-refusing cultivation of the *utile* that he had so meticulously denounced in the *Supplément au voyage de Bougainville*? Indeed not; he was tempted by the (La Grenée–provoked) *marche naturelle* of his ideas, as Condillac would say, to conclude this, but his own instincts prevented him.

Mais là...je vous entends. Astuce, mauvaise foi, nulle grande vertu, nul héroisme, une foule de petits vices, enfans de l'esprit économique et de la vie contentieuse. . . . Il faut l'avouer....où irai-je donc? où trouverai-je un état de bonheur constant? Ici, un luxe qui masque la misère, là, un luxe qui, né de l'abondance, ne produit qu'une félicité passagère. Où faut-il que je vive? Où est la demeure qui me promette et à ma postérité un bonheur durable? . . . Vous êtes un insensé. . . . Dans l'empire, le ciel suscite un maître qui amende ou qui détruit; dans le cycle des races, un descendant qui relève ou qui renverse. Voilà l'arrêt immuable de la nature. Soumettez-vous-y. (125)

But there...I've got you. Ruse, bad faith, no great virtue, no heroism, a horde of minor vices, children of the economic and contentious life. . . . I have to admit it...Where will I go, then? Where will I find a state of constant happiness? Here luxury masking misery, there luxury that, born from abundance, produces only transitory felicity. Where must I live? Where is the home that promises for me and my posterity an enduring happiness? . . . You are unreasonable. . . . In the empire, heaven brings forth a master who corrects or destroys; in the cycle of races, a descendant who raises up or throws down. Such is the unchangeable decree of nature. Submit to it.

Clearly Tahiti was not the answer, although Diderot here seemed unable to provide one that would give him faith in the future. He seemed to be saying, In a world where money will eventually hold sway, why even try?

The Modern Arcadia

Diderot's text is misleading if we take it at face value. Moreover, it is logically self-contradictory: Diderot had said at the beginning of his diatribe that "partout où [les arts] tireront leur origine de cette sorte de luxe ils fleuriront et fleuriront à jamais" (119; "wherever the arts derive their origin from this sort of luxury, they will flower, and flower forever"). In the passage just quoted he clearly contradicted this original optimism. There are two ways to interpret this contradiction: on the one hand, perhaps the original position was merely an impossible utopian dream, like Tahiti or the perfect *Encyclopédie*; maybe it was only an oneiric hypostatization, misguided with respect to the continual change characterizing the physical world. On the other hand, perhaps the argument was pessimistic not because Diderot himself subscribed to the position he finally came up with but because his conclusions were natural philosophical reactions to a series of bad paintings, bad precisely because they provoked the fatalism arising from the false view of luxury that gave them their meaning. The paintings are bad for more than failing to work the way good paintings do (which Diderot has not yet explained to his reader) or being only simulacra of paintings. They are bad also because, no matter how obvious their falsity is to the beholder, they truly pervert his vision of the world and the things he can produce in response to it.

La Grenée's paintings make Diderot morally as well as physically sick. After being subjected to these paintings, he in effect could not have faith in his powers of creation. Diderot did not say this; he demonstrated it by his outburst and by a significant change in its structure. It began as typical wholesome Diderotian dialogue but degenerated into logical argument. The second half of his diatribe is a point-by-point restatement of the initial dialogue. It follows the relentless rules for logical argument belonging to "the opposition," to those who, like d'Alembert, subscribed to the mind-body opposition that permits the representational construal of language and from which false luxury and thus false painting derive. Diderot had been partly turned into one of the corrupt, so naturally he could not think his way out of the impasse. He had lost his tools to do it.

How do we know this? Through a structural mechanism: the heart of the *Salon* is a step-by-step encounter with concrete examples of the duality of luxury. Diderot was soon to encounter the truly luxurious paintings of Joseph Vernet, which would quite literally provide both the counterpoint and the antidote to the paintings of La Grenée. But first, he made a short passage through his beloved Chardins, a passage that would begin the healing process.

> Commençons par dire le secret de celui-ci. . . . Il place son tableau devant la nature, et il le juge mauvais tant qu'il n'en soutient pas la présence. . . . Ses compositions appellent indistinctement l'ignorant et le connaisseur. C'est une vigueur de couleur incroyable, une harmonie générale, un effet piquant et vrai, de belles masses, une magie de faire à désespérer, un ragoût dans l'assortiment et l'ordonnance. Eloignez-vous, approchez-vous, même illusion, point de confusion, point de symmétrie non plus, point de papillotage; l'oeil est toujours recréé, parce qu'il y a calme et repos. On s'arrête devant un Chardin comme d'instinct, comme un voyageur fatigué de sa route va s'asseoir, sans presque s'en appercevoir, dans l'endroit qui lui offre un siège de verdure, du silence, des eaux, de l'ombre et du frais. (128–29)

> Let me start by telling you this one's secret. . . . He compares his painting with nature and judges it poor as long as he cannot stand its presence. . . . His compositions attract equally the ignorant and the connoisseur. They have an incredible vigor of coloring, general harmony, a piquant and true effect on the observer, beautiful masses, an unbeatable magical touch, an appetizing variety and order. Stand back, draw near, same illusion, no confusion at all, no symmetry at all, either, no blurring; one's eye is always refreshed, because there is calm and rest. One stops in front of a Chardin as if by instinct, like a traveler tired from the road who sits down, almost without being aware of it, in the one spot that offers him a seat amid greenery, silence, running water, shade, and coolness.

The still life may have been conventionally considered a low genre; nonetheless (or perhaps as a result), Chardin was masterful at using it to slow down the frenetic activity of the observer. The La Grenées had left Diderot fatigued but overexcited, hence depressed and nihilis-

La Source abondante, by C.-L. Vernet. Engraving by Le Bas (Photo: Bibliothèque nationale).

tic. The Chardins soothed his spirit; their contemplation transmitted the calm and rest essential to the successful still life (as its name clearly indicates). One minor but revealing observation is that Diderot did not describe these paintings. He was not drawn into an analytic description of them as he had been with the La Grenées; he merely told Grimm the effect that they had on him. For his reader in turn, the passage through the Chardins serves the purpose of the *airs* in a Fragonard: they are the still spaces in a painting where the observer's eye can go to rest for a moment before returning to the dynamic machine of the shapes and forms. This indirect evocation of the *effect* of a Chardin rather than the description of the paintings themselves also prepares the reader for the abrupt change in painting criticism that Diderot would introduce with the Vernets.

After the Chardins, Diderot was once again able to confront real paintings. With characteristic bravura, he dropped his reader into his conceit with no introduction, no warning, no explanation. "J'avais écrit le nom de cet artiste au haut de ma page, et j'allais vous entretenir de ses ouvrages, lorsque je suis parti pour une campagne voisine de la mer et renommée par la beauté de ses sites" (129; "I had written the artist's name at the top of my page and was going to hold forth on his works, when I left for a countryside bordering on the sea and renowned for the beauty of its sites"). The Vernets seized him. He claimed to be immediately absorbed into the experience of interacting with them; so absorbed, in fact, that he "forgot" to tell us that he was describing his reaction to them. In this Salon, Vernet exhibited seven landscapes. Diderot pretended each was a *beau site* that he was going to visit with an old abbé and his two pupils. In each case the old abbé led Diderot to a vantage point where he suddenly sprang the view on him. Diderot was astonished: "à l'aspect d'un nouveau site, non moins admirable que le premier, ma voix coupée, mes idées confondues, je restai stupéfait et muet" (133; "at the view of this new site, no less admirable than the first, finding myself speechless, my ideas in a tumult, I remained stupefied and mute"). In general, although with exceptions to which I will return, Diderot began his interaction with each painting by attempting a Condillacean analytic description worthy of the perfection it reached in his *Salon de 1765*. In each of his attempts to use this type of analysis to describe Vernet paintings in the *Salon de 1767*, however, a transformation occurred. The more Diderot analyzed the landscape, the less his description

Les Occupations du rivage, by C.-L. Vernet. Engraving by Le Bas (Photo: Bibliothèque nationale).

designated objects and the more it described the effect that the objects had on him. In several cases he even entered into the landscape and described it not from the position of a dominant exterior analytic eye but from the positions he successively held as he wandered from point to point. He experienced the paintings as events rather than describing them as objects. More than a site, each was really a promenade; the initial visual unity effaced itself immediately before the activity of exploring the landscape, of interacting with, even critiquing, each of its beauties to maximize the affect.

The best overall description of this phenomenon in painterly terms is found in Michael Fried's *Absorption and Theatricality*:

> [We find] in Vernet's art a tension or contradiction between, on the one hand, a subtle but forthright mode of decorative integration, capable of being taken in at a glance, and, on the other, a network of relationships among multiple disparate centers of interest whose separation from and connection with one another within an imaginary space can be apprehended only in time . . . In the superb *Vue du golfe de Naples* (1748), the interplay among variously tilting masts, sails, oars, the tree, the anchor at the left, etc., serves both to foster a perception of the painting as a decorative whole and, by virtue of the presence of numerous subtle disaccords between those elements—I am thinking of the way in which they often seem to tilt or curve *against* one another—to slow down and in effect to fragment our imaginary experience of the painted scene. (134–35)[7]

The most striking example of this occurred in Diderot's evocation of the second site; his astonishment emblematizes the decorative unified moment; his four-page excursion, the serial experience of the multiple disparate centers of interest. What I would like to focus on is not the painterly aspect itself but the transformation that occurs in

---

7. Michael Fried's *Absorption and Theatricality. Painting and Beholder in the Age of Diderot* (Berkeley: University of California Press, 1980) is especially fine on the *Salon de 1767*. The notion of absorption that he develops to pinpoint the primary mechanism of painting and theater for Diderot can be subsumed, I believe, into the mechanism of mutual seduction-coordination that characterizes the operation of the physical dynamic world described in the first half of this book. In that sense, my analysis of Diderot's response to the Vernets can be considered complementary to Fried's: the absorption he describes is half of a larger process. What distinguishes the *Salon de 1767* from the other *Salons* is, I think, that it turns its attention from absorption considered as an esthetic end in itself to the interactive relationship.

the observer's event of experiencing the painting as seen through Diderot's reactions: he moves from the initial moment of unified *astonishment* first to the dynamic exploration characteristic of *admiration*, and finally to the moment of *poetic creation*. The observer reacts, then interacts, then acts.

So, as we would expect, Diderot and the abbé are impelled by their admiration to discuss a series of philosophical questions. These were not, of course, well-ordered debates. "Toute cette conversation se fesait d'une manière fort interrompue. La beauté du site nous tenait alternativement suspendus d'admiration, je parlais sans trop m'entendre, j'étais écouté avec la même distraction" (131; "All this conversation was carried out haltingly. The beauty of the site kept us alternately suspended in admiration; I spoke without paying much attention to what I was saying, I was listened to with the same distraction"). The reader is in the presence of two Dorvals, each being tuned by the landscape under observation to emit *des torrents d'idées*, each through conversation with the other transforming initial *bizarreries* into coherent plausible interpretations.

Was this really any different from what had already occurred in Diderot's submission to the paintings of La Grenée? When looking at those paintings as well, he had certainly been driven to produce a text, even if it was a long and exquisitely articulate diatribe against bad painting. In fact, there was a difference. One might say the *essential* difference. For from site one through site seven, the dialectical play between the fragmenting effect of the nature-provoked associations of ideas and the continuity provided by the ongoing conversation yielded a logic of a new sort, a logic that for Diderot was a great deal more convincing in its affective seduction than the pure march of reason.

Nous abandonnâmes les débris de notre repas aux domestiques qui nous avaient servis et, tandis que nos jeunes élèves se livraient sans contrainte aux amusemens de leur âge, leur instituteur et moi sans cesse distraits par les beautés de la nature, *nous conversions moins que nous ne jettions des propos décousus.*
    Mais pourquoi y a-t-il si peu d'hommes touchés des charmes de la nature? —C'est que la société leur a fait un goût et des beautés factices. —*Il me semble que la logique de la raison a fait bien d'autres progrès que la logique du goût.* —Aussi celle-ci est-elle si fine, si sub-

tile, si délicate, suppose une connaissance si profonde de l'esprit et du coeur humain, de ses passions, de ses préjugés, de ses erreurs, de ses goûts, de ses terreurs, que peu sont en état de l'entendre, bien moins encore en état de la trouver. Il est bien plus aisé de démêler le vice d'un raisonnement que la raison d'une beauté; d'ailleurs, l'une est bien plus vieille que l'autre. *La raison s'occupe des choses, le goût de leur manière d'être.* (152; my emphasis)

We abandoned the debris of our meal to the servants who had attended to us and, while our young students indulged in the amusements typical of their age, their tutor and I, ceaselessly distracted by the beauties of nature, *conversed less than we uttered disjointed remarks.*

But why are there so few men touched by the charms of nature? —It's because society induced in them a factitious taste and beauty. —*It seems to me that the logic of reason has made more progress than the logic of taste.* —Which is so fine, so subtle, so delicate, assumes such a profound knowledge of the human mind and heart, of its passion, prejudices, errors, tastes, and terrors, that few are capable of understanding it, much less capable of discovering it. It is much easier to figure out a mistake in reasoning than the reason why something is beautiful; moreover, one is much older than the other. *Reason deals with things, taste with their mode of being.*

This passage serves to sum up the preceding many pages of dialogue, which focus less and less on the paintings themselves and more and more on how the observer's perception of each new painting is guided by the preceding argument and how the twists and turns of the succeeding argument are provoked by the observation of each new painting. The interactive momentum that builds up is in its own structure a mirror image of the Vernet experience as Fried describes it. The initial disparate fragments of argument eventually add up to a coordinated whole that cannot be reduced to a logical argument. This coordinated whole is the combination of the absorptive moment with its complementary creative moment. The initial unity of astonishment turns into experiential fragmentation to produce fragmented conversation that resolves into a unity of coordinated interpretation. The conversation thus represents not the thing's appearance but a way of being with the thing, as Diderot had already foreshadowed in his discussion of the problem with portraits. In this case the "thing" is the extraordinarily dynamic Vernet paintings.

Diderot's whole thesis is therefore contained in this self-reflexive passage, in which the logic of taste is both discussed and exemplified by the behavior of the two conversants. Their logic of taste reveals itself to be the same natural philosophical logic that Diderot had elaborated years before in the *Interprétation de la nature* and the article "Encyclopédie." When finally adapted to the art object, it produces the transformation of art criticism that Diderot was introducing, or rather that he was finally foregrounding and justifying, in the *Salon de 1767*. In the *Salon de 1765*, he had already hesitantly yielded to it (for example, in his discussion of the paintings of Le Prince and of Greuze's "Jeune fille qui pleure son oiseau mort"): "Un tableau avec lequel on raisonne ainsi, qui vous met en scène, et dont l'âme reçoit une sensation délicieuse, n'est jamais un mauvais tableau" (2:173; "A painting that you argue with like this, that inserts you into the action and from which the soul receives such a delicious sensation, is never a bad painting"). The 1765 introduction was uncertain, even apologetic, though, for in that *Salon* he was developing the analytic method applied to art to its apogee. In the *Salon de 1767*, however, he leapt beyond the analytic to embrace the absorptive interaction and not only made it the central feature of his art theory but in fact used it to elaborate that theory. He seemed to have realized that only thus could he develop an esthetic theory consonant with his long-established material dynamism. He emphasized the importance of the very real physical reactions that the observer will have to paintings: in case the reader had missed his none too subtle point, Diderot appended a long sketch of the still to be written *Rêve de d'Alembert*, a passage whose writing was supposedly provoked by Diderot's dream reaction to the Vernets the next night (162–65). Diderot the natural philosopher was reacting to the paintings as though they were nature.

Can we indeed say that for Diderot paintings were distinct from nature, that they represent it but do not reproduce it? What *is* the relationship of a great painting (not a simulacrum painting) to nature? In effect, this was the central issue of the philosophical ruminations of Diderot and his abbé; it was what provoked their very first *torrents d'idées*, when exploring their very first site:

> Quel est celui de vos artistes, me disait mon *cicerone*, qui eût imaginé de rompre la continuité de cette chaussée rocailleuse par une touffe

d'arbres? —Vernet peut-être. —A la bonne heure; mais votre Vernet
en aurait-il imaginé l'élégance et le charme? Aurait-il pu rendre l'effet
chaud et piquant de cette lumière qui joue entre leurs troncs et leurs
branches? —Pourquoi non? . . . Je répondais de distraction; car mon
attention était arrêtée sur une masse de rochers couverte d'arbustes
sauvages, que la nature avait placeés à l'autre extrémité du tertre
rocailleux. . . . Eh bien! dis-je à mon *cicerone*, allez-vous-en au Sal-
lon, et vous verrez qu'une imagination féconde, aidée d'une étude
profonde de la nature, a inspiré à un de nos artistes précisément ces
rochers, cette cascade et ce coin de paysage. . . . —Vous avez beau
dire Vernet, Vernet, je ne quitterai point la nature pour courir après
son image; quelque sublime que soit l'homme, ce n'est pas Dieu.
—D'accord; mais si vous aviez un peu plus fréquenté l'artiste, il vous
aurait peut-être appris à voir dans la nature ce que vous n'y voyez
pas . . . si Vernet vous eût appris à mieux voir la nature, la nature, de
son côté, vous eût appris à bien voir Vernet. (130–31)

Which of your artists, my *cicerone* said to me, could have thought to
break the continuity of this rocky pathway by a clump of trees?
—Vernet, perhaps. —That's possible; but could your Vernet have
thought up its elegance and charm? Could he have captured the hot
and piquant effect of this light playing among their trunks and
branches? —Why not? . . . I answered distractedly; for my attention
was caught by a mass of rocks covered with wild scrub that nature
had placed at the other end of the rocky knoll. . . . Well then! I said
to my *cicerone*, go to the Salon and you will see that a fertile imagination, aided by a profound study of nature, has inspired one of our
artists to paint precisely these rocks, this cascade and that corner of
the countryside. . . . —You can go on saying Vernet, Vernet; I will
still not leave nature to chase her image; no matter how sublime
man may be, he's still not God. —All right, but if you knew the
artist a bit better, he might have taught you to see in nature what
you don't see . . . if Vernet could have taught you to see nature better, nature, on her side, would have taught you to see Vernet well.

The joke, of course, is that the "nature" being discussed is all the
while a Vernet painting. The point that must be emphasized is that
the joke is effective only because Grimm will *know* that Diderot's
absorption is only feigned. Diderot is not claiming that the Vernets
are so realistic, such perfect representations of reality, that he is actually fooled by them into thinking that he is in the countryside. On
the contrary, the entire argument will come to center on the issue of

a double experience: the evocation of nature that the paintings effect in the observer coexists with his awareness that they are constructed physical objects. Like Falconet's statue, they are not representations of existing things. As a theatrical execution (143-44) differs in its effect on the audience from a real execution, so an effective landscape affects its witness differently from the way that a real landscape would. In other words, a valid art object does not represent an event any more than it represents objects. As the end of the above quotation suggests, nature evokes the art object as much as the art object evokes nature. The observer's experience of them is in each case an event in its own right. However, when the observer is able to hold both in his mind at the same time, each becomes greater from its comparison with the other (which was what Diderot meant when he said in the article "Encyclopédie" that comparison was the fundamental gesture of true philosophy). The coordinated whole formed by painting, nature, and observer is, like the multiple thinking minds of the *Rêve*, greater than the sum of its parts. This is what it meant for Diderot to *bien voir*. This double event replaces the action of the Condillacean analytic eye; it fills in the empty space created by analytic representational language's designation of absent referents.

Now, Diderot was not saying that analytic procedures should never have been invented. Indeed, they served their purpose admirably.

L'esprit philosophique veut des comparaisons plus resserrées, plus strictes, plus rigoureuses, sa marche circonspecte est ennemie du mouvement et des figures. Le règne des images passe, à mesure que celui des choses s'étend. Il s'introduit par la raison une exactitude, une précision, une méthode, pardonnez-moi le mot, une sorte de pédanterie qui tue tout: tous les préjugés civils et religieux se dissipent, et il est incroyable combien l'incrédulité ôte des ressources à la poésie. . . . [Mais] la discipline militaire naît quand il n'y a plus de généraux; la méthode, quand il n'y a plus de génie. (153-54)

The philosophical spirit wants closer, stricter, more rigorous comparisons; its circumspect progress is the enemy of movement and figures. The reign of images passes away as that of things grows. Reason introduces an accuracy, precision, and method, and—excuse the word—a sort of pedantry that kills everything: all civil and religious prejudices dissipate, and it is unbelievable how much incredulity removes the resources of poetry. . . . [But] military discipline arises when there are no more generals; method, when there is no more genius.

Precisely as Condillac had intended in the *Traité des sensations*, the analytic language had banished figurative language and its illusions so as to banish superstition and thus undermine the arbitrary authority of religion. But along with God had gone the moral meaning of natural sites and the impetus behind poetic creation.

What had bothered the abbé so much in the first pages of Diderot's imagined promenades was that God was being banished—but not by analytic language. He was being replaced by Vernet. We find the abbé silly and naïve in his concern; how could anyone seriously think that Diderot's praise of Vernet constituted heresy, or even that the good Enlightenment atheist reader could take the issue of heresy seriously? This philosophical Enlightenment reader, however, is the one who is naïve. In a passage resonating strongly with Voltaire's panegyric of Newton, Diderot exclaims,

> Ce qu'il y a d'étonnant, c'est que l'artiste se rappelle ces effets à deux cents lieus de la nature, et qu'il n'a de modèle présent que dans son imagination; c'est qu'il peint avec une vitesse incroyable; c'est qu'il dit: Que la lumière se fasse, et la lumière est faite; que la nuit succède au jour et le jour aux ténèbres, et il fait nuit et il fait jour; c'est que son imagination aussi juste que féconde lui fournit toutes ces vérités; c'est qu'elles sont telles que celui qui en fut spectateur tranquille et froid au bord de la mer en est émerveillé sur la toile, c'est qu'en effet ses compositions prêchent plus fortement la grandeur, la puissance, la majesté de Nature, que la Nature même:[8] il est écrit: *Caeli enarrant gloriam Dei*, mais ce sont les cieux de Vernet, c'est la gloire de Vernet. (160)

What is astonishing is that the artist recalls these effects two hundred leagues from nature and his only model is in his imagination; that he paints with unbelievable speed; that he says, "Let there be light," and there is light; "Let night follow day and day the shadows," and there is night and day; that his imagination, as correct as it is fertile, furnishes him with all these truths; that the spectator who saw them tranquilly and cool at the seaside is enchanted when he sees them on the canvas; that in effect his compositions proclaim more strongly the grandeur, power, and majesty of Nature than

8. Diderot does not usually capitalize *nature*.

Nature herself: it is written: The heavens interpret the glory of God, but these are Vernet's heavens and Vernet's glory.

There is a god function, but the poet performs it. The poet inspires coordination with the natural world. By doubling the event, by turning mere need into the agreeable, by substituting pleasure for the merely sufficient, the poet restores the philosopher's ability to perceive the world's dynamic complexity that had been taken from him by analytic language. Diderot had said that "il y a dans la poésie toujours un peu de mensonge; l'esprit philosophique nous habitue à le discerner, et adieu l'illusion et l'effet" (157; "In poetry there is always some falsehood; the philosophical mentality accustoms us to discerning it, and goodbye to illusion and effect"). Yet, "jamais, depuis que le monde est monde, deux amans n'ont dit identiquement *je vous aime*; et dans l'éternité qui lui reste à durer, jamais deux femmes ne répondront identiquement *vous êtes aimé*; depuis que *Zaïre* est sur la scène, Orosmane n'a pas dit et ne dira pas deux fois identiquement: *Zaïre, vous pleurez*" (157; "never, since the world was made, have two lovers ever said, 'I love you' in the same way; and in the eternity that it will still endure, two women will never identically answer, 'You are loved'; for as long as *Zaïre* has been staged, Orosmane has not said and never will say the same way twice: 'Zaïre, you're crying'"). The poet and the artist, in their performance of nature, do not restore the illusion or the lie banished by analytic language. They restore the dynamic, what Diderot calls the accent, the singularity of each event as event, and thus its affect. They do this by demonstrating the complementarity made possible by the difference between the art object and the world it expresses and by demonstrating the difference between art object and representative language.

> Cependant deux hommes ont la même pensée et la rendent par les mêmes expressions, et deux poètes ont quelquefois fait deux mêmes vers sur un même sujet. Que devient donc l'axiome? —Ce qu'il devient? il reste intact. —Et comment cela, s'il vous plaît? —Comment? C'est qu'il n'y a dans la même pensée rendue par les mêmes expressions, dans les deux vers faits sur un même sujet, qu'une identité de phénomène apparente, et c'est la pauvreté de la langue qui occasionne cette apparence d'identité. (156)

And yet two men have the same thought and turn it into the same expressions, and two poets have sometimes written the same two lines on the same subject. What happens to your axiom then? —What happens to it? It remains intact. —And how does that come about? —How? It's because there is only an apparent identity to the same thought turned into the same expressions and the two lines written on the same subject, and it is the poverty of language that causes this appearance of identity.

Diderot had said that "une nation est vieille quand elle a du goût" (159), but clearly the old age that he means here is the old age of the culture that produced Bougainville, not that of the old man of Tahiti. The European culture contains its own renewal and can become young only by growing older and older. Therefore it cannot return to the innocence of the preanalytic utopia, to a progress-denying arcadia, nor can it remain within the analytic clarity without falling prey to an analogous and equally fatal rigidity. Early on, before explaining its full implications, Diderot had already evoked the modern order to come. Without even understanding its own processes, it continually regenerates a modern arcadia, which is old and new at the same time.

Enchaînés dans l'enceinte étroite des villes . . . nous allons contrefaire un moment le rôle du sauvage, esclaves des usages, des passions, jouer la pantomine de l'homme de Nature. *Dans l'impossibilité de nous livrer aux fonctions et aux amusemens de la vie champêtre, d'errer dans une campagne, de suivre un troupeau, d'habiter une chaumière, nous invitons à prix d'or et d'argent le pinceau de Wouwermans, de Berghem ou de Vernet à nous retracer les moeurs et l'histoire de nos anciens aieux.* Et les murs de nos somptueuses et maussades demeures se couvrent des images d'un bonheur que nous regrettons. (139; my emphasis)

Chained within the narrow confines of cities . . . we counterfeit for a moment the role of the savage; slaves to custom and passion, we mime the man of Nature. *In the impossibility of our giving ourselves over to the functions and amusements of country life, of our wandering in the countryside, following a herd, living in a hut, we pay in gold and silver for the paintbrush of Wouwerman, Berghem, or Vernet to retrace the story of our ancient ancestors.* And the walls of our sumptuous and gloomy homes are covered with images of a happiness that we miss.

So, if Diderot's men of merit have bought the right paintings, if they have placed Oudry's ugly little dog just inside their sumptuous drawing rooms and Mlle. Collot's bust of Diderot in their study, or especially if they set off their windows overlooking Paris with a series of Vernet landscapes, they will continually compare their own physical surroundings with the experiences provoked by the paintings. This comparison will not make them nostalgic for a lost past but will lead them to exciting and productive philosophical reflections of the sort that Diderot was producing before his reader's very eyes when studying the Vernets. Unlike the simulacrum paintings, which were merely empty objects to be owned, which merely pointed toward past riches to remorselessly remind their owners of their lack of merit, the real works of art inspire a form of action. In other words, the esthetic complex formed by civilization and art object functions for the public men of talent analogously to the way the *Encyclopédie* was supposed to work for the men of knowledge. Rather than informing them of already existing knowledge in order to tie them to the past, it provided the machine to drive toward the future. The men of merit who bought great paintings, the people who were exposed to the great paintings in their visits to the Salons, would be impelled, like Diderot and his fictional abbé, to work with rather than against their culture, to reform and transform it. This is why Diderot here, as he had at the end of the *Supplément* (and foreshadowing the *Essai sur les règnes de Claude et de Néron*), rejects the notion of revolutionary change. Sudden chaotic disruption destroys the hard-won layers of self-transforming organization and coordination built up over the centuries. The real *philosophe* who succeeds the classical *savant* philosopher and the man of merit who exposes the venal amateur will, like Aristippe confronting Socrates, say,

Je me soumettrai à la loi, de peur qu'en discutant de mon autorité privée les mauvaises lois, je n'encourage par mon exemple la multitude insensée à discuter les bonnes. Je ne fuirai point les cours comme toi, je saurai me vêtir de pourpre; je ferai ma cour aux maîtres du monde, et peut-être en obtiendrai-je ou l'abolition de la loi mauvaise, ou la grâce de l'homme de bien qui l'aura enfreinte. (147)

I will submit to the law for fear that by using my own private authority to challenge bad laws, I might encourage by my example the senseless masses to challenge the good ones. I will not, like you, flee the court, I will be able to dress in purple; I will court the masters of the world and maybe I will obtain either the abolition of the bad law or the amnesty of the good man who broke it.

Still, how does one know what the good is? By judging what it was in the past? Clearly not, as all of Diderot's texts indicate. Further, how does one predict if there are no universal rules; how does one then know what is a reliable judgment rather than merely bizarre? The answer is that the inability to predict does not mean an inability to act. The Diderotian philosopher who succeeds the classical *savant* and the man of merit who exposes the venal amateur do indeed act with respect both to the past and to the present and are indeed able to make ethical judgments. To show the mechanism underlying such judgments and to bring out the ethical consequences of his esthetic system, Diderot had to introduce the notion of the *modèle idéal.*

The *Modèle Idéal:* Plato versus Diderot

Diderot's *modèle idéal* has often been reduced to a sophisticated version of Platonic form. Many passages in the "Préambule" (where he tried to present a coherent theory of it) seem to lend themselves to this interpretation.[9] However, I think it is just as plausible to say that Diderot was historicizing the notion of ideal model and thereby producing a notion as much opposed to the common construal of Platonic ideal form as Vernet's poetics was to mannerism and the *Supplément*'s strategic adaptation was to fixed social law.

Diderot's development of the concept went as follows: Modern taste is corrupt (for all the reasons I sketched above). As a result, no modern equivalent of the antique imitation of beautiful nature exists to provide the artist with his ideal model. Anyway, what does one mean by an ideal model? Does one take for model the most beautiful example of an object that one knows within existing nature—for example, the most beautiful woman one has seen? No, indeed for the result would be merely a portrait. What if one were to combine the most beautiful example one knows of each of the elements that make up a woman (nose, mouth, fingers, nails, bust, feet, hands)? The

9. Cf. Herbert Dieckmann's astute situating of the problem in his *Cinq Leçons sur Diderot* (Geneva: Droz, 1959), chap. 4 ("Questions d'esthétique"), esp. 114–16; and Fried's discussion of the related issue of history painting in chap. 2 of his *Absorption and Theatricality.*

result would be merely a composite portrait, and ideal beauty is not a composite of individual beauties. "Vous avez senti la différence de la chose générale et de la chose individuelle jusques dans les moindres parties," Diderot tells his imaginary artist, "puisque vous n'oseriez pas m'assurer depuis le moment où vous prîtes le pinceau jusqu'à ce jour, de vous être assujetti à l'imitation rigoureuse d'un cheveux" (57; "You have sensed the difference between the general and the individual thing down to the smallest part . . . since you would not dare assure me that, from the moment you picked up the brush until this day, you have put yourself to the rigorous imitation of a single hair"). The ideal model was called by Plato the truth or the archetype; the modern Plato would call it the general idea. It exists nowhere in physical nature, but only in the understanding; it is in this sense an ideal being.

Or notre philosophe prétend que c'est jusqu'à cette idée générale, jusqu'à cette vérité qu'il faut que le peintre s'élève dans ses productions, sans quoi il ne serait que le copiste de la chose individuelle, un portraitiste, et son tableau ne serait qu'une chose du troisème rang, après la vérité ou l'idée générale et la chose individuelle qui en est une émanation ou une copie; son tableau ne serait alors qu'une copie de cette copie. (58)

Now our philosopher claims that it is to this general idea, this truth, that the painter has to rise in his productions, otherwise he will be the mere copyist of the individual thing, a portraitist, and his picture will be only a third-rate thing, coming after the truth or general idea and the individual thing that is an emanation or copy of it; his picture will thus be only a copy of this copy.

If it does not exist anywhere, then how do we learn it? Unfortunately, some people try to learn it from studying the great art of the ancients, especially the Greeks. The Greeks learned it somehow, and the modern artist's comparison of their works with the real objects around him begins to show him what is going on. This procedure is ultimately doomed to failure, though, because the Greek statues in the long run are for the modern artist only objects among other objects, and the artist using them still falls into the trap of the composite portrait painter. Why? Because the servile copyist is not "pénétré des vues, des procédés, des moyens de ceux qui ont fait la chose, [il ne fait que] voir simplement la chose faite" (62; "penetrated by the opinions, procedures, and means of those who made the thing, [he only manages to] see simply the realized object"). "Maître La Grenée" was an artist of this sort; the elements he took from his (Condillacean) analysis of the great works of his predecessors were not the *vues, procédés,* or *moyens* that created the objects; they were mere conventions he extracted from the dead objects, the frozen masks produced by prior artists' inspired gestures. They were again the dead objects that for the men of no merit replace the activity of the men of merit. The men of no merit share the misapprehension that they learn by looking at the fixed appearance of the object in itself rather than by focusing on the activity that produced it.

What could the activity that produced a painting have to do with the *modèle idéal*? Think again of the beautiful object, the beautiful woman, this time no longer as a fixed object but as a dynamic and changing object.

> Ne convenez-vous pas que tout être, surtout animé, a ses fonctions, ses passions déterminés dans la vie; et qu'avec l'exercice et le tems, ces fonctions ont dû répandre sur toute son organisation une altération si marquée quelquefois, qu'elle ferait deviner la fonction? (58) . . . Si ce que je te disois tout à l'heure est vrai, le modèle le plus beau, le plus parfait d'un homme ou d'une femme, seroit un homme ou une femme *supérieurement propre à toutes les fonctions de la vie,* et qui seroit parvenu à l'âge du plus entier développement, sans en avoir exercé aucune. (60)

> Do you not agree that every being, especially an animate one, has its functions and passions determined in life; and that with use and time, these functions sometimes extend throughout its organization such a marked alteration that we can guess its function? . . . If what I said to you a minute ago is true, then the most beautiful, perfect model of a man or woman would be a man or women *superiorly adapted to all the functions of life,* one who would have arrived at the age of most complete development without ever having carried out any [of those functions].

Diderot's argument was highly elliptical, but it begins to make sense when placed in the context of his natural philosophy ("Convenez que, si vous n'êtes pas frappé de ces observations, c'est que vous n'avez pas la première teinture d'anatomie, de physiologie, la première notion de la nature" [59; "Agree that, if you are not struck by these observations, it's because you haven't the slightest inkling of anatomy or physiology, not the first notion of what nature is"). Notice first that for him the paradigm for an object was not an inanimate object— that is, it was not reactive and unchanging. It was an animate object. It was characterized by its capacity to change. This change is predetermined to a certain extent, especially change manifested as activity— for example, the exercise of its functions, the effects of its passions. The paths these changes might take are predetermined by its initial organization, as Diderot had insisted from early days in the *Interprétation de la nature* and would continue to say through the *Rêve de d'Alembert* and the *Eléments de physiologie*. Of course, the changes themselves *alter* this initial organization. Think of poor d'Alembert in the *Rêve*, caught in the sway of his intellectual passions, sweating and hallucinating during his dream. The alterations in his physical state were so marked that Mlle. de l'Espinasse thought that he was quite ill. The alterations are both determined to an extent and determining to an extent for each actual object. Therefore each object will alter itself away from its initial organizational similarity with the other objects in its class.

The kind of organization Diderot meant was, as we have seen in so many other of his texts, the organization through which any object interacted with the rest of the physical world. As he had so carefully tried to work out in the *Interprétation de la nature*, the defining characteristic of all matter and thus of all objects was its organization. It seems that for Diderot, in the animate object, the notion of organization complements the notion of function. Function is an activity whose point is to maintain the survival of the object. (As the first half of the above quotation shows, the survival of the organism depends on how well it incorporates rather than prevents change, so the organism's function does not serve to maintain the initial organization per se. It maintains continuity through change.) The organization of an animate object instantiates its ability to function. The "better" its organization, the better it will function, and the better it will survive (by evolving). In other words, the value judgment "better" applied to an animate object is a measure of its survival activity.

Now we can understand the second half of the quotation: the beauty of a man or woman is an index of that body as "supérieurement propre à toutes les fonctions." This gives us a starting place for understanding what Diderot meant by beauty. In direct opposition to his contemporaries within the Aristotle-Bacon-Condillac tradition, who conceptualized all objects by generalizing from a definition of the inanimate object as the instantiation of a category, Diderot generalized his conception of the animate object to characterize all objects in nature. If we keep this in mind, his concept of beauty begins to take form: it is a value judgment never representable or even explainable, because beauty, rather than being a quality, is the sign of an aptitude for efficient activity. As soon as an object begins to be acted upon and to act itself, it alters its initial organization; therefore, any fixed physical instantiation of the ideal model is impossible. Diderot argues here that it would require that the complete elaboration of the entire organization inherent in an animate object ("[son] plus entier développement"), which requires passage through time, be simultaneous with the organization's never having altered. For an animate object to avoid change requires, on the other hand, that it *not* pass through time. The combination is logically impossible. This is why the model, although it can be understood, can never really exist. This is why, in Diderot's terms, it must be qualified as ideal.

He held, however, that the ideal model can be extrapolated from experience. From the Condillacean analysis of many objects? No, from interaction with them. The language Diderot used was a perfect recall of the program for the training of the natural philosopher in the *Interprétation de la nature*:

Par une longue observation, par une expérience consommée, par un tact exquis, par un goût, un instinct, une sorte d'inspiration donnée à quelques rares génies. . . . Avec le tems, par une marche lente et pusillanime, *par un long et pénible tâtonnement, par une notion sourde, secrète, d'analogie, acquise par une infinité d'observations successives dont la mémoire s'éteint et dont l'effet reste* . . . s'éloignant sans cesse du portrait, de la ligne fausse, pour s'élever au vrai modèle idéal de la beauté, à la ligne vraie . . . ligne vraie que ces grands maîtres ne peuvent *inspirer* à leurs élèves aussi rigoureusement qu'ils la conçoivent . . . ligne vraie *non traditionelle* qui s'évanouit presque avec l'homme de génie, qui forme pendant un tems l'esprit, le caractère, le goût des ouvrages d'un peuple . . . selon le climat, le gouvernement, les loix, les circonstances qui l'auront vu naître (60–61; my emphasis)

Through long observation and consummate experience, through exquisite tact, through a taste, an instinct, a sort of inspiration given to a few rare geniuses. . . . With time, through a long and pusillanimous progress, *through long and painful groping, through a mute and secret analogy acquired through an infinity of successive observations the memory of which disappears but whose effect remains*, . . . ceaselessly moving away from the portrait, the false line, to rise to the true ideal model of beauty, to the true line . . . that these great masters cannot *inspire* in their students as rigorously as they conceive of it . . . *nontraditional* true line that almost disappears with the man of genius, which for a time forms the spirit, character, and taste of the works of a people . . . according to the climate, government, laws, and circumstances that brought it about.

The reason that the ancients were able to produce such great art is ironically that they were primitive. They were forced to develop their ability to *subodorer*, as Diderot called this special interactive rational but alogical intuition, because they were spared the distraction caused by modern man's two complementary cultural artifacts: analytic logic and the existing body of Greek and Roman art objects. In this way the Greeks were analogous to the European men of merit and the opposite of venal speculators.

The two cultural artifacts, as the prior example of La Grenée's paintings showed, force modern imitators to conceptualize objects as inanimate and unchanging. They therefore think of beauty as an isolable thing and not as an interactive function carried by an object. Moreover, the imitation procedure was nonsense, a form of circular reasoning: it cannot produce the ideal model, because its operation already supposes the ideal model.

C'est un vieux conte, mon ami, que pour former cette statue, vraie ou imaginaire que les Anciens appeloient la Règle et que j'appelle le modèle idéal ou la ligne vraie, ils aient parcouru la nature, empruntant d'elle, dans une infinité d'individus, les plus belles parties dont ils composèrent un tout. Comment est-ce qu'ils auroient reconnu la beauté de ces parties? (62)

It's an old wives' tale, my friend, that to make this real or imaginary statue that the ancients called the Rule and that I call the ideal model or the true line, they scoured nature, borrowing from her, in an infinity of individuals, the most beautiful parts, out of which they composed a whole. How could they have recognized the beauty of these parts?

Therefore, the only effective way to become a great painter is, whether one likes it or not, to adopt the "vues, les procédés, les moyens de ceux qui ont fait la chose." Diderot believed that

ce n'est point à l'aide d'une infinité de petits portraits isolés, qu'on s'élève au modèle original et premier ni de la partie, ni de l'ensemble et du tout; [les Grecs] ont suivi une autre voie, et ... celle que je viens de prescrire est celle de l'esprit humain dans toutes ses recherches. (62)

it's not by using an infinity of tiny isolated portraits that one rises to the original and primary model either of the part, of the ensemble, or of the whole; [the Greeks] took another path, and ... the one I just prescribed is the one taken by the human mind in all its research.

In a long passage that calls on the entire vocabulary of the *Interprétation de la nature*, Diderot claims that the process of *tâtonnement* is the only way to reach the *modèle idéal*, and one must achieve some sort of contact with the ideal model to produce work that is genuinely creative. Mere copying, mere portraiture, mere mannerism are not art. Moreover, the *modèle idéal* is reached in the *beaux arts* in the same way that all genial training takes place. The man of agricultural genius, the great natural philosopher, the great doctor, the great painter, they all *tâtonnent,* they all *subodorent.* Their abilities are not limited to the objects they produce, for they all have this ability to interact with nature to intuit latent organization from reading its responding activity.

This is how they interact with one another's productions, as well. Because they read the activity of a production the way they read nature, men of merit recognize one another. The Baron d'Holbach was able to perceive Oudry's genius because he looked at Oudry's painting of the little dog not as an object in the analytic sense or even as the representation or the portrait of an animate object but as an animate painting by analogy with the dynamic philosophical systems that were his subjects of study. This is the mechanism that allows the man of merit to recognize in an object the hand of another man of merit. Without this, one cannot recognize merit directly; one can see only the masks it leaves behind. It is the same mechanism that allowed Diderot to enter into and literally to animate Vernet's paintings.

If one agrees to "tâtonner" (and Diderot argued that, whether his genial interlocutor recognizes it or not, this is in fact what he has done), then "nous serions arrivé comme eux [the Greeks] à un modèle original et premier, à une ligne vraie qui aurait été bien plus nôtre, qu'elle ne l'est et ne peut l'être" (63; "we would have arrived like the Greeks at an original and primary model, at a true line that would have been much more our own than it is or can ever be"). But notice the construction: the result will not be a rediscovery of an already existing ideal model. The *modèle idéal* is not an idea eternally the same, a Platonic form always already existing in the understanding of a god figure. So the *modèle idéal* that the French come up with will be essentially and even locally French. As the article "Encyclopédie" had suggested years before in the argument concerning Greek euphony and the Italian lover's hundred portraits of his mistress, one cannot recapture the "original" because there is no original. Each time and place has its own ideal model. The Greek ideal model was the one specific to the Greeks' own general physical organization, the one that functioned superiorly in their particular geographical context. The "Vénus Tahitienne n'est pas notre Vénus galante," as the Almoner had understood in the *Supplément au voyage de Bougainville*. Although there might be a historical relationship between the Greek ideal model and the eventual French ideal model because the two cultures were geographically and historically continuous, the Greek was only historically, not esthetically, prior to the French. To think that the Greek could be more esthetically valid or even think that the French ideal model could be the same as the Greek would be to make the same mistake about the definition of the ideal model that the analytic man makes about the definition of an object: that would be to reduce it to merely another portrait, whereas it is in fact always only a form of activity—to *faire beau*.

> Convenez donc que, quand vous faites beau, vous ne faites rien de ce qui est, rien même de ce qui puisse être. Convenez donc que la différence du portraitiste et de vous, homme de génie, consiste essentiellement en ce que le portraitiste rend fidèlement Nature comme

elle est, et se fixe par goût au troisiéme rang [in the hierachy formed by ideal model, natural object, copy of object], et que vous qui cherchez la vérité, le premier modèle, votre effort continu est de vous élever au second. (59)

Agree then, that when you construct something beautiful, you create nothing of what is, nothing even of what could be. Agree that the difference between the portraitist and you the man of genius, is essentially that the portraitist renders Nature faithfully the way it is and chooses to stay at the third level, and that you who seek truth, the first model, your continual effort is to raise yourself to the second.

Thus the poet creates not representations but real (animate) objects. Here, as in many of his other texts, Diderot held an entity's value, both ethical and now esthetic, to be an index of the harmony it manifests with the always changing natural dynamic around it. Art objects are no exceptions—if anything, they set the clearest examples. Because in this sense Vernet's paintings embodied the *modèle idéal*, Diderot could equate him with God: Vernet was a creator of real objects, of objects that exist and act in the material world. Because the paintings are both a result of and a call for the natural philosopher's *tâtonnement*, Vernet induces a productive harmony with nature. "Si Vernet vous eût appris à mieux voir la nature, la nature, de son côté, vous eût appris à bien voir Vernet" (131; "If Vernet could have taught you to see Nature better, Nature on her part could have taught you to see Vernet well").

The modern *modèle idéal*, however, is continually shifting (although almost imperceptibly at any one point in time) so as to stay "ahead" of the actual state of nature. It is thus the opposite of a Platonic form, which is always the same, embedded in a utopian past, never recuperable. The modern *modèle idéal* is never attainable, because its very nature is to adapt to the adaptations made to reach it.

The *modèle idéal* was, one could say, the peculiarly Diderotian alternative to the scientific empiricist's notion of scientific truth. A scientific law is a modern version of a Platonic form: it also can never be experienced purely and directly, but it is perceivable through multiple trials and errors, a pure form approached through a statistical generalization of many impure measurements. Like the Platonic form, it is assumed to be universal and unchanging, to predate and explain the approximate world. Diderot, while clearly an empiricist in that he was interacting continually with physical nature to divine a truth within it, did not conceive of his form of truth as universal or fixed, and therefore he sought not fixed knowledge but the activity provoked by the search. Diderot's particular form of empiricism led not to science but to esthetic production.

The link between the esthetic activity here evoked and ethical judgment lies in Diderot's omnipresent notion of an underlying physically active coordination that all forms of intellectual production make accessible. Virtue he defined as acting in accordance with and promoting this harmony with nature. That much at least the *Supplément*'s Tahitians had understood, but their way of trying to achieve that virtue was counterproductive. Even though they knew that the world was continually changing, they thought that an ideal harmony could still be attained if their system of sexual-economic exchange were made permanent. In terms of the *Salon de 1767*, we could say that their mistake was to have tried to make their ideal form of social organization Platonic instead of general, ahistorical instead of locally determined and contingent.

For two reasons demonstrated by the functioning of its real art, Diderot believed that European "virtue" would never be counterproductive. First, the attempt to reach a *modèle idéal* required constant *tâtonnement* with not only nature, but also the resulting art objects. Art is the insurance policy of the natural dynamic. As the Vernets showed, art does more than manifest this beauty itself by serving as a cultural artifact. It also returns its spectator to the world of nature in such a way that the spectator is forced continually to reevaluate the art object's fidelity in generating the experience of the dynamic it portrays. Moreover, art induces the spectator to judge (actual) Nature's adequation to an intuited notion of superior coordination and thus not only to judge how effectively it functions but also to see what it could become from there, to judge what it therefore should become. The consequence of the *modèle idéal* thus was the creation of a supple judgmental capacity, a judgmental capacity that, rather than being chained to its past findings, could adapt its values to the changes in the world. The art object shows the philosopher where to start to modify nature to make it better and, complementarily, how to make man's productions accord more fully with nature's improved coordination. This is how Diderot thought that the esthetic produced an ethical program. This is why Oudry wanted d'Holbach to keep the painting of the little dog. Every art object is a way of imitating nature's action rather than its appearance: it is a way of acting on nature itself, or of provoking action on nature by others.

The second reason for modern Europe's cultural efficacity is that art objects go beyond acting on nature to act also on the men of merit in other disciplines to get them to construct ideal model functions—in other words, standards for judgment—in their own fields. All art forms, indeed all creative activities, including philosophy, agriculture, and governance, do this both for themselves and for their sister disciplines. This is why Diderot was welcome in the studios of the great painters: his philosophical insights helped them make "truer" paintings, as he never tired of telling us, just as much as their paintings (witness his reactions to the Vernets) stimulated philosophical production in him or, presumably, motivated economic reform for a Turgot.

It has often been said that the *Salon de 1767* was a turning point for Diderot. I think this is so, but I think this evaluation has to be understood in terms of Diderot's philosophical achievement more than in terms of his ability to describe paintings. For description, the breakthrough clearly occurred in the *Salon de 1765*. The much more consequential innovations of the *Salon de 1767* may have actually been brought about by the *Salon de 1765*, in fact: once his coherent perception of the art object and of artistic activity had been achieved—that is, once Diderot himself had attained a point of interaction with an ideal model of his own—then, motivated by it, he could let it function by analogy within his own philosophical activity. The *Salon de 1767* was the empirical demonstration of his philosophical theory of the ideal model. The recording of his empirical reactions to the paintings, as must by now be clear, gave way before the philosophical activity it produced: Diderot's whole *Salon* was focused on authorizing the creative ethical activity it embodied. The effect of the Vernets was not merely to produce an esthetic theory but to force Diderot to use this esthetic theory to generate a luxurious morality.

SIX

The Nephew's Natural Morality

At first glance, *Le Neveu de Rameau* seems to be a work in direct opposition to Diderot's entire Enlightenment project. The *Encyclopédie* had proposed an optimistic mechanism for improving social structure by concerting the intellectual activity of a community of *savants* engaged in writing its articles. The couple formed by the *Supplément au voyage de Bougainville* and the *Salon de 1767* seemed to present a picture of European culture irresistibly renewing itself in the ruins of its own failures, driven by a productive affinity with its special geographical context. The *Neveu*, on the other hand, depicts a seemingly pessimistic and fatalistic, because natural, human community. It is indeed held together by intellectual and physiological affinities, but in this text they all manifest themselves as forms of appetite, as lusts or hunger. Intellectual as well as physiological drives appear as forms of physical greed rather than need, as negative excess rather than the positive excess that underlies the European esthetic drive in the other texts. We may judge the Nephew's community immoral, but it is just as cohesive as that of the encyclopedic scholars or the Baron d'Holbach's philosophical salons—perhaps more so. Accordingly, when we remember that the Enlightenment's social project aimed to derive its social worth and ultimately also its political authority by redefining virtue as the attempt to conform to the structure of nature, the question of which is the morally superior structure becomes especially trenchant. Bordeu as spokesman for Diderot had argued in the *Rêve* that nature drives toward material organization and cohesion; this vector was essential to Diderot's dynamic materialism. Therefore, in materialist terms, at least, the Nephew's society cannot be dismissed. From Diderot's characteristically uncompromising standpoint, the social

order dissected in the *Neveu* suffers no loss of coherence or naturalness when its values are judged to be corrupt and pessimistic even by
conventional Enlightenment standards—as explained by Diderot's
supposed stand-in in this text, the encyclopedist MOI. Diderot
would seem to be saying that however unpalatable, the social changes
brought about by natural development must be accommodated. The
result is a confrontation between the apparently naïve optimism of
Diderot's works from the 1750s and the fatalistic detachment prompted
by a disturbing realization of seeing the social consequences of accept-
ing such a materialism. It is true that the contemporary *Salon de 1767*
could be misread as envisioning a perfection point for the arts (for
who could surpass Vernet?), a point at which the harmony between
world and observer is complete and unsurpassable. Implicitly posed
in the also contemporaneous *Supplément au voyage de Bougainville* as
well, this dilemma of the illusory endpoint is finally investigated in
depth and, I think, successfully resolved in the *Neveu de Rameau*,
where even the rules of harmony become dynamic.

Sometimes readings of the *Neveu de Rameau* as a Manichean or
Nietzschean celebration of the amorality of the material universe are
used to justify the power of passion to free man from the constraints
of mediocrity and reason.[1]

Other and more typical readings see it as revealing a dark side to
Diderot's own character, thus evidencing a pessimism and consequent modernity that rescue his otherwise naïvely optimistic philosophy.[2] I would propose, however, that both such judgments almost
inevitably result from certain particularly eloquent passages spoken
by LUI, but that these passages should be carefully interpreted within
their rhetorical context before the resulting judgments can be generalized. The *Neveu*'s structure and dynamics prove to be the filter
through which any particular quotation must be observed before its
meaning can be reliable. In this way, of course, it resembles Diderot's

1. Two good recent readings in this vein are James Creech, "Le Neveu de Rameau: 'Diary'
of a Reading," *MLN* 95, no. 4 (1980): 995–1004; and Elisabeth de Fontenay, *Diderot ou le matérialisme enchanté* (Paris: Grasset, 1981), chaps. entitled "Un fond lyrique inaliénable" and
"Après la pluie le beau temps."

2. Cf. Roland Desné's introduction and overview of this tradition in Denis Diderot, *Le
Neveu de Rameau. Le Rêve de d'Alembert*, ed. Roland Desné and Jean Varloot (Paris:
Messidor/Editions Sociales, 1972; reprint, 1984). DPV 12 is the edition of the *Neveu* that I
will be citing. Cf. also Jack Undank's deconstruction of this position running *en filigrane*
throughout his *Inside, Outside and In-Between* (Madison, Wis.: Coda Press, 1979), esp. 138–53.

other works and hews to the notion of interpretation that Diderot demonstrated in the *Pensées sur l'interprétation de la nature*.

The *Neveu*, however, goes beyond the earlier works. Not only does its particular structure demonstrate the ideas explicitly presented as did that of the *Rêve*, but also it is itself an artifact to be judged as a work of art by the reader while he is instructed about what works of art essentially are and how they function. It is from this perspective that we can consider the most provocative although usually unexplained characterization of the *Neveu*: that it serves as Diderot's literary testament. I suggest that a more appropriate characterization is to see it as Diderot's song aimed at posterity. The *Neveu*, as we shall see, is a fugue, a many-layered fugue, not merely by analogy with musical form, but as an ambitious extension of the very notion of a musical entity and of musical activity. The two main lines of the most evident fugal pattern are those of the two main subjects of discussion. Interwoven throughout the text are a discussion of the superiority of the new Italian music compared to the French (reflecting the *Querelle des Bouffons* of the mid 1750s), and a second discussion of the Nephew's complicity with a corrupt social order. Let us begin with the most striking and best-studied subject, the social message.

All the World's a Fool

The curious thing about this text is the social message the Nephew transmits along with his discussion of music. The two seem antithetical, dissonant to the conventional Enlightenment ear—what does the charm of the Italian opera have in common with the cynicism of the sordid social groups the Nephew frequents? These social groups embody everything that La Grenée's paintings displayed in the *Salon de 1767*. Their members are the venal speculators who would not be able to experience a Vernet even if they had the wit to buy one, who could not understand the virtues of the Italian operas even while performing them. MOI says to the Nephew, "Vous me ramenez des moeurs à la musique dont je m'étais écarté malgré moi; et je vous en remercie; car, à ne vous rien celer, je vous aime mieux musicien que moraliste" (170; "You bring me back from morals to music, which I had gotten away from in spite of myself; and I thank you; for, to hide nothing, I like you better as a musician than as a moralist"). But as we shall see, the Nephew's depravation is continuous with the music he loves: "Ce sont les dissonances dans l'harmonie sociale qu'il faut savoir placer, préparer et sauver. Rien de si plat qu'une suite d'accords parfaits. Il faut quelque chose qui pique, qui sépare le faisceau, et qui en éparpille les rayons" (177; "It is the dissonances in the social harmony that you have to know how to set up, prepare, and maintain. Nothing is as dull as a series of perfect chords. There has to be something that pricks, that separates the cluster and scatters the rays"). To show the solidarity between the Nephew's behavior in the two domains, to see that the dissonance perceived by MOI is in fact a fugue, and a productive one at that (this is one reason the text is structured as a dialogue and the Nephew is designated not by his name but by the relational *LUI*), consider first the way LUI functioned in the Bertinhus household.

Let us recall the situation. M. Bertin and his mistress, Mlle. Hus are two grotesque characters: she is an obese, incompetent actress; he is a tall scarecrow, a venal speculator. They "hold court" at feeding time, packing their table with the *rapaces* of the *Salon de 1767,* who drain them of the money they have squeezed out of people of real merit. The social contract in this minisociety is the following: those who eat pay in flattery and humiliating services for what they eat and spend. Bertin and Hus provide the concrete illustration of the social category presented only abstractly in the *Salon*: these people of money rather than merit pursue a sysiphean goal of buying the signs of a merit that their very buying shows they can never reach. Although Bertin and Hus see themselves as the rulers of this little society, they do so only because they purchase the behavior of their subjects to read as the sign of their own superiority. Since those who take the sign for the thing pay their own price, Bertin and Hus must continually buy more and more sycophants to fill the table when those who have had (or gotten) enough leave. In what seems a parody of Diderot's Enlightenment monastery model in the *Rêve*, the remaining sycophants must train the newcomers to fill the vacant places, to fit in, to harmonize with the dominant theme.

This is where the Nephew enters. The Nephew defines his role within this parody of a court as having been that of the "fou du roi" (139).[3] But what is a fool? In general terms, the fool is the one person

3. The Nephew as fool has been studied from other points of view. See for example Heather Arden, "Le fou, la sottise et *Le neveu de Rameau*," *Dix-huitième siècle* 7 (1975): 209–23.

in a court who can dare to utter the unspeakable truths, for everyone laughs at him. He plays the role of a standard scapegoat, but such a simple definition hides a more important fact. Like the scapegoat, whose exclusion from a social group either creates or reaffirms the architecture of distinct identities of its other individual members, the fool as fool exists only as a position within a structure. Outside this structure, the fool's same behavior would have a different meaning. The utterances that amused the courtiers become the dangerous words of a traitor.

Diderot is often uncomfortable with the notion of the singular individual, and it is replaced with an antithetical notion. We have already seen analogous manifestations. In his anti-d'Alembertian reversal of the *Encyclopédie,* for instance, the articles are primarily the substrate on which to build a resonant structure of fertile cross-references. The mind-body tradition that Diderot rejects defines presence in terms of essentially discrete things with everything void between them, whereas Diderot's dynamic materialism holds that the relations between things are as present and as necessary to perception as the notion of "thingness" that normally founds the paradigm of presence. In fact, both things and relations are present and are forms of presence. This emphasis is critical, because Diderot's entire strategy is to play on the presence of what is normally assumed to be absence to build an entire world out of a materialism of the relational (as, for example, in the *Salon de 1767,* where the problematic of expression replaced the problematic of representation). In the *Neveu* he deals with the most complex form of the relational, the world made up of both public and private interpersonal relations.

To elaborate the difference, let us perform as a thought-experiment a Diderotian shift on our normal point of view. Rather than construing a social group as a collection of distinct individuals, as a pre-polyp *grappe d'abeilles* formed of people, let us, extrapolating from the mechanophysical model developed in chapter 1 view it as a resonant organic structure, a vibrating network of events in which the "people" are only illusorily discrete. Not by accident is Jean-François Rameau himself almost never referred to in the text by name but consistently by relational tags: he is called either Rameau's nephew, or LUI. Let us consider people, therefore, as positions held within a network of interlocking social forces (I shall define the forces later), as people whose personal identities come not from their being considered as enduring discrete essences but from the history of their inter-actions with the positions around them. They are less individuals in the modern sense of being psychically distinct than they are social functions. We are encouraged in this direction not only by Diderot's previous works but also by the *Neveu*'s name for the position of the head of the court in which the Nephew serves: it is not a single per-son, but a polyp, the combination of Mlle. Hus and M. Bertin that LUI refers to repeatedly as Bertinhus. What is important to Diderot is not the distinct personage of either Bertin or Hus but the function of head of the court itself, whether performed by one, the other, or both together.

In the court the lowly fool holds a very special social position, one defined precisely in functional terms, namely, his relation to the king. He is the king's polar opposite and his mirror image. The king has the power of decision—all his words are actions affecting the entire group. Because they are, because the king is the voice not of a private person but of a judge and the arm of the state, his power is supposed to be understood to be disinterested. This is, perhaps, what defines the public as opposed to the private: the public is the domain of the relational, the private that of "thingness"—of d'Alembertian dis-crete essences. Man in his public nature is as he exists with respect to others. As a private person he is separate and distinct and not defined by his interrelations, which, for Diderot, are interrelations of self-interest.[4] In theory, the king's interest is everyone's interest; he is the royal "we." The fool, on the other hand, can make no decisions. Lack-ing in some quality considered necessary to make him a competent member of society (size, birth, regular conformation, or most typi-cally, intelligence), the fool originally was merely an outlet for frustra-tions: to abuse a fool, therefore, is safe because he is powerless. The fool can never act on and therefore benefit from his own words, which are therefore considered to be without self-interest. Unlike the

4. Diderot's loyalty to the relational and his abhorrence of the consequences of a philos-ophy of "thingness" thus perhaps explain his difficulty in ever really generating convincing portraits of characters as having psychological interiorities. It is not just that we do not see them but that the characters do not even seem to have them. Think not only of MOI and LUI but also of Mlle. de l'Espinasse and d'Alembert in the *Rêve*. Think especially of Suzanne Simonin in *La Religieuse*. Diderot's loyalty to the relational ultimately also explains his inability to understand Rousseau's isolated man as other than perverse—his own notion of private is still relational: it is the bourgeois family rather than the state.

king (who speaks for all when he speaks for himself) and unlike the other members of the court (who speak for themselves), the seemingly paradoxical result is that he can say things no one else can say because he speaks for no one. Interest defines the private. Disinterest defines the public. Therefore the fool is not the opposite of the public king in serving as the epitome of the private. He is, by being no one, as absolutely public, as disinterested, as the king.

Historically, because the fool spoke for no interest, his function went from serving merely as the passive scapegoat to embodying, ironically, a very active social force. This shift transformed the fool into the jester. The jester's privileged subject of discussion became, of course, the one thing that no one else could speak of and live. The jester's role was to criticize the king's actions when they slipped into serving self-interest rather than the public interest. The jester did this by evoking the underlying structure of power relations that was supposed to determine the king's actions and opposing them to the king's actual self-serving motivations. The king was the arm of this network of power relations, but the fool served as the voice of this relational nature. He restrained the king from speaking or acting as a private individual to keep him speaking only as king or judge. He continually reimposed upon the king his identity as a social function with respect to his subjects rather than as a private person. The jester said without power exactly what the king said with it. (To prove my point, consider the case of Lear: when he loses his power, he sounds to our ears just like his fool. In fact, because we can hear him only relationally, he actually becomes a fool.) The personal powerlessness of the jester allowed him to serve as the social safeguard: the king without a fool was a tyrant, a person using public power to further private ends. But the king was equally important to the fool's having a real social function, for a fool without a king is a madman. Together, however, they formed a couple that maintained the social dynamic: the entire social network of relations of power and rank was stretched between these two endpoints.

One last point: laughter plays a critical role in this mechanism. One would certainly never laugh at the king's serious words, but the appropriate response to the jester is to laugh at him. This laughter has a well-known structure: although what he says hits home as true, it is not funny. What is funny is that the power of the statement puts into relief the powerlessness of the speaker. This laughter at the disparity between message and speaker makes the impersonal, purely relational nature of power brutally obvious. Certainly, this shift in perception could not happen were the speaker not himself totally powerless. While the jester seems to mock the king, what he is first of all fundamentally mocking is himself—as powerless, as fool. This is the condition of his speaking; without it, he would not be funny. To transmit his message, he must continually devalue himself in the eyes of his audience. He ensures the viability of the jester role as author function, therefore, by masking it with the fool.

From this general discussion of the role of the fool we can now return to the Nephew. At first sight he certainly fits all the qualifications. His job is to flatter and obey, indeed, but primarily it is to make Bertinhus laugh, most often at his own expense. The critical event, however, is the jester scene that fails. Rameau follows precisely the formulas outlined above: he lays bare the ugly social mechanisms of the Bertinhus table by insulting himself first of all and makes Mlle. Hus swallow it by making her laugh at his own expense.

> LUI C'est ce chien de petit prêtre avare, puant et usurier qui est la cause de mon désastre. . . . On sert; on fait les honneurs de la table à l'abbé, on le place au haut bout. J'entre, je l'aperçois. Comment, l'abbé, lui dis-je, vous présidez? voilà qui est fort bien pour aujourd'hui; mais demain, vous descendrez, s'il vous plaît, d'une assiette; après-demain, d'une autre assiette; et ainsi d'assiette en assiette, soit à droite, soit à gauche, jusqu'à ce que de la place que j'ai occupée une fois avant vous, Fréron une fois après moi, Dorat une fois après Fréron, Palissot une fois après Dorat, vous deveniez stationnaire à côté de moi, pauvre plat bougre comme vous, *qui siedo sempre come un maestoso cazzo fra duoi coglioni*. L'abbé, qui est bon diable et qui prend tout bien, se mit à rire. Mademoiselle, pénétrée de la vérité de mon observation et de la justesse de ma comparaison, se mit à rire; tous ceux qui siégeaient à droite et à gauche de l'abbé et qu'il avait reculés d'un cran, se mirent à rire. (140–41)

> LUI It's that dog of a stinking, avaricious, usurious little priest that caused my disaster. . . . Dinner is served; the abbé is asked to do the honors at table; he is placed at the head. I come in, I see it. "What, abbé," I say to him, "You're presiding? This is great for today; but tomorrow, you'll go down one place, if you please; the day after

tomorrow, another place; and thus from place to place, either to the right or the left, until from the place that I occupied before you, Fréron after me, Dorat once after Fréron, Palissot once after Dorat, you will come to rest at my side, poor dull devil that you are, who always sits like a majestic prick between two balls." The abbé, who is a good sort and who takes everything well, laughed. Mademoiselle, struck by the truth of my observation and the acuity of my comparison, burst out laughing; everybody sitting on the right and left of the abbé and those who had gone down one place, broke into laughter.

The Nephew's viewpoint is from the bottom of the table, the fool's position. His recounting of what he sees from his absolute position is thus a structuring act. No one can resent it or him because everyone is placed at least higher than Rameau. Everyone reacts correctly and the jester's job of putting the guests in their places is accomplished.

excepté monsieur qui se fâche et me tient des propos qui n'auraient rien signifié, si nous avions été seuls: Rameau, vous êtes un impertinent. —Je le sais bien; et c'est à cette condition que vous m'avez reçu. —Un faquin. —Comme un autre. —Un gueux. —Est-ce que je serais ici, sans cela? —Je vous ferai chasser. —Après dîner, je m'en irai de moi-même. (141–42)

except *monsieur*, who got angry and made cracks that would have meant nothing had we been alone: Rameau, you're impertinent. —I know that full well; and that is why you receive me. —A fraud. —Like anybody else. —A beggar. —Would I be here otherwise? —I'll have you thrown out. —After dinner I'll go by myself.

This is the insolence of the desperate jester trying to make the master understand that insolence is his job. When Bertin does not accept it, Rameau does not understand why: "Mais mademoiselle, qu'est-ce qu'il y a donc d'extraordinaire? Ai-je été différent aujourd'hui de moi-même? . . Monsieur, voilà ce fou . . . est-ce qu'il ne sait pas que je suis comme les enfants, et qu'il y a des circonstances où je laisse tout aller sous moi?" (142; "But mademoiselle, what's so unusual? Have I been different from myself today? . . . Monsieur, take this fool . . . am I not like a child, and aren't there times when I let everything go around me?"). He knows that he has played his role perfectly. The

curious result is that he suddenly sees for the first time the real importance that the fool has in a court.

Au milieu de cet imbroglio, il me passa par la tête une pensée
funeste, une pensée qui me donna de la morgue, une pensée qui
m'inspira de la fierté et de l'insolence: c'est qu'on ne pouvait se passer
de moi, que j'étais un homme essentiel.

MOI Oui, je crois que vous leur êtes très utile, mais qu'ils vous le
sont encore davantage. Vous ne retrouverez pas, quand vous vou-
drez, une aussi bonne maison; mais eux, pour un fou qui leur
manque, ils en retrouveront cent.

LUI Cent fous comme moi! Monsieur le philosophe, ils ne sont pas
si communs. Oui, des plats fous. On est plus difficile en sottise qu'en
talent ou en vertu. Je suis rare dans mon espèce, oui, très rare. A
présent qu'ils ne m'ont plus, que font-ils? Ils s'ennuient comme des
chiens. (143–44)

In the middle of this mixup, a fatal idea ran through my head, a
thought that made me arrogant, a thought that inspired pride and
insolence: they couldn't do without me—I was an essential man.

MOI Yes, I think you are useful to them, but they are even more so
to you. You will not easily find as good a household; but they, for
one fool they lack, they can find a hundred.

LUI A hundred fools like me! Mr. philosopher, they are not so common. Sure, dull fools. But one is pickier about foolishness than
about talent or virtue. I am a rare example of my type—indeed, very
rare. Now that they no longer have me, what are they doing?
They're as bored as dogs.

The Nephew is right; he is unique in just the way that the king's
jester must be unique in order to function. Yet MOI is also right, this
is not just a case of "Le fou est mort, vive le fou." What the Nephew
fails to see is that the classic jester, the real king's fool, is not called
for in these circumstances. He is not dealing with an authentic king,
nor is there an authentic architecture of power. He is dealing, as we
have already seen, with people who live in the shadow world of
signs, with simulacra of people of merit for whom the most undesir-
able event is to have the emptiness behind their carefully constructed
images revealed. When the jester speaks to a real king, he reveals a real

and fearful power. When Rameau speaks to Bertin, he reveals that the relational structure implied by the appearances is not there, that the courtiers are attracted not by a real king's real merit but by a pseudo king's pseudo merit: by his money. "[LUI.] Je ne lui ai point manqué. —[BERTIN.] Pardonnez-moi; on invite monsieur l'abbé, et... —[LUI.] C'est lui qui s'est manqué à lui-même en invitant l'abbé, en me recevant et avec moi tant d'autres bélîtres tels que moi" (142; "[LUI:] I wasn't disrespectful to him. —[BERTIN:] Excuse me, but we invite the abbé, and... —[LUI:] He failed himself by inviting the abbé, by receiving me and with me so many other rascals like me"). By removing momentary illusions, a real jester actually restores the real king to his real power. The Nephew shows, however, that nothing backs up Bertin's carefully purchased illusions. He has indeed betrayed himself by inviting sycophants, betrayed his own nullity; he is no one. He is not a master, and this is no court. The simulacrum has been exploded, and LUI's succeeding descriptions of Bertinhus turn to the grotesque the more MOI urges him to abase himself and return. The "king" has been transformed into the incarnation of no one, into a fool.

It is not that the Nephew is unwilling to be servile, base, and craven. To get food or money, he will without resentment perform the meanest tasks; they are part of the job. However, by playing the fool he pays for the right to be the jester: "Il faut que je les désennuie; c'est la condition; mais il faut que je m'amuse quelquefois" (143; "I have to distract them; that's the condition; but I have to amuse myself sometimes"). The Nephew amuses himself by provoking certain social truths, by being the *grain de levain* in a social setting. The "plats fous" mentioned above by LUI recall the "accords plats" that he so detests in music. Bertinhus had asked him to be a *plat fou:* Rameau was to coddle but not shake the masters, to maintain a simulacrum of social harmony rather than to inject dissonance. He was, in effect, to be the simulacrum of a fool the way Bertinhus was a simulacrum of a king.

This seems to be logically inconsistent, for isn't the task of the real jester to restore social accord rather than to disrupt it? Yes, but the harmony desired by Bertinhus and the harmony restored by the traditional jester are not the same. We here are in the same dual structure that is already present in the article "Encyclopédie" with the opposition between the *joli* and the *beau* styles and that structures the entire *Salon de 1767* in the opposition between decadent art and the *modèle idéal*. Like the *beau* and the *modèle idéal*, the jester's performances in general are supposed to pierce through artifice to provide a vision of natural truth. In traditional terms or even for the d'Alembertian Enlightenment, this natural social truth would indeed be a fixed structure of power relations, thought to be preordained, so the jester's job would indeed be to reimpose the same political harmony, the same *accords,* no matter how boring. As we have seen in the *Supplément au voyage de Bougainville*, however, the Diderotian world no more permits an ideal eternal social or political structure than it does an unchanging physical world. Therefore Diderot's jester, to reaffirm continually the true social structure, must continually show new and different truths. The political or social *modèle idéal* he induces is no more fixed than the *modèle idéal* driving the work of the great painters. Thus he will have to take his place among those other speakers of nature, the great experimenter, the great painter, the great philosopher. Diderot adjusted the standard Enlightenment notions of these roles and their products to match his materialist dynamics; so too he redefined the jester's role and the vision we can have of the "product" his performances generate. Clearly the Nephew is out of his element in the Bertinhus household. He is like Oudry surrounded by the venal amateurs.

A great difference separates Diderot's jester and his other natural philosophers, however. The jester is only one half of a couple; he needs a king figure in order to project his social model. Bertinhus obviously would not, and moreover could not, serve as his counterpart. Where is the effective master figure for Rameau? The simple answer would be that none exists, for he has outlived the age of the jesters in the same sense that from Diderot's point of view the age of even the Enlightened monarch has passed. Catherine would turn out to be a disappointment, Frederick the Great was already a deception, and Louis XV was the shadow of a king. Indeed, Rameau speaks of himself as a genius whose time has passed or whose time has not yet come (176). The more serious answer starts with recognizing that even trying to look for a straightforward analogue of the traditional king figure is a mistake, like succumbing to the Tahitian nostalgia. The answer lies in shifting the question. We understand the role of the jester and that he does not exist in isolation. What was the function served by the king that had to be harnessed by the king-jester couple? What part of that function endures through the continuing natural change? In fact, we already know, and not just by analogy with Diderot's other texts: "LUI. Au reste, souvenez-vous que dans un sujet aussi variable que les moeurs, il n'y a d'absolument, d'essentielle-ment, de généralement vrai ou faux, sinon qu'il faut être ce que l'*intérêt* veut qu'on soit" (139; my emphasis; "LUI: But still, remember that in a subject as varied as morals, there is nothing absolutely, essen-tially, or generally true or false except that you have to be what *inter-est* wants you to be"). The king restrains self-interest, the relational form of appetite—it is what one attempts to take from, or in spite of, others. Self-interest is the private motivation lying behind a search for power. It is the primordial social force mentioned at the begin-ning of this chapter. In other words, for the Nephew all political power is simply the public manifestation of what is paradigmatically a physical, even physiological drive for survival.[5] These physiological drives for survival are of two sorts: needs and passions. From the chapter on the passions in the *Eléments de physiologie* (compiled around 1778), one can divine the following schema: Needs, as we also know from elsewhere, especially from the *Rêve*, are functions of the organization of each body, in man particularly of the specific organs. Each organ has its own functions and its own tasks. This organiza-tion is going to determine what it is in its own interest to seek or to avoid in order either to survive or to operate. "L'intérêt naît dans chaque organe de sa position, de sa construction, de ses fonctions" (DPV 17:486; "Interest arises in each organ as a function of its posi-tion, construction, and functions"). Interest, then, or self-interest, is a natural consequence of physical organization. Although Diderot is not entirely consistent either in this chapter or in the chapter on the

5. For a clever reading of the *Neveu de Rameau* as the incarnation of body (appetite) set in opposition to MOI's pure rationality, see Aram Vartanian, "Diderot, or the Dualist in Spite of Himself," in Jack Undank and Herbert Josephs, eds., *Diderot: Digression and Dis-persion* (Lexington, Ky.: French Forum, 1984), 250–68. As is by now obvious, I disagree with Vartanian's thesis that Diderot is a closet dualist; I am unsure that binary thematic struc-tures always imply an unconscious or unresolved dualist tendency. On the contrary, I think that often Diderot uses such oppositions paradoxically, in other words, to force his reader to transcend such initial positions. Here in the *Neveu*, especially, I think Diderot is con-sciously setting up an opposition in order to change the commonsense negative moral eval-uations of appetite. Nonetheless, the textual evidence Vartanian brings to support this thematic opposition, no matter what Diderot's epistemological purpose may have been, is both very funny and convincing.

stomach (DPV 17, pt. II, chap. 16), in practice he tends to distinguish hunger from appetite. Hunger is merely the pain caused by the sensation of lack. It is a necessary component of, but is not synonymous with, appetite. It is merely a need. Appetite, however, he (usually) defines as a passion, for example, "la fureur de la faim" (DPV 17:494; "the furor of hunger"). But what is passion? Diderot at first gives a very simple definition: "Il n'y a qu'une seule passion, celle d'être heureux. Elle prend différents noms suivant les objets" (DPV 17:486; "There is only one passion, and that is to be happy. It takes on different names according to its objects"). Passions seem to be a compound sensation—desire added to the physical pain of need. Appetite, therefore, is a good example of a passion. "En toute passion il y a vue de l'objet, besoin qui naît des organes mus, désir, désir involontaire, quelquefois permanent" (DPV 17:492; "In every passion there is an object in view, a need arising from the affected organs, desire, involuntary desire, sometimes permanent"). But the organ feels only the need, not the passion. The pain of the need in the organ induces a state of passion in the whole: "Différence du tout et de l'organe; le tout prévoit, et l'organe ne prévoit pas. Le tout s'expérimente, l'organe ne s'expérimente pas; le tout évite le mal, l'organe ne l'évite pas, il le sent et cherche à s'en délivrer" (DPV 17:486; "Difference between the whole and the organ: The whole foresees, the organ does not. The whole experiments; the organ does not. The whole avoids pain; the organ does not—it feels it and tries to get rid of it"). Desire, which can only be felt by the whole, is the critical addition: desire added to need provokes action, and action provokes movement—even involuntary movement. Two good examples, moreover, show that passion need not be cognitively acknowledged: Mlle. de l'Espinasse's very distinct erotic reaction to d'Alembert's orgasm in the *Rêve* and Diderot's idiosyncratic take on Bordeu's theory of the pulse. "Je ne doute point que chaque passion n'ait une espèce de pouls qui lui soit propre, ainsi que chaque organe ou maladie. Chaque passion a son action propre. Cette action s'exécute par des mouvements du corps" (DPV 17:487; "I have no doubt that each passion has its own pulse, just like each organ and disease. Each passion has its own action. This action is carried out by the movements of the body"). Diderot defines passions as having only two structural forms of movement, no matter what the object: love (which he sometimes also calls desire) or aversion. Desire is a movement-toward that he defines as literally a swelling of the body or the consciousness, and aversion is a movement-away-from that he defines as a collapsing: "les parties se rapprochent, se raccourcissent, deviennent denses comme la pierre" (DPV 17:488; "the parts come together, get shorter, become as dense as stone"). Appetite is the synonym for the impetus behind "passion-toward."

Whether passion is morally good or bad depends entirely on the context. "Elle est vice ou vertu selon sa violence, ses moyens et ses effets" (DPV 17:486; "Passion is vice or virtue according to its violence, its means and effects"). The form of passion that is called desire or love or appetite can be many things depending on how it is handled, for it is primarily a dynamic force. "Le désir est importun, il sollicite, il est impatient. Borné dans la brute, immense dans l'homme, il s'accroît en raison directe de l'importance réelle ou idéale de l'objet, et inverse des obstacles, et quelquefois en raison composée des deux selon le caractère" (DPV 17:493; "Desire is importunate; it solicits, is impatient. Limited in the brute animal, immense in man, it grows in direct proportion to the real or ideal importance of the object and inversely to obstacles, and sometimes as a combination of the two according to the characteristics"). When such a force is kept in line, when its results are brought into perfect harmony with the needs of its physical or mental substrate, then true beauty has been achieved. In animals, as in Tahiti, adequacy is the goal. In man, whose desire is immense or open-ended (as suggested by the opposition with *borné*) because ideal (here ideal means, as he explains elsewhere (DPV 17:493), a projected construct in the imagination resulting from the memory of a previous satisfying experience), the beauty has to be equally open-ended and ideal, in the same sense that the *modèle idéal* was in the *Salon de 1767*. In a passage that, in fact, evokes the *Salon* almost literally, Diderot says, "Donnez à la chose que vous faites toute l'utilité dont elle est susceptible, ou toute sa bonté: faites en sorte que l'effet utile soit produit de la manière la plus simple, et soyez sûr que vous atteindrez en même temps la grâce et la beauté, cette règle me paraît sans exception" (DPV 17:494; "Give the thing that you make all the utility it is capable of, or all goodness: make it so that the useful effect is produced in the simplest way, and be sure that you will attain at once grace and beauty; this rule seems to me to have no exceptions"). How do you take appetite and bend it to the *modèle idéal*? In effect, that is the Nephew's whole task. As we saw above, the king-jester couple was a way of rendering public and thus disinterested the appetite of the one person who had the power to be infinitely impatient: the king. In a physical body the organization and balance of the whole must preclude disruption by the singular organ. In the body of the state, the dominance of the interest of the whole over the interest of each separate part, of the public over the appetites and passions of the private, defines the balance. There may indeed no longer be a functional king figure in the Nephew's view of France, but there are certainly socially active appetites. In fact, the lack of a single effective king figure necessitates generalizing the power to satisfy the appetite. This power is clearly recognizable as such, however, because it carries the simulacrum of the king embossed on it: it is money. It can pass from one person to another; it is power quantified. In fact, the social rank of the traditional kingdom has been replaced by a "degree of kingship" determined by how much money one has. In the "Louis d'or" pantomime (*Neveu*, 166), the Nephew kisses the coin, bows to it, and in fact performs all the acts of obesience to a king. Then, when he "owns" it—puts it in his pocket—he becomes a bit kinglike himself: "Je me promène avec fierté; je relève la basque de ma veste; je frappe de la main sur mon gousset; et c'est ainsi que je lui [his son] fait concevoir que c'est du louis qui est là, que naît l'assurance qu'il me voit" (175; "I walk around with pride; I raise the tail of my jacket; I tap my waistcoat pocket with my hand; this is how I make him understand that it is from the *louis d'or* that I have there that the assurance he sees in me arises"). Louis the king becomes Louis the coin, becomes LUI. Whereas MOI thinks the Nephew worships money, we see that his vantage point as jester makes him unique in understanding it. He knows it as the power to fulfill self-interest concretized. He knows also, as in the *Salon*, that power is separate from the merit that justifies wielding it. Money itself, like passion, has no intrinsic moral value but is good or bad only according to what is done with it. Justice is the use of power—or money—to maintain or restore a balance of competing self-interests. Injustice is the instigation of imbalance that results from unmeritorious people having power—or money—that they don't deserve. This, in effect, is the Nephew's message at the table of Bertin-hus; its other side is that injustice is by nature self-correcting. This inevitable correction is, according to the Nephew, the law of nature (149, 191).[6] The other side of the law of appetite is the law of a natural

---

6. As has been well commented, the Nephew's many statements of this position are directly taken from Diderot's readings of Hobbes. But a provisional warning: his words

redress of imbalances. Nature "connaît tous les vices qui échappent aux lois. Vous vous livrez à la débauche des femmes; vous serez hydropique. Vous êtes crapuleux; vous serez poumonique. . . . Le plus court est de se résigner à l'équité de ces jugements . . . et de s'amender ou de rester ce qu'on est, mais aux conditions susdites" (150; "knows all the vices that escape the laws. You debauch women, you'll get dropsy. You're dissolute, you'll be consumptive. . . . The quickest solution is to resign yourself to the justice of this judgment . . . and to reform or stay what you are, but on the above conditions"). The Nephew siphons money from those who have it without deserving it, but nature itself is the ultimate jester.

In the decadent world that the Nephew portrays, the jester is still the teacher and the balance restorer, but he no longer restores a prior hierarchical order. In a world where everyone has appetite and can exercise it, where everyone risks being invaded by someone else's insistence, the jester ends, like nature, by being curiously egalitarian. From this point of view, Rameau's speech at Bertinhus's table was not a failure at all; its results were just what they should have been. Rather than continuing to enjoy their own unmerited position, Bertinhus will have to face their own lack of merit and "s'ennuyer commes des chiens." LUI has denounced their "vile pantomime," which thus no longer constitutes a "dance" (a constructed movement intended to provoke pleasure), but merely an agitation.

MOI Je ne connais personne qui ne sache quelques pas de votre danse.

LUI Vous avez raison. Il n'y a dans tout un royaume qu'un homme qui marche, c'est le souverain. Tout le reste prend des positions.

MOI Le souverain? encore y a-t-il quelque chose à dire? Et croyez-vous qu'il ne se trouve pas, de temps en temps, à côté de lui, un petit pied, un petit chignon, un petit nez qui lui fasse faire un peu de la pantomime. *Quiconque a besoin d'un autre, est indigent et prend une position.* . . . Ma foi, ce que vous appelez la pantomime des gueux, est le grand branle de la terre. (190–91; my emphasis)

should not be taken at face value as defining Diderot's own position. We will return to this question at the end of the chapter.

MOI I don't know anyone who doesn't know a few steps of your dance.

LUI You're right. In the whole kingdom there's only one man who walks, that's the sovereign. Everyone else strikes poses.

MOI The sovereign? And you want me to tell you? You think that from time to time he doesn't find himself next to a little foot, a little chignon, a little nose that pushes him into a little pantomime? *Whoever needs another is indigent and strikes poses.* . . . In faith, what you call the pantomime of rogues is the great impetus of the earth.

In this exchange, MOI holds the jester's position. MOI and LUI have reversed roles. Or as LUI will say elsewhere, "Moi je suis le vôtre [his fool] peut-être dans ce moment; ou peut-être vous, le mien. Celui qui serait sage n'aurait point de fou. Celui donc qui a un fou n'est pas sage; s'il n'est pas sage, il est fou; et peut-être, fût-il roi, le fou de son fou" (139; "Maybe I'm your fool at this moment; or maybe you're mine. He who would be wise can have no fool. So he who has a fool is not wise; if he isn't wise, he's a fool; and maybe, be he a king, the fool of his fool"). The fool figure has become generalized. Just as the sociopolitical structure is no longer focused on two visible and unchanging human endpoints, the jester function is no longer synonymous with one man. MOI's is not a cynical or pessimistic statement, however, for just as in the modern arcadia of the *Salon de 1767*, the positive role of the jester outweighs its seeming uselessness. MOI may have taken on the role of the jester for a moment, but as such he becomes, as LUI will say, the midwife to LUI's intellectual productions.

LUI [after having succeeded in a particularly difficult pantomime of the passions]. C'est cela, je crois. Voilà que cela vient; voilà ce que c'est que de trouver un accoucheur qui sait irriter, précipiter les douleurs, et faire sortir l'enfant; seul, je prends la plume; je veux écrire . . . le dieu est absent; je m'étais persuadé que j'avais du génie; au bout de ma ligne, je lis que je suis un sot, un sot, un sot. (181)

LUI [after having succeeded in a particularly difficult pantomime of the passions] That's it, I think. It's coming; that's what it means to find a midwife who knows how to irritate, precipitate labor pains and make the child come out; alone, I take my pen; I want to write . . . the god is absent; I have persuaded myself that I had genius; at the end of my line I read that I am a fool, a fool, a fool.

In turn, MOI says that LUI, for all his seeming depravation:

> est un grain de levain qui fermente et qui restitue à chacun une por-
> tion de son individualité naturelle. Il secoue, il agite, il fait
> approuver ou blâmer; il fait sortir la vérité; il fait connaître les gens
> de bien; il démasque les coquins; c'est alors que l'homme de bon sens
> écoute, et démêle son monde. (72)

> is a grain of yeast that ferments and restores to each a portion of his
> natural individuality. He shakes, he agitates, he makes people
> approve or disapprove; he makes the truth come out; he publicizes
> good people; he unmasks scoundrels; this is when the man of good
> sense listens and figures out his world.

What better definition of the role of the jester? In a world without kings, the jester and the philosopher—the sage, not the *savant*—play the same role. In a world that continually changes, the role must continually shift to another agent.

But MOI is uncomfortable with this arrangement. Although he clearly acknowledges LUI's special talent, he still despises him and tells him so repeatedly throughout their discussion. It would seem difficult to both admire and despise someone. We know that MOI also admires LUI's command of music. "Je vous aime mieux musicien que moraliste" ("I like you better as a musician than as a moralist"), he had told him, but LUI's response was, "Je suis pourtant bien subalterne en musique, et bien supérieur en morale" (177; "And yet I am thoroughly mediocre in music and superior as a moralist"). And yet the above quotation shows that what MOI prized above all at the beginning of his description of the Nephew was LUI's ability to bring out moral truths.

To resolve this seeming paradox we turn to the question of music, for only by exploring in some depth Diderot's concept of musical performance can we uncover the actual mechanisms that the Nephew uses to transmit his jester message.

Musical Variations

Already in the article "Encyclopédie" and the *Rêve de d'Alembert*, the problems and potential that music had held for Diderot were striking. In the *Neveu* the nature of music—as mechanophysical vibration, as physiological resonance and mental patterning—determines both the subject matter and the structure of discussion as well as the process of interpretation proposed to the reader by Diderot. Music thus becomes the dominant instantiation of creative resonance, with special emphasis on the notion of harmony. I would argue that this notion constitutes the musical version of the intellectual-physical coupling demonstrated in the *Rêve* and of the *modèle idéal* in the *Salon de 1767*. In "Encyclopédie," two forms of harmony induction were at play: the harmony induced in the encyclopedists' minds by their writing and discussion in producing the *Encyclopédie* and the harmony with the material world attained and manifested by the genius. In the *Supplément au voyage de Bougainville*, the notion of sexual harmony underlay a theory of economic order. In texts I have not discussed, like *La Religieuse*, singing or chanting creates a medium or background essential to the transmission of information through regular speech.[7] In the *Neveu de Rameau*, however, all forms of musical resonance are generalized into (rather than reduced to) their original analogue. Sound is polarized vibration; music is complex living sound. Music is thus the most complex model for vibration that structures. However, music is sound that is not just harmony but a form of activity made up of an interplay of melody, harmony, and dissonance. Interestingly, the *Neveu*'s investigation of music shows that music is not the metaphor from which the other models are derived, as is sometimes claimed about Diderot. The notion of music can indeed be extended, but Diderot extends it so as to cast the other forms of resonance as *material* subsets of music. In the *Neveu*, Diderot deals with the most complex and dynamic of these analogues: pantomime, dance, and laughter.

Let us therefore confront music, but through what may seem at first to be an indirect approach. The Nephew is an astounding mime. One way to describe the structure of this work is to say that it is a contrapuntal succession of discussions (these are not "just" conversations) and pantomimes about music: the speculative or anecdotal arguments spark "demonstrations" in the form of the Nephew's pantomimes, which themselves bring about shifts—sometimes unexpected—in the subject matter of the continuing discussion. The early pantomimes are simple and very short character sketches, each pro-

7. See Rosalina de la Carrera's meticulous presentation of this mechanism in the *Religieuse* in her "Paradoxes of Communication in Diderot's Fictional, Historical and Philosophical Writings" (dissertation, Johns Hopkins University, 1985), chap. 3.

voking a moment of laughter for MOI. But they gradually become longer and less theatrical. During a long digression, the Nephew describes the parasitic symbiosis characterizing the Bertinhus household and the behavior that forces his dismissal. In his recital the Nephew describes dialogues, tells cruel jokes about himself and the others, but curiously desists from pantomime. The sixth pantomime, which starts up the series again after this long digression, breaks with its predecessors: it proves to be no laughing matter. The Nephew has just recounted the story of a criminal genius in order to force MOI to acknowledge that crime can be sublime in spite of its immoral essence. His intention is to focus parallel attention on the fact that the esthetic value of his own talent for storytelling is likewise not dependent on subject matter.

LUI L'atrocité de l'action [of the criminal genius] vous porte au-delà du mépris; et c'est la raison de ma sincérité. J'ai voulu que vous connussiez jusqu'où j'excellais dans mon art; vous arracher l'aveu que j'étais au moins original dans mon avilissement. . . .

Et là-dessus, il se mit à faire un chant en fugue, tout à fait singulier. Tantôt légère et folâtre; dans un instant il imitait la basse; dans un autre, une des parties du dessus; il m'indiquait de son bras et de son cou allongés, les endroits des tenues; et s'exécutait, se composait à lui-même, un chant de triomphe, où l'on voyait qu'il s'entendait mieux en bonne musique qu'en bonnes mœurs.

Je ne savais, moi, si je devais rester ou fuir, rire ou m'indigner. Je restai, dans le dessein de tourner la conversation sur quelque sujet qui chassât de mon âme l'horreur dont elle était remplie. Je commençais à supporter avec peine la présence d'un homme qui discutait une action horrible, un exécrable forfait, comme un connaisseur en peinture ou en poésie, examine les beautés d'un ouvrage de goût; ou comme un moraliste ou un historien relève et fait éclater les circonstances d'une action héroique. Je devins sombre, malgré moi. Il s'en aperçut, et me dit:

LUI Qu'avez-vous? Est-ce que vous vous trouvez mal?

MOI Un peu; mais cela passera.

LUI Vous avez l'air soucieux d'un homme tracassé de quelque idée fâcheuse.

MOI C'est cela.

Après un moment de silence de sa part et de la mienne, pendant lequel il se promenait en sifflant et en chantant; pour le ramener à son talent, je lui dis . . . (157)

LUI The atrocity of his action carries you beyond scorn; that's the reason for my sincerity. I wanted you to see how much I excell in my art; to wrest from you the admission that I am at least original in my degradation. . . .

And with that, he started to sing a fugue, quite singular. Sometimes light and fanciful; at one instant he imitated the bass; at another the high parts; he showed me, with his outstretched arm and neck, the held notes; and he performed, composed to himself, a song of triumph in which one saw that he understood good music better than good morals.

I didn't know if I should stay or flee, laugh or be indignant. I stayed, intending to turn the conversation to a subject that would chase from my mind the horror that filled it. I began to have a hard time putting up with the presence of a man who discussed a horrible action, an execrable crime, as a connoisseur in painting or poetry examines the beauties of a work of taste; or as a moralist or historian brings out and puts into relief the circumstances of a heroic action. I became somber in spite of myself. He noticed and said to me:

LUI What's wrong? You don't feel well?

MOI A bit, but it will pass.

LUI You have the worried look of a man harassed by a troublesome idea.

MOI That's it.

After a moment of silence on his part and mine, during which he walked about whistling and singing, to bring him back to his talent, I said to him . . .

Until this moment, the relationship of pantomime to the discussion has been to reaffirm the commonplace judgments spoken by either LUI or MOI at moments of potential disagreement. In other words, the pantomimes have harmonized with the melody of the conversation. MOI laughs, usually in spite of himself, and the concord between the Nephew and MOI is maintained or even restored. The discussion can go on. This time, however, the Nephew takes a chance. This is the first example of an unamusing pantomime, in fact of an openly dissonant pantomime: the "music" he is miming is dissonant, and the relationship of the pantomime itself to MOI's state of mind is dissonant. As the end of the passage shows, the conversation almost terminates. MOI has to reinitiate the dialogue, during a moment described by MOI as one of mutual silence but in which LUI in fact sings and whistles. MOI interprets his singing as silence because LUI is not using the music to reinstitute conversational harmony. LUI's singing is anything but noncommunicative, however; it decidedly produces a cognitive effect on MOI, an effect reminiscent of the ecstatic absorptive state experienced by that other MOI contemplating Dorval in the *Entretiens sur le fils naturel*.[8]

What is MOI's state? Having already been emotionally disturbed by the dissonance between subject and tone in the Nephew's description of the appalling actions of the Renegade of Avignon, he now describes his state as one of horror. Horror is a particular mental state of dissociation from an event, a form of refusal to assimilate that results in paralysis. This had always been a key notion for Diderot, tightly bound to his materialist psychology. Let us turn, for example, to the article "Horreur" that he wrote for the *Encyclopédie*. In it he tells us that horror not only designates "l'aversion, quand elle est extrême," but also that:

> nous appliquons encore la même expression à une sorte de sensation particulière, mêlée de frémissement, de respect, & de joie, que nous éprouvons à la présence de certains objets, ou dans certains lieux; & nous disons alors *le sombre d'une forêt épaisse, le silence & l'obscurité qui y règnent, nous inspirent une* horreur *douce & secrète.* ... *L'horreur* prise en ce sens, vient moins des objets sensibles, que des idées accessoires qui sont réveillées sourdement en nous. (DPV 7:428–29)

> We apply further the same expression to a kind of specific sensation, mixed with shivering, respect, and joy, that we feel in the presence of certain objects or in certain places; and we then say *the obscurity of a thick forest, the silence and darkness that reign there, inspire in us a sweet and secret horror.* ... *Horror* in this sense comes less from sensible objects than from the accessory ideas mutely awakened in us.

One may plausibly posit that horror begins as the limit form of the perception of what elsewhere Diderot calls the bizarre, but which

8. See chapter 3, esp. 115–18.

here he names the dissonant. However, horror is actually not a state but a process with several stages. It may begin in aversion—the recognition of the intolerable disparity of two objects brought into relationship with each other—but it can just as well end in joy and respect, in either the creation or the reaffirmation of the physical structure of knowledge, in a newly created harmony between knowledge and the passions (the "horreur douce"). In its Diderotian construal, then, horror has the potential to yield a form of intuitive understanding or a form of cognitive induction that operates from initial dissonance.

The horror pantomime is not, as had been the preceding ones, an illustration or acting out of some described behavior. In other words, it is no longer representational. It is an explicitly musical performance: the fugue the Nephew is miming is supposed to express passions rather than represent things. It expresses both the dissonance felt by an observer in the structure of the Renegade's behavior and the disparity between the quality of the Nephew's storytelling and the atrocity of the story itself. MOI's reaction is a rendering physical of his prior judgment of the recited actions, this time felt as an involuntary ("je devins sombre, malgré moi") repugnance for the Nephew's physical presence, strong enough itself to mimic physical sickness: "Vous vous trouvez mal?" asks the Nephew. Either MOI does not acknowledge it in his account of the pantomime, or he is unaware of it, but LUI has produced the effect he desired, and he whistles and sings as he waits, confident, for his victim to return of his own accord. "J'ai voulu que vous connussiez jusqu'où j'excellais dans mon art," he had said after the recital, "que j'étais au moins original" (*Neveu*, 156; "I wanted you to know how much I excell in my own art; that I was at least original"). It is the pantomime, though, more than the storytelling that shows how he is in fact *singulier*. (We can interpret *singulier* here not only as "unique," but also as "composing a unity"—in Diderot's terms, "coherent.") He is thus effective in his operations on MOI's passions. Although MOI physically processes the dissonance in his body so as to manifest a sort of physiological understanding somewhat like Diderot's reaction to the paintings of La Grenée, his mind rebels: "pour le ramener *à son talent*, je lui dis: Que faites-vous à présent?" (157; "to bring him back to his talent, I said to him: What are you doing now?"). The Nephew has in fact just provided his philosopher with the first and a quite blatant concrete experience of LUI's real talent, but the philosopher avoids understanding by refusing to allow the horror processing to develop into *admiration*, in the Diderotian sense. He refuses to allow his passions to construct a bridge from his physiological understanding to his intellectual awareness. MOI respects LUI's talent but refuses to acknowledge it, so he changes the subject.

Refusing to recognize that the Nephew has carefully constructed the horror experience does not allow the philosopher to escape its effects entirely, however. This first dissonant pantomime backs MOI into a discussion of the expressive nature of music, epitomized by the Italian opera's innovative shattering of Lully's and Rameau's speech-mimicking structures solidly grounded in Rameau the uncle's greatest achievement, his theory of the *basse fondamentale*. It is this notion of representational music, not only its consequences but also its conceptual warrant, that is under attack in *Le Neveu*.

From the starting point of the *basse fondamentale*, we can posit that for an Enlightenment musical theorist, music contains an implicit spatial architecture. The fundamental bass, what we would now call the key, provides a fixed reference point against which all the other relations between sounds are rationalized. To take a very simple case, from this standpoint harmony in a simple chord (two synchronous tones) involves more than the relation existing between the two tones: it is this initial tonal interval as perceived in the larger space created by the listener's awareness of each tone's distance from the fundamental bass—octave, third, fifth, and seventh. Each chord thus manifests both the explicit harmony of the actual struck tones and their implicit harmony with respect to an overall stable system of sounds.[9] In order to keep in mind the stakes peculiar to Diderot's text, we might say that the explicit harmony is always a relative harmony whereas the implicit reveals an absolute harmony. For Rameau, the relative carries its full musical weight only when perceived in the context of the absolute harmony.

The consequence is that the possible relations between tones are determined by the rules of harmony—some combinations are acceptable and some are not. Melody is merely the harmonic relations performed diachronically; dissonance, whether in chord or syntagm, is

9. Jean-Philippe Rameau, *Traité de l'harmonie* (1722), preceded by "Rameau, et les méprises de la tradition" by Joseph-François Kremer (Paris: Meridiens Klincksieck, 1986). Rameau worked out the abstract theory in bk. 1, 1–48.

the performing together of two sounds that are not related to each other by one of the accepted intervals. Rameau was working from what is generally recognized as having been an empirically derived harmonic system, a system that had been used for at least a hundred years and characterized French baroque music (especially Lully's). Rameau's innovation, a profoundly influential one, was to have grounded it in mathematics (really an arithmetic) and thus to have rationalized it—almost a Newtonian version of the old idea of the music of the spheres. What had before been merely rules were now considered to be natural laws, generated as consequences from a single principle, the fundamental bass. Rameau did for music what Condillac would try to do for language and the senses, what d'Alembert was doing for algebra, what Newton had done for mechanics: he provided a fixed and absolute basis for explaining, for judging, and for generating the phenomena.

This rationalizing was extended even farther in French opera, which had to be able to deal with the content as well as the sound of the words being sung. A fairly elaborate theory of the relationship of melodic use of harmonic intervals—in other words, syntagmatic harmony—to language statements was worked out in order to "naturalize" the music of opera. The music was supposed to represent naturally rather than conventionally the intonation patterns of speech. Rameau and his contemporaries felt that Lully's work had been a step in the right direction. Rameau went one step farther, however, by inverting the cause and effect relation: he felt that the intonation patterns conveyed emotional responses because they were created by emotional responses. In other words, a universal natural psychological music existed that itself had to be a function of the universal natural harmonics. Rousseau, in his *Essai sur l'origine des langues humaines*, argued that this natural music was at the origin of all human languages. Many of his contemporaries agreed with him. But it is in the ensuing step that divergences arise: how did the priority shift from expression (natural music) to representation (the words as signs)? For Rousseau, the corrupting effect of human interaction is conventionalization; as soon as it begins, the ear deafens to the natural music, which is nonetheless always there and always the same. One of the principal advantages of opera would then be that it restores the emphasis on the natural music by rationalizing and thus standardizing rather than conventionalizing the harmonic intervals to be used to convey a part of the cognitive message. From the point of view of these rationalists (including, I would argue, Rousseau, even though he argued against Rameau's theories), the passions thus solicited serve to recratylize language and to remove some of the arbitrary from the representational side of language. The consequence that I would like to focus upon is that, contrary to what one might at first expect, such a move revalidates a representational view of language and thus conforms to the epistemological underpinnings of Condillac, for example. Like the *Traité des sensations*, it naturalizes by depsychologizing the cognitive content. Rameau's own operas and songs consciously attempted to embody this principle.

Against this background, Rameau the Nephew situates his own ideas on Italian opera as the counterpoint to his uncle's. When he does so, he reveals the stakes that had been implicit in a long preceding treatise on the nature of nature and the nature of imitation. As has been well documented, the esthetic position outlined by the Nephew coincides closely with Diderot's own quite original position among the theoreticians of the baroque.[10] What I would like to emphasize is not so much what Diderot's musical theory was for its own sake, but how he here links the very idea of musical theory to the notion of all imitation of nature. He makes it clear that such imitation is an expressive operation, not, as Lully and Rameau the uncle had thought, a representative operation. It is expressive because, rather than attempting to convey recognition of passion, it expresses through *acting on* the passions to bridge the physical and the cognitive modes of understanding. Music thus becomes here a particularly effective, because affective, mode of imitation. As both Diderot and Grimm would cast it in the early 1750s, melody and harmony soothe because the body registers harmonic resonance smoothly; dissonance excites because the body must struggle and adapt to bring the tones into arithmetic resonance.

> LUI Le chant est une imitation, par les sons d'une échelle inventée par l'art ou inspirée par la nature, comme il vous plaira, ou par la voix ou par l'instrument, des bruits physiques ou des accents de la passion; et vous voyez qu'en changeant là-dedans, les choses à changer, la définition conviendrait exactement à la peinture, à l'éloquence, à la sculpture, et à la poésie. (158)

10. Desné, intro. to *Neveu*, in Diderot, *Le Neveu. Le Rêve*, 15n.

LUI Song is an imitation using the sounds of a scale invented by art
or inspired by nature, as you wish, performed by voice or instrument, of physical noises or the accents of passion; and you see that
changing the right things in this definition will make it fit exactly
either painting, eloquence, sculpture, or poetry.

Art is nature, nature is art. One expresses the other and they inter-
twine, as we know already from the *Interprétation* and the *Salon de
1767*. In the way that the paintings of Vernet did for the *Salon de
1767*, music here sets the paradigm for the other *beaux arts*. Does this
differ from Rameau? Or Rousseau? Yes, in two critical ways. Harmony is complemented for Diderot by accent; they both can be transformed by dissonance. First, accent: "L'accent est la pépinière de la
mélodie. . . . On nous accoutumera à l'imitation des accents de la passion ou des phénomènes de la nature, par le chant et la voix, par
l'instrument, car voilà toute l'étendue de l'objet de la musique" (159–
62; "The accent is the heart of melody. . . . Using either song and
voice or instruments we get accustomed to the imitation of the
accent of passion or natural phenomena, for this is the whole point
of music"). Accent, in other words, rhythm—like pulse, another analogue of vibration—is the complementary constituent of affective
music. The other constituents are all variations of both its vibration
structure and its effect. Accent's effect is to transmit, in the most
efficient way possible, an experiencing of internal (*la passion*) or external (*les phénomènes*) material nature, rather than the grasp of it as
either a thing or its objectification. Diderot construes true music to
be a construction that under ideal circumstances should be experienced as an event in the same way that the natural philosopher's
student experiences an experimental demonstration in Diderot's
observational physics or a spectator undergoes a Vernet painting.
Music becomes an event precisely through the intervention of
accent. For example, melody in the spatial model of harmony outlined above was harmony read on the time axis rather than spatially,
but its meaning, its effect, derived from the listeners' act of restoring
in their own mind the spatial construct. Moreover, accent is more
than just rhythm, which reaffirms periodic architecture. Accent
serves also as a temporal punctuation that never lets the listener for-
get duration, and duration is at the heart of the notion of experiencing, of knowledge understood as event. Accent also continually

emphasizes certain notes over others in order to bring the listener back from music as spatial construct to music as provoked noise, as voice, as the unpredictable. In this way accent becomes the least spatial and the most time-oriented of the components of music. In fact, it unhinges the spatial harmony by continually setting up competing resonances, by juxtaposing harmony with dissonance.

Let us posit that the definition of music can be expressed as a linear relation: harmony → melody → accent. Harmony is the most spatial and accent the most temporal; music results from a dialectical operation of one on the other. Melody, then, is both the synthesis of the two and the path from understanding one to the other. The end at which we start determines the result, however. If, with Rameau and his colleagues, we set harmony as the paradigm notion, we must read the other two as functions of harmony. Accent then is reduced to rhythm, the form of temporal emphasis integratable to the architectural. It forces the listeners to hear together in their memory the notes occurring in the same position in each measure. Rhythm, too, will have its occurrence determined by the universal laws determining acceptable resonances. If, however, we begin with accent as event, melody becomes the site where we learn to hear harmony as frozen event. Accent, by forcing tones to resonate together that are not normally considered in harmony, can develop the intervening melody to create a relation between two tones where one could not have been understood before. The reason that such a reversal matters is that a frozen event is, of course, only that: it is a memory trace like the ones in the *Rêve de d'Alembert*, a provisional understanding, not a universal and atemporal law. Music and, by extension, all of the *beaux arts* are thus merely additional modes of the overall model of interpreting nature that Diderot had already proposed in 1753. To transmit understanding, one does not represent, but one expresses—causes events to occur—and thus interprets nature. The music of Lully and Rameau failed because it attempted to represent, but the Italian opera succeeds in replacing imitation as representation with imitation understood as reanimation of expression.[11] The cognitive procedures of understanding through inductive experience therefore resurface. As one might by now expect, the same epistemological vocabulary struc-

---

11. Another indication of this difference is the Italian opera's reliance on the singers' improvising from a musical sketch rather than on fixed musical scores.

turing such discussion from the *Interprétation* on returns here to describe the procedures of judging music, a vocabulary now given its full weight by the notion of the *modèle idéal* from the *Salon de 1767*:

> LUI ... Le vrai, le bon, le beau ont leurs droits. On les conteste, mais on finit par *admirer*. Ce qui n'est pas marqué à ce coin [in other words, as Italian music], on l'admire un temps; mais on finit par bâiller. Bâillez donc, messieurs; bâillez à votre aise. Ne vous gênez pas. L'empire de la nature, et de ma trinité, contre laquelle les portes de l'enfer ne prévaudront jamais: le vrai qui est le père, et qui engendre le bon qui est le fils; d'où procède le beau qui est le saint-esprit, s'établit tout doucement. (163)

> LUI The true, the good, and the beautiful have their rights. We may contest them but we end up *admiring*. What isn't in this corner [the corner of Italian music] we may admire a while, but we end up yawning. So yawn, messieurs; yawn as much as you want. Don't restrain yourselves. The empire of nature and my trinity, against which the doors of hell will never prevail—the true, which is the father, who engenders the good, which is the son; from which proceeds the beautiful, which is the holy spirit—establishes itself calmly.

"On les conteste. . . ." To contest something is to resist it with logical arguments. The d'Alembert voice had attempted to contest the Diderot voice's positions in the *Rêve de d'Alembert*, but as we saw there, the logical is an ineffective bulwark against the material invasion of ideas: d'Alembert "finit par admirer." Diderot's article "Admirer" in the *Encyclopédie* argues that admiration is the state of cognitive and physical comprehension resulting from the observer's being brought into harmonic configuration with the natural phenomenon he is observing. From astonishment and rejection of the bizarre, possibly even from horror, one proceeds through Diderotian interpretation to admiration of the beautiful as recognition of the true and the good. As the Nephew's theological conceit reveals, admiration leads to a form of comprehension that goes beyond mere cognitive understanding both in scope and in feeling. Just as with "la douce horreur," the passions are called in to reinforce the intellect, so we more than know: we believe.[12]

---

12. Two peripheral comments are in order here. First, the article "Admirer" can usefully be compared to the article "Adorer," also written by Diderot. Second, here is where we

But do we *believe* this construal of music? The Nephew has spent a fair amount of time outlining this extension of Diderot's overall materialist dynamic into music theory. He has been quite eloquent and logical in explaining his preference for the Italian opera. His argument is not difficult to understand, but MOI (and theoretically, therefore, the reader) needs something more than words to make him believe it. That is the purpose of the great absorptive pantomime that forms the high point and climax of the work.

Diderot had already shown in the horror pantomime the outline of the complex machine for working on the knowledge-passion complex that he is deriving here. There MOI avoided understanding and showed that he could dissimulate with his reader to avoid facing the full consequences of his or the Nephew's behavior when he could not accommodate the new to his old cognitive structure. He will no longer be able to avoid the Nephew's persuasion in the absorptive pantomime. Like the horror pantomine, instead of being a pantomime in the normal sense, it is a performance that imitates various phenomena by expressing them in music. It is, in fact, the experimental demonstration, the performance of the *Interprétation's grand manouvrier,* intended to complement and *faire passer* the content of the theoretical discussion that preceded it.

The absorptive pantomime reveals to the reader the nature of the MOI voice in this text. *Le Neveu de Rameau* is written as a first-person recounting of a dialogue because MOI is in the position of the experimented-upon. MOI is not the Diderot voice, any more than the Nephew is. Nor is MOI intended to be a reliable witness or detached observer that the reader can take at face value. He indeed provides a strategic observation point, but only because, when we see the action through him, we are forced to observe his reactions as well. He is the subject of the Nephew's experimental manipulations, and as the horror pantomime has already made clear, we have to interpret his descriptions of the events not as neutral objective accounts

---

understand just how seriously Diderot took Locke's axiom that one can believe only what comes from the senses. He has redefined not only the operation of the senses but also the structure of belief in materialist terms. This last redefinition provides, I think, the under-pinning for the shift in meaning of the term *certitude* that Jean Starobinski discusses in a recent article on Diderot, "Diderot: Le Démontrable et l'indémontrable," in *L'Età dei lumi. Studi storici sul settecento europea in onore di Franco Venturi* (Naples: Jovene, 1985), 261–84.

242 ≈ DIDEROT'S HUMANISM

but as the reactions of the observer being brought into resonance with a system he does not yet understand.

The Nephew begins by stringing together a series of refrains from the Italian operas.

> Et puis le voilà qui se met à se promener, en murmurant dans son gosier, quelques-uns des airs de *L'Ile des fous*, du *Peintre amoureux de son modèle*, du *Maréchal-ferrant*, de *La Plaideuse*; et de temps en temps, il s'écriait, en levant les mains et les yeux au ciel: si cela est beau, mordieu, si cela est beau! Comment peut-on porter à sa tête une paire d'oreilles et faire une pareille question. Il commençait à entrer en passion, et à chanter tout bas. Il élevait le ton, à mesure qu'il se passionnait davantage. (164)

> And then he started to walk around, murmuring in his gullet some of the airs of the *Ile des fous*, of the *Peintre amoureux de sa modèle*, of the *Maréchal-ferrant*, of *La Plaideuse*; and from time to time, he cried out, raising his hands and eyes to the heavens: if that isn't beautiful, zounds, if that isn't beautiful! How can one have a pair of ears on one's head and ask such a question? He started to become impassioned and to sing under his breath. He raised the tone as he became more impassioned.

Like the great experimenter, the Nephew first induces in himself a controlled state of passion, a resonance with his subject matter's physical instantiation that will allow him to express, rather than represent it. He first creates what appears to MOI to be a chaos of musical phrases and characters, an impossible and unbalanced vibrating dissonance of sounds and actions.

> Il entassait et brouillait ensemble trente airs, italiens, français, tragiques, comiques, de toutes sortes de caractères; tantôt avec une voix de basse-taille, il descendait jusqu'aux enfers; tantôt s'égosillant, et contrefaisant le fausset, il déchirait le haut des airs. . . . Il s'apaise, il se désole, il se plaint, il rit; jamais hors de ton, de mesure, du sens des paroles et du caractère de l'air. Tous les pousse-bois [chess players] avaient quitté leurs échiquiers et s'étaient rassemblés autour de lui. Les fenêtres du café étaient occupées, en dehors, par les passants qui s'étaient arrêtés au bruit. (165)

> He piled up and mixed together thirty airs—Italian, French, tragic, comic, all types; sometimes *basso cantate*, he descended into hell;

sometimes bawling a falsetto, he tore apart the high notes. . . . He calms down, he gets distressed, he complains, he laughs; never at odds with the tone, the measure, the meaning of the words, or the characteristics of the air. All the chess players had left their chess-boards and congregated around him. The windows of the café were crowded by passersby who had stopped at the noise.

Out of the dissonance the Nephew has already created a spellbind-ing, absorptive group attentiveness. We would have expected this absorption to have required harmony, but his audience resonates to the rightness, the sureness of his expression.[13] The Nephew is able to transmit the precision, the capacity to judge when music is great or genial; he functions as the great experimenters did, but according to MOI, he does this in spite of himself. The untrustworthiness of MOI's portrayal of the Nephew in this passage, however, shows through when he alternates a curious unwillingness to perceive the effectiveness and virtuosity of the Nephew's performance with a reluctant step-by-step admission of seduction.

> On faisait des éclats de rire à entrouvrir le plafond. Lui n'apercevait rien; il continuait, saisi d'une aliénation d'esprit, d'un enthousiasme si voisin de la folie, qu'il est incertain qu'il en revienne; s'il ne faudra pas . . . le mener droit aux Petites-Maisons. . . . Il répétait avec une précision, une vérité et une chaleur incroyable, les plus beaux en-droits de chaque morceau; . . . il l'arrosa d'un torrent de larmes qui en arrachèrent de tous les yeux . . . s'il quittait la partie du chant, c'était pour prendre celle des instruments qu'il laissait subitement, pour revenir à la voix; entrelaçant l'une à l'autre, de manière à con-server les liaisons, et l'unité du tout; s'emparant de nos âmes, et les tenant suspendues dans la situation la plus singulière que j'aie jamais éprouvée...Admirais-je? oui, j'admirais! Etais-je touché de pitié? j'étais touché de pitié; mais une teinte de ridicule était fondue dans ces sentiments, et les dénaturait. (165–66)

---

13. The relationship of this passage to the absorptive mechanism esteemed in painting by Diderot and analyzed in Michael Fried's *Absorption and Theatricality: Painting and Beholder in the Age of Diderot* (Berkeley: University of California Press, 1980) is obvious. I would add that this passage demonstrates that the absorption mechanism was always intended to function as the primary vehicle of the esthetic mode of comprehension, but must be understood as directly derived from the physical model of knowledge underlying all of Diderot's work, not just his work on painting.

They laughed fit to tear open the ceiling. He noticed nothing; he continued, seized by an alienation of the spirit, by an enthusiasm so close to madness that it wasn't clear he could come out of it; if it wouldn't be necessary to take him straight to the insane asylum. . . . He performed the most beautiful sections of each piece with unbelievable precision, truth, and warmth; . . . he watered them with a torrent of tears that drew them from all of our eyes . . . if he dropped the voice part, it was to take up the instrumental, which he left immediately to return to the voice; intertwining them so as to keep the links and the unity of the whole; taking possession of our souls and holding them suspended in the most singular situation I have ever experienced...Did I admire? yes, I admired! Was I touched with pity? I was touched with pity; but a hint of the ridiculous was mixed in with these feelings and denatured them.

Most interpretations of this passage read it, as does Desné, from MOI's point of view filtered through the *Paradoxe sur le comédien*: the Nephew is like the mediocre actor or Mlle. de l'Espinasse in the *Rêve*.[14] He is a creature of sensibility, who feels deeply and whose feeling is absorptive. He cannot be as effective as the great actor, however, because he does not maximize the outward appearance of feeling by rigidly controlling his own internal feelings and consciously using them as an instrument to manipulate his audience's feelings. He is, like Mlle. de l'Espinasse, always at the mercy of his own diaphragm. I would argue, however, that this reading is crucially misguided. The indication of the Nephew's incompetence is supposed to be the insistent recurrence of laughter and the sensation of the ridiculous felt by the observer. I see two reasons to resist immediately applying the *Paradoxe's* "vous aurez beau verser des pleurs, vous serez ridicule, on rira" ("you can cry as much as you want, you will be ridiculous and people will laugh") to this passage.[15] The first is that MOI's pronouncements cannot be taken at face value. We must leave open the possibility that the "teinte de ridicule," which is tellingly situated not in a description of the Nephew's performance but in MOI's reaction to it, tells us more about MOI's resistance than about the Nephew's actual performance. The notion of "dénaturé" is even more significant: if the natural is the comfortable harmony of

14. Desné, intro. to *Neveu*, in Diderot, *Le Neveu, Le Rêve*, n. 157.

15. Denis Diderot, *Paradoxe sur le comédien* in *Oeuvres esthétiques*, ed. Paul Vernière (Paris: Classiques Garnier, 1968), 314.

the already digested, then anything that either does not live up to its structure *or goes beyond it* will be seen as *dénaturé* until it has been accommodated into the existing structure. In other words, this judgment, coming from MOI, may provide another bit of information about his preconceptions but tells us little about the Nephew. In spite of all of MOI's pronouncements about the Nephew's seeming "aliénation d'esprit," we do not at this point in the pantomime have sufficient data to decide what form of denaturing is occurring here.

The second and more important reason for rejecting the standard interpretation of this passage is that, as we have seen, the Nephew makes his living by making other people laugh. He is a past master of it: he provokes laughter on purpose, whereas the laughter provoked by the *Paradoxe*'s mediocre actor's performance is the opposite of the effect he is seeking. It is most plausible to assume here that the audience, and MOI, are laughing at the Nephew not because of his failure as a mime but precisely because of his success. It is in fact crucial for the Nephew to make MOI laugh if he wants his persuasion to succeed. Laughter is his tool. When he is effective, laughter occurs at the exact moment when what had previously been experienced as dissonant is suddenly transformed into a new harmonic relationship. Notice that this is not a gradual process in which a chain of logical steps slowly incorporates a seemingly dissonant notion into a preexisting harmonic structure. On the contrary, it functions through a demonstration of incommensurability. It works by putting into sharp relief the contrast between two modes of understanding. The two, for an instant simultaneous in the observer's mind, provide a double pleasure: that of understanding both the old and the new harmony while appreciating the impossibility of maintaining both. Laughter is the physical expression of the pleasure felt; it is the physiological manifestation of a gestalt switch and thus a passionate form of understanding. Not by accident are the last two pages of Diderot's chapter on passions in the *Eléments de physiologie* devoted to laughter. The second half of the pantomime, where the Nephew does succeed in transmitting his esthetic vision (literally, as we shall see) to MOI, is fittingly introduced by laughter.

Mais vous vous seriez échappé en éclats de rire, à la manière dont il *contrefaisait* les différents instruments. Avec des joues renflées et bouffies, et un son rauque et sombre, il *rendait* les cors et les bassons;

il prenait un son éclatant et nasillard pour les hautbois . . . criant, chantant, se démenant comme un forcené; *faisant* lui seul, les danseurs, les danseuses, les chanteurs, les chanteuses, tout un orchestre, tout un théâtre lyrique, et se divisant en vingt rôles divers, courant, s'arrêtant, avec l'air d'un énergumène, étincelant des yeux, écumant de la bouche. . . . (166; my emphasis)

But you would have broken into laughter at the way he *counterfeited* the different instruments. With swollen and puffed out cheeks and a raucus and somber sound, he *rendered* the French horns and bassoons; he adopted a piercing and nasal voice for the oboes . . . crying, singing, acting like a madman; *creating* all by himself the dancers, singers, a whole orchestra, a whole lyric theater, and multiplying himself into twenty diverse roles, running, stopping, with the air of an energumen, eyes flashing, foaming at the mouth.

The transformation of MOI has begun: what he thinks he is describing is an impossible pantomime. How can the Nephew be all the members of an orchestra at once? How can MOI tell us that he has become an entire theater and that he plays twenty different roles at once? The physical state of the Nephew, described by MOI as *incroyable,* indicates to the Diderotian reader that something unusual is occurring here; an impossible, that is, *dénaturé,* message is being attempted. "Que ne lui vis-je pas faire? Il pleurait, il riait, il soupirait; il regardait, ou attendri, ou tranquille, ou furieux; *c'était* une femme qui se pâme de douleur; *c'était* un malheureux livré à tout son désespoir" (166; my emphasis; "What didn't he pull off? He cried, he laughed, he sighed; he looked at you either tenderly, tranquilly, or furiously; *he was* a woman who faints with pain; *he was* a wretch drowned in despair."). MOI has gone from describing acting as represention to describing acting as expression. The Nephew is no longer engaged in a process of counterfeiting (representing), or even doing, but is engaged in being. He does not act a role, for his music has caused him to *become* that person for MOI. The performance is so convincing that MOI does not even notice that the Nephew moves from representing to imitating to being people to being nature itself.

[C'était] un temple qui s'élève; des oiseaux qui se taisent au soleil couchant; des eaux ou qui murmurent dans un lieu solitaire et frais, ou qui descendent en torrent du haut des montagnes; un orage; une tempête, la plainte de ceux qui vont périr, mêlée au sifflement des vents, au fracas du tonnerre; c'était la nuit, avec ses ténèbres; c'était l'ombre et le silence; *car le silence même se peint par des sons.* (167; my emphasis)[16]

He was a temple being built; birds quieting at the setting sun; streams either murmuring in a solitary and cool place or falling in a torrent from the heights of the mountains; a storm; a tempest; the cries of the dying, mixed with the whistling of the wind, with the fracas of thunder; he was night with its gloom; he was shadow and silence; *for even the silence can be painted by sounds.*

So effective is the Nephew's pantomime that even silence has been not represented, which is impossible, but expressed. The experience of silence has been transmitted. Through sound, the Nephew has *fait passer* silence to MOI, seemingly the most impossible performance of all. On reflection this oxymoron is not one at all, for the Nephew is representing, which would imply creation of a simulacrum of silence through silence itself. He is bringing MOI into resonance with him so that MOI can understand what silence feels like—and this form of understanding is brought about through vibration, through sound, through accent. Because the Nephew is expressing, not representing, MOI cannot describe the Nephew's actual performance. Just as with the laughter process, the mode of understanding is a perceptual experience, not the acquisition of an intellectual content. MOI can only indicate to us what his reaction was; in effect, what he understood by being in contact with the Nephew's intense activity. LUI had said in the earlier theoretical discussion that internal nature, the passions, was linked to external nature, the phenomena. Here the Nephew has shown what he meant by making MOI move through his passions to a "vision," a new perception, of the phenomena. MOI no longer tells us what he feels, but what he "sees."

MOI has understood here precisely the Nephew's message that he was trying to avoid before, the second form of horror from the article in the *Encyclopédie*. Even the images are the same: the temples, the deep forests full of darkness and silence. If we look again at that article, however, we see the mechanism by which the expression operates: "*L'horreur* prise en ce sens [the sublime transcendent horror],

16. *Peindre* has to be taken here in its Vernetian sense: in Diderot's art experience paradigm, painting is not representation but expression. In other words, even silence can be expressed by sounds.

vient moins des objets sensibles, que des idées accessoires qui sont réveillées sourdement en nous" (DPV 7:429; "*Horror* in this sense comes less from sensible objects than from the accessory ideas they awaken mutely in us"). The association of ideas, as we have seen so many times over, functions in both directions for Diderot: the wild dissonance of the Nephew's music was so effective that it instantaneously provoked the association with the objects with which MOI connects horror. MOI may have recoiled to begin with, but by this point in the pantomime, he can no longer perceive the music or its dissonance with aversion, as *dénaturé*. Or rather, LUI has turned dissonance into harmony by restructuring MOI's aesthetic models by subjecting him to the intense performance of the essence of the Italian opera. MOI is in a state of both belief in and mastery of the principles of the new music, for he is in resonant congruence with the Nephew. He has passed through horror to admiration: "Plus un être créé & pensant voit loin dans la nature, plus il a de discernement, & plus il admire" (DPV 5:277). MOI is not aware that he now understands the principles of the new music, however. The end of his depiction of the pantomime suggests this in an indirect way.

> Sa tête était tout à fait perdue. Epuisé de fatigue, *tel qu'*un homme qui sort d'un profond sommeil ou d'une longue distraction; il resta immobile, stupide, étonné. Il tournait ses regards autour de lui, *comme* un homme égaré qui cherche à reconnaître le lieu où il se trouve. ... *Semblable à* celui qui verrait à son réveil, son lit environné d'un grand nombre de personnes; dans un entier oubli ou dans une profonde ignorance de ce qu'il a fait, il s'écria dans le premier moment: Hé bien, messieurs, qu'est-ce qu'il y a? d'où viennent vos ris, et votre surprise? qu'est-ce qu'il y a? Ensuite il ajouta: Voilà ce qu'on doit appeler de la musique et un musicien. (DPV 12:167; my emphasis)

> He was out of his head. Exhausted *like* a man coming out of deep sleep or a long reverie; he sat immobile, stupid, astonished. He looked about him, *like* a dazed man who tries to recognize where he is. ... *Like* someone who awakens to see his bed surrounded by numerous people; in profound amnesia or ignorance of what he had done, he at first cried out: "Well, messieurs, what's wrong? Why are you laughing and surprised? What is it?" Then he added, "That is what one should mean by music and a musician."

MOI's last line unknowingly suggests to the reader that the Nephew was quite in control of his performance, even if it was a particularly energetic and exhausting one. MOI *interprets* the exhaustion as the sign of an unbalanced mind; as though the Nephew were in fact the *homme de sensibilité* decried by the *Paradoxe sur le comédien*. The Nephew's own words show instead an ironic detachment from his audience's reactions, a detachment supported precisely by MOI's inability to perceive the effectiveness of the pantomime on himself. The effectiveness came from his being able to do something that even the great actor of the *Paradoxe* had not been able to accomplish and only music and its analogues can realize: a synthesis of intellect and passion. He has performed a demonstration. A few lines later, he sums up.

> C'est au cri animal de la passion, à dicter la ligne qui nous convient. Il faut que ses expressions soient pressées les unes sur les autres; il faut que la phrase soit courte; que le sens en soit coupé, suspendu; que le musicien puisse disposer du tout et de chacune de ses parties; en omettre un mot, ou le répéter; y en ajouter un qui lui manque; la tourner et retourner, comme un polype, sans la détruire. (169)[17]

> It is up to the animal cry of passion to dictate the appropriate line. Its expressions must rush on each other; the phrase must be short; the meaning cut up, suspended; so that the musician can organize the whole and each of its parts, omit a word or repeat one, add a missing one, turn and overturn it, like a polyp, without destroying it.

Once the pantomime ends, the audience breaks up and drifts away. The continuation of the theoretical argument that follows, being merely a dispassionate logical elaboration, cannot inspire passionate interest, transmit a perceptual experience, and hence induce belief the way the Nephew's physical activity had. Logical argument does not have the accent—in other words, the resources of physical resonance to call on—to construct a complete, functional, and dynamic unity in the listener.

The Nephew's most effective mode of communication is thus his pantomimes, determined by or congruent with his affinity with Italian opera. Still, because of the way his pantomimes operate, MOI can-

---

17. Notice the return of the polyp and the idea that a musical "object" is a dynamic organic organization whose effect is maintained even if the internal components change.

not see him as creator or teacher. As he says at the very beginning, "je n'estime pas ces originaux-là" (72; "I have no respect for those eccentrics"). In other words, the admiration MOI feels is not for LUI himself but for what MOI has learned. He admires nature as LUI has allowed him to perceive it, but LUI himself remains "ridiculous" or at least *singulier*. That is, LUI remains capable of inducing laughter and thus capable of introducing change, but the catalyst is not itself affected by the reaction.

LUI "fait sortir la vérité; il fait connaître les gens de bien; il démasque les coquins" (72; "brings out the truth, publicizes good people; unmasks scoundrels"). MOI figures out his world after contact with LUI, but he neither figures out LUI nor sees LUI as continuous with either that world or its disentangling. The fact that MOI sees the Nephew only as an irritant to his own self-sufficient reflection and not as a creator-author does not prevent the Nephew from being effective, however. Nor does it mean that LUI is not aware of the quality or the consequences of his own performances. He does, indeed, see them as intellectual productions and sees that they require an audience to be in dissonance or harmony with, to work upon.

LUI uses the passions to transform and tame the passions, especially one state that we do not think of as a passion, but which Diderot qualifies, in the *Eléments de physiologie*, as one of the most powerful passions of all: admiration. The great pantomime is LUI's real jester scene, the one that validates his efficacity as jester (he makes people laugh, he transmits his message about the nature of the passions) and, more importantly, shows that he still has a worthy audience for his performances—not just the philosopher MOI, but even the people in the street.

The passage from the *horreur douce* to admiration is the tool not only of Dorval and Vernet, then, but of the Nephew. Rameau's subject is different from theirs, however, different in one critical way: he "hits people where it hurts the most," in their self-interests, their passions, and their perceptions of their own power. The old problem of conflict of interest arises again; in order to get people to accept his message, he must hide his own merit and thus the benefits he could possibly derive from his accomplished performances. He must continually make himself look like a fool. Note that he is not a martyr to his role. He manages to get his food, his snuff, his lemonade, but without seeming to have "earned" them, to have "merited" them. As we saw above, Rameau was perfectly in control of his performance, but MOI was convinced that he was ripe to be sent to the Petites-Maisons. LUI hides his merit both for the reasons that motivated the old jester and for an even more important new reason already suggested above: he is not merely reiterating a preexisting commonly shared view of power structures; he is, by introducing the social dissonance as he does *chez* Bertinhus or in his succeeding discussions about money with MOI, creating new ones.

MOI senses this at one level. His entire introduction moves back and forth between this insight and a recurring insistence on LUI's *nature vicieuse.* The Nephew himself maintains a running joke with himself and MOI about his primordial defectiveness, continually making MOI laugh at his pantomimes of his own vices and faults, continually playing with a determinist "biology" that would have him doomed by his heredity. At the same time he alternates these characterizations of himself with much more serious statements and hints that indicate that in fact LUI considers himself to be a rather special form of genius—the genius of dissonance. He never allows MOI to quite grasp it, because to do so would be to unmask the jester and destroy his ability to function. In order to ensure admiration for the message he is transmitting, the Nephew must make himself look ridiculous and provoke the gestalt-shifting laughter. As we have seen, the lines are there.

MOI A votre place, je jetterais ces choses-là sur le papier. Ce serait dommage qu'elles se perdissent.

LUI Il est vrai; mais vous ne soupçonnez pas combien je fais peu de cas de la méthode et des préceptes. Celui qui a besoin d'un protocole n'ira jamais loin. Les génies lisent peu, pratiquent beaucoup, et se font d'eux-mêmes. (129)

MOI In your position I would put all this on paper. It would be a shame for it to be lost.

LUI True; but you have no idea how little I care for precepts and method. He who needs a protocol will never go far. Geniuses read little, practice a lot, and form themselves.

Then he immediately makes himself ridiculous in classic jester fashion, thereby preventing MOI from realizing what his words imply.

The whole structure of the text is based on it being the reader and not MOI who perceives this doubling of the Nephew's description of himself. The first task of the reader is to perceive the incompatible statements and resolve them into harmony. To do this he has to take LUI at his word—he has to judge him not according to accepted protocol but according to process, process understood not passively but actively. The reader has to process the text himself. This is, in effect, what the fugal patterns of the text demand: the Nephew's statements about himself form a strange, dissonant fugue where neither "strand" is entirely correct, for each is partially correct. They have to be taken together, have to be forced into a new harmony, before the reader can see who the Nephew really is. Once the reader sees this, the lesson can be applied to the other fugal patterns in the work. The alternations between discussion and pantomime tell the same sort of story about logical and passionate modes of transmitting information. The shocking transitions of subject matter between music and social power also work this way. They all require that the reader maintain throughout the text the doubled perception inherent in the jester's laughter. Laughter basically signifies the recognition of the shift from the dissonant to a new harmonic. The text even displays an example of the convergence toward the new harmonic: by its end, some of MOI's arguments sound strangely like LUI's, but he is afraid that it is an accord only in appearance. "Si nous entrons une fois dans la discussion des périls et des inconvénients à éviter, nous ne nous entendions plus" (179; "If once we enter into a discussion of the perils and inconveniences to be avoided, we will no longer agree").

MOI has been profoundly changed by LUI's pantomimes, but not into LUI; he will think in a new register, but his own. Still, it is this same MOI who is able to answer, "Hélas oui, malheureusement" when LUI asks him on the last page, "Monsieur le philosophe, n'est-il pas vrai que je suis toujours le même?" (196; "Mr. philosopher, am I not always the same?"). Indeed LUI is the same, but not the same in the way that MOI thinks: he is the same in his maintenance of his dissonance and his ability to provoke, to change minds and comportments without people knowing it, and his ability to dance the vile dance that flatters and insults at the same time. Today's dissonance is tomorrow's harmony. Because dissonance is always relative, the Nephew's role is to continually displace the harmony, but he can do this only by a transforming interaction of his own with MOI.

Together, and only together, they form a machine for guiding social change. What is the final message? Obviously none exists in simple terms; as we have seen so often in Diderot's other texts, "tout change, tout passe, il n'y a que le Tout qui reste" ("Everything changes, everything passes away, only the Whole remains"). What remains is the Nephew as a critical figure. His very presence both is and invites a reflection on the nature of the network of interpersonal relations in which he finds himself. His message is an imperative to the reader to continue this open-ended fugue with the future: "Rira bien qui rira le dernier" ("He who laughs last laughs best") is the last line of the work. Laughter, as I have tried to show, is not a passive reaction in Diderot's world. It is an active form of cognitive processing of the very substance of that which motivates actions, or which might even be qualified as the essence of motivation; namely, the passions underlying self-interest.

In fact, Diderot's entire social argument is not an apology for vicious behavior; it is a plea for a clear-eyed understanding of the nature of the passions and a pragmatic adaptation to them that allows them to be channeled for the benefit of the maximum number of people. As the first sentence of Diderot's chapter in the *Eléments* on the passions had said, the passions themselves have no intrinsic moral value, positive or negative. What has is what one does with them. Bertinhus abused the same passions that MOI would use in a more positive vein. So the reader need not, any more than had MOI, become the Nephew. He is indeed his intellectual "progeny" due to the "midwifing" of the pantomimes or their disembodied form, the fugal structure of the work. Even so, as the Nephew's indirect denunciation of the determinism of the *molécule paternelle* had suggested, the child is not trapped in the vices of his father. MOI inherits from the Nephew an ability to perceive social forces more neutrally, to judge the nature of power. It is the understanding of the nature of power that justifies its use. Bertin and Hus wielded money, but one word from the penniless Nephew, who alone understood its significance, was sufficient to destroy their power. The readers (whom Diderot in most of his other texts calls his "nephews") inherit from Diderot this same disabused but not pessimistic view, a view in which self-conscious and thus Enlightened self-interest provides the force behind a finally virtuous social structure. Diderot's political goal is the creation of this enduringly virtuous social structure.

But what is virtue? Surely not the Nephew's program . . . and yet the last lines of the *Eléments de physiologie* are, "Il n'y a qu'une vertu, la justice; qu'un devoir, de se rendre heureux" (DPV 17:516; "There is only one virtue—justice; one duty—to make oneself happy"). In any other ethical system of his era, the drive to personal happiness would lead to social injustice; the private is by nature in constant conflict with the public need. In Diderot's relational world picture, where the world of mind is continuous with the world of matter, the private is continuous with the public, because reason is continuous with the passions. Social justice, which is a balancing of the desires of the many, can only really be achieved if the naturalness of self-interest is acknowledged. But in this, surprisingly, MOI is further evolved than LUI. MOI has understood that in a world where self-interest is acknowledged as both inescapable and as the only morally neutral social force (as it is, after all, in the Tahiti of the *Supplément au voyage de Bougainville*), the man who sees his own self-interest increased by his dialectical interaction with the self-interests of the people around him can interact in such a way that everyone's drive to happiness is maximized. Interest is personal virtue. Justice is interpersonal virtue. MOI's enlightened version of Shaftesbury answers LUI's Hobbes.

Self-interest is satisfied, however, only by interaction, mutually beneficial interactions of the sort that MOI and LUI undergo all through the *Neveu de Rameau*. Their relationship provides the concrete demonstration of the sort of interactions that were theorized in the *Salon de 1767*'s modern arcadia as resulting from the mobilization of the *modèle idéal*. This kind of interaction, which incorporates both the demands and the processes of the passions into the functioning of reason, is particularly well embodied in the open-ended literary evolutions of Diderot's texts. What distinguishes Diderot's texts from those of d'Alembert or Condillac, what makes his literature different from their philosophy, is that he openly calls upon the passions. What makes him different from Rousseau's hypnotic because passion-directing texts is that he foregrounds the cognitive results so that the reader can only maintain his critical independence, can never take the easy dogmatic way out. As such, literature for Diderot is indeed consciously amusing, but that amusement makes it neither trivial nor a flight from reality. To *bien rire* is, in the Diderotian world, to assume one's responsibilities. It is the manifestation of a satisfaction of self-interest and a realization of critical thought that forms the basis for constructive and thus virtuous behavior. It is, as the Nephew should know (for he is the only one who almost never laughs), the road to happy virtue. Diderot's testament to his reader is a lesson revealing what he thought were the natural mechanisms that could produce his modern arcadia, the social realization of the active material determinism already worked out in his mechanophysical texts written a full twenty-five years before.

By Way of Conclusion

I have tried to accomplish two things in this book. One, the explicit project, was to present Diderot's thought in such a way that its special coherence, which in some ways also constitutes its special tautology, would be foregrounded and opened up to modern readers. Diderot was unique not so much because his work was, in our terms, interdisciplinary; this was true of many, perhaps most of the Enlightenment thinkers. But Diderot was special in terms of the vast range of disciplines he drew on and the extent to which he conceived of his project as necessarily all-encompassing. This latter quality has to be taken seriously if we are to understand what he thought the purpose of his writing was; it motivated what we recognize as his literary production in the same way that it fueled his less easily definable works.

If I have succeeded in making the conceptual field underlying Diderot's work accessible and coherent, then the most appropriate conclusion to this goal of the book would not be one that I would write. If my pulling the reader through this trajectory of Diderotian texts has been effective, it should indeed help open up such relatively unsatisfying or intractable works as the *Essai sur les règnes de Claude et de Néron* and suggest pertinent new interpretations for more familiar works such as *Jacques le fataliste* and *La Religieuse*. But more importantly, it should result in the reader's exposure to an intellectual activity that I think both characterizes Diderot's work and that his work was intended to transmit the ability to engage in. It does not contain quite the same esthetic values that we hold, but that content is not what determines its effect. Diderot's work attempts to provide and valorize mechanisms for the continual challenging and shifting of values that bring about the new to displace the old. The Nephew shows MOI that the guarantee of this always-new order is for him to be MOI's intellectual midwife just as MOI must be his. Diderot's dream was to be the eternal midwife of future generations of thinkers and for that role to be continued by his readers for each other in further generations. He tried to establish a paradigm of the antiparadigmatic, an institutionalization of the critical. This is the legacy he intended to leave his descendants, and it is in this sense that Diderot's work may, I think, most responsibly be called modern.

But my second, albeit implicit, goal in writing this book was to replace Diderot in his own historical context in such a way that his work might eventually serve as a lens to bring his larger intellectual context into focus as well. Diderot, the writer of interaction, of conversation, was in constant interaction and conversation with just those authors we think of as essentially Enlightenment thinkers. Through his interactive texts we the readers are also drawn into reflection on his contemporary interlocutors; we see them through his eyes. In fact, we see his work fully only if we take into account that it is an intellectual pantomime, a not so vile dance sparked by the literary activity of these other writers. The crucial literary-critical dialogues underlying Diderot's work were set up between what, from the vantage point of his critiques, we can isolate as three distinct strains of the French Enlightenment project.

The best-known construal of the Enlightenment, the first strain, if you will, I have studied elsewhere. In this book I have used d'Alembert, at some length and in detail, as the spokesman for this strain because he is the interlocutor that Diderot singled out and addressed explicitly in his own work. This strain is typified by the work of Condillac and leads into the work of the French chemists and Auguste Comte; I characterize it as the Enlightenment of knowledge. The second strain is typified by the coherence underlying Diderot's thought that I have tried to illustrate in this book as a whole. Drawing on the definition of the term that he himself derives in the texts discussed in chapters 1 and 2, I would say that Diderot's Enlightenment is an Enlightenment of operational poetics. It intended to replace the oligarchy of men of knowledge with the community of creators activated by the *modèle idéal*. The third strain is more difficult to characterize. It is the strain that the programmatic works of Diderot that are analyzed in the second half of this book directly address. This strain is not, like d'Alembert's and to some extent Diderot's, knowledge oriented. I will call it, for want of a better word, politically oriented. Here Diderot's antagonist, his goad, his constructive opposition, is Rousseau. Rousseau's work is often described as constituting a sort of anti-Enlightenment. In that it sets itself in opposition to the first, or knowledge-oriented strain, and eventually also to Diderot's work, such a characterization may in some senses be valid. Rousseau's writing does not aim to transmit knowledge as does d'Alembert's, nor to create it, as does Diderot's. I posit that his Enlightenment project is centered on questions of power because he aims to affect and effect, to create and impose conceptual machines whose subject matter is less important than the demonstrations of their capacity to manipulate by creating uniquely powerful speaking voices. As he does this sharing the vocabulary and many of the positions of the other two strains, I would reclaim Rousseau for the Enlightenment. Although he remains a latent and not explicit presence in Diderot's work, I think that part II of this book suggests, at least, how much he was an essential if detested interlocutor for Diderot. In this work I have been primarily interested in Diderot's response to Rousseau not for what it can tell us about Rousseau but for elaborating the positive program that Diderot developed as a result. However, Diderot's work, as it is by nature interactive, serves not only as a counterpart to, but also as the hinge between the other two strains. It should provide a strategic point of departure for a detailed complementary analysis of Rousseau's intellectual project.

I think that as late as the mid-1750s, these three strains, because they shared a vocabulary, a belief that merit is based on intellectual activity, and an opposition to the social forces then governing France, thought themselves identical. However, these similarities were countered by profound dissimilarities resulting from epistemological differences at first invisible. The terms in the shared vocabulary—terms such as *reason, knowledge, art, judgment,* or *philosopher*—actually indicated different concepts, as we have seen, especially in chapters 3 and 4. The more intellectual activity that occurred—the more the Enlightenment authors either wrote and argued with one another or attempted to bring about social change—the more these differences became evident. The resulting tension was productive and is, I think, possibly a much better overall characterization of the Enlightenment than would be a descripton of any one strain, even as interactional a one as Diderot's. I have attempted to paint a picture of the strain to which Diderot belonged in its interactions with the other two, because its very nature as interactional allows it to serve as a starting point for the larger project of evoking the entire activity that characterized the Enlightenment, not as a simple monolithic theoretical program, but as this essentially complex historical event.